Missing Data

Methodology in the Social Sciences

David A. Kenny, Series Editor

This series provides applied researchers and students with analysis and research design books that emphasize the use of methods to answer research questions. Rather than emphasizing statistical theory, each volume in the series illustrates when a technique should (and should not) be used and how the output from available software programs should (and should not) be interpreted. Common pitfalls as well as areas of further development are clearly articulated.

SPECTRAL ANALYSIS OF TIME-SERIES DATA
Rebecca M. Warner

A PRIMER ON REGRESSION ARTIFACTS
Donald T. Campbell and David A. Kenny

REGRESSION ANALYSIS FOR CATEGORICAL MODERATORS
Herman Aguinis

HOW TO CONDUCT BEHAVIORAL RESEARCH OVER THE INTERNET: A BEGINNER'S GUIDE TO HTML AND CGI/PERL
R. Chris Fraley

PRINCIPLES AND PRACTICE OF STRUCTURAL EQUATION MODELING, SECOND EDITION
Rex B. Kline

CONFIRMATORY FACTOR ANALYSIS FOR APPLIED RESEARCH
Timothy A. Brown

DYADIC DATA ANALYSIS
David A. Kenny, Deborah A. Kashy, and William L. Cook

MISSING DATA: A GENTLE INTRODUCTION
Patrick E. McKnight, Katherine M. McKnight, Souraya Sidani, and Aurelio José Figueredo

MULTILEVEL ANALYSIS FOR APPLIED RESEARCH: IT'S JUST REGRESSION!
Robert Bickel

MISSING DATA

A GENTLE INTRODUCTION

Patrick E. McKnight
Katherine M. McKnight
Souraya Sidani
Aurelio José Figuredo

Series Editor's Note by David A. Kenny

THE GUILFORD PRESS
New York London

First Indian Sub-Continent Edition : 2008
by New Age International (P) Ltd., Publishers

This special low-priced edition is for sale in India, Bangladesh, Bhutan, Mayanmar (Burma), Sri Lanka, Nepal and Pakistan only.

Originally Published in the *United States of America.*

Printed in India at Saras Graphics, Rai.
1 2 3 4 5 6 7 8 9 10
C-07-08-1939

ISBN(13): 978-81-224-2203-0
ISBN(10): 81-224-2203-9
Original Edition Price: $ 38.00
Indian Edition Price: Rs. 295.00

PUBLISHING FOR ONE WORLD
NEW AGE INTERNATIONAL (P) LIMITED, PUBLISHERS
(formerly Wiley Eastern Ltd.)
4835/24, Ansari Road, Daryaganj, New Delhi - 110002
Visit us at **www.newagepublishers.com**

About the Authors

Patrick E. McKnight, PhD, is Assistant Professor in the Department of Psychology at George Mason University, Fairfax, Virginia. The majority of his work focuses on health services outcomes and, in particular, on measuring those outcomes to make them readily interpretable. He has worked and published in the health-related areas of asthma, arthritis, cancer, speech, pain, low vision, and rehabilitation. Dr. McKnight is an active member of the American Evaluation Association, serving as co-chair of the quantitative methods topical interest group for the past 4 years.

Katherine M. McKnight, PhD, teaches statistics at George Mason University, Fairfax, Virginia, and is Director of Evaluation for LessonLab Research Institute, part of Pearson Achievement Solutions. She has published numerous articles reflecting a wide range of interests, with the common underlying framework of the thoughtful use of research methods, measurement, and data analysis for addressing research and evaluation questions. She is a member of the American Evaluation Association and the Association for Psychological Science.

Souraya Sidani, PhD, RN, is Professor in the Faculty of Nursing, University of Toronto. Her areas of expertise are in quantitative research methods, intervention design and evaluation, and measurement. Her research areas of interest focus on evaluating interventions and on refining research methods and measures for determining the clinical effectiveness of interventions. She is a member of the American Evaluation Society and the Canadian Evaluation Society.

Aurelio José Figueredo, PhD, is Professor of Psychology at the University of Arizona. He is the director of the graduate program in Ethology and Evolutionary Psychology (EEP), a cross-disciplinary program integrating the studies of comparative psychology, ethology, sociobiology, and behavioral ecology, genetics, and development. His major areas of research interest are the evolutionary psychology and behavioral development of life-history strategy and sex and violence in human and nonhuman animals, and the quantitative ethology and social development of insects, birds, and primates. In the EEP he regularly teaches the graduate year-long course in Statistical Methods in Psychological Research.

Series Editor's Note

The topic of missing data is one that has been neglected for many years. I think many of us followed the advice (perhaps apocryphal) of R. A. Fisher of what to do with missing data: "The best solution to handle missing data is to have none." Missing data were present in every study but researchers tended to act as though they had complete data. All of this has changed. There are three related developments in statistics that have moved the topic of missing data out of the repressed unconscious to a topic of focused conscious interest.

First, statisticians—most notably Rubin, Little, and Shaffer—have developed a classification scheme for missing data. We now have the tools to diagnose and correct our analyses for missing data. No longer do we have to pretend that our data are complete.

Second, in a not unrelated development, researchers have begun to think that differences in design are really differences in missing data. So, for instance, the way a between-subjects design differs from a within-subjects design (i.e., a repeated-measures design) is not so much that they are different types of design; rather, a between-subjects design is the same as a within-subjects design with a measurement missing for each person. A related idea is to analyze data from very different types of groups as if there were missing data. As an example, data from one-child families can be analyzed with data from two-child families if we treat the measurements of the second child as "missing" in the one-child families.

Third, statistical methods have been developed to estimate models with missing data. As one example, growth-curve analysis (i.e., measuring change in individuals) can be conducted even for subjects who have only a single measurement. Additionally, structural equation models can be estimated, even if some of the people do not have measurements on all of the variables.

Although conceptual frameworks and analytic methods have been developed by statisticians, these methodologies have not yet been fully absorbed by applied data analysts. This book represents the first attempt to provide practitioners with an introduction to this topic. It provides some of the technical details and references to advanced sources. An important and useful focus is on conceptual and design issues. Moreover, the authors clearly emphasize the difficulties created by missing data and provide the reader with strategies for anticipating and reducing, if not eliminating, the problem. With this book, we can now acknowledge that we have missing data, we can determine how much harm the missing data cause, and, finally, we can perform the analyses that we wish to perform, after making our missing data adjustments.

DAVID A. KENNY

Preface

My works are like water. The works of the great masters are like wine. But everyone drinks water.

—MARK TWAIN

Our interest in missing data came about from our own individual, as well as our collective, concerns. The available literature on missing data was confusing to us. We felt the literature did not address the specific concerns we had with *our* data. After identifying the problems we were having as missing data problems, we found that our uncertainty and frustration were shared with other social scientists, who were equally baffled by missing data and began to seek our help. Though we knew little about the topic, we helped others as best we could.

It was at the annual American Evaluation Association conference of 1994 that we began to focus our energies on missing data. The four of us each presented papers detailing our current understanding of missing data problems and we offered some general suggestions for solving them. Later, we attempted to test our recommendations and found ourselves less certain than we had been before about suitable treatment strategies. This caused us to realize that the only way out of our quandary was to carefully review the extant literature on missing data. This entailed collecting articles from a wide variety of sources, but the mathematical notation and cumbersome presentation of much of the material prevented our study of the material from being very enlightening to us. Through it all, however, our sense of the complexity of missing data issues grew. We realized that if we were struggling with these concepts while focusing considerable attention on the matter, other social scientists who thought about missing data less than we did would not likely grasp what they were up against. This book is the result of our efforts and our concern for other social scientists and anyone who faces missing data problems with the same uncertainty we had in 1994.

OUR THANKS

We owe a great deal of gratitude to our colleague Lee Sechrest. Without his support, suggestions, and continued interest in missing data, we might have drifted into other areas of inquiry and left missing data for others to solve. Lee has come up with four "laws" that were recently published by Bradley Smith (2006). All four laws influenced our way of thinking, so we wanted to present them in our book,

Lee's Law Number 1: Everything eventually turns up. This law says that missing data often are not missing. If the data are simply misplaced on our desk, a thorough search may very well turn up data we believed to be missing.

Lee's Law Number 2: More is better than less. We view this law not from the perspective of missing data but from the perspective of data. If we have more actual data, that can offset missing data. More *missing* data, however, we would not want!

Lee's Law Number 3: Rarely is there such a thing as a true catastrophe. Unless all information is lost, most missing data situations can either be prevented or treated. Catastrophic data loss is rare enough that we do not need to prepare ourselves for that outcome.

Lee's Law Number 4: Nothing in statistics or research methodology requires you to do something stupid. This last law is our guiding principle. Thoughtful approaches should always be preferred. No procedure warrants using unsound data-handling methods. People who have misused or performed contraindicated analyses should own up to the mistakes and not blame an approach. At the heart of it all, we embrace a philosophy where researchers calmly approach missing data as an interesting question rather than as a catastrophe. The researcher acts as a detective, "solving" the problem without compromising the integrity of the study.

OUR MISSION

Providing a readable text on a technically complex topic presents a challenge that few writers ever volunteer to undertake. The technically adept often consider these efforts wasteful, error prone, or oversimplified, while the intended audience often fails to see the point of the contribution. We accepted this challenge either ambitiously thinking that we were capable of surmounting it or ignorant of the difficulties that lay ahead. Regardless, we felt that a clear and comprehensive, nonmathematical discussion of missing data was sorely needed. We do not present ourselves as experts in statistics nor as mathematicians bringing these complexities to the masses, but rather as social scientists who have come to an understanding and appreciation of missing data. In short, we come from the same population as the intended audience but with some of the technical capabilities to explain these concepts to our peers. Germane to our expertise and our intended readers' expertise is a study conducted well over 70 years ago that showed that novice rats learned maze running more quickly by watching novice rats than by watching expert rats. We are novices and we expect that most of our audience are novices. While we would not typically style our lives or perspectives around a single analogy like that, the findings in that study are consistent with our experience of missing data. Researchers are more likely to learn from other researchers who are fumbling around with the complexities of missing data than from experts whose grasp of the complexities is so handy that they assume that others understand the issues equally well. Our work in this volume constitutes Twain's water and we hope researchers come to drink.

In this text we have tried to distill much of the information already available in the statistical literature as well as contribute a broader perspective on missing data in general. Students and researchers in social and medical science ought to benefit from reading this book and using it as a research reference. Our aim is to present missing data in a fashion that stimulates students, reviewers, researchers, and editors to address the conceptual and analytical issues presented by missing data. The book is a comprehensive reference for the detection, diagnosis, and treatment of missing data. It is written in plain, nontechnical language, accessible to nonmathematically oriented readers. The book can be read from start to finish or in individual chapters, according to the reader's preferences. Each chapter relies somewhat on the explanations in earlier chapters, but cross-references are provided. The chapters are organized so that the reader can become familiar with (1) missing data in general, (2) likely problems stemming from missing data, and (3) methods to describe, prevent, diagnose, treat, and communicate missing data. On the book's website (reachable through *www.guilford.com/pr/mcknight.htm*), we offer a fairly comprehensive list of references annotated to guide readers in their search for more specific information. We put the guide on the website because the literature in this area changes rapidly. We chose to host the supplementary material on the Internet because printed material would not allow us to dynamically update the material to keep interested readers abreast of these new developments. The material in this book ought to serve as a sufficient reference, however, for most researchers.

OUR INTENDED AUDIENCE

Given that we believe most researchers would benefit from this book, we wrote it for all scientists—from students to experts. We did not make assumptions about readers' prior knowledge of the missing data literature, but some familiarity with empirical science would certainly be helpful. The book ought to be useful as a supplemental text in graduate-level statistics seminars or as a stand-alone reference for researchers. Again, we hope you find the book more like water than wine.

Contents

1

A Gentle Introduction to Missing Data

As the old saying goes, the only certainties are death and taxes. We would like to add one more to that list: missing data. As any social scientist can attest, missing data are virtually guaranteed in research studies. However, why data are missing, how missing data may affect research outcomes, and what to do about missing data are far less certain. Although the problem of missing data has been addressed in the statistical literature for decades, it still remains a significant conundrum for social scientists who are not methodologists or statistical experts. This state of affairs is at least partially due to their lack of familiarity with the statistical literature on missing data. This lack of familiarity is likely due to a variety of reasons, including a lack of understanding about the importance of missing data and an inability to interpret what is generally a complex and technical literature. The purpose of this book is to bridge the gap between the technical missing data literature and social scientists. The purpose of this introductory chapter is to both familiarize the reader with the concept of missing data and stress the importance of missing data when interpreting research results. In addition, we provide the reader an overview of the remainder of the book.

THE CONCEPT OF MISSING DATA

Broadly, the term *missing data* means that we are missing some type of information about the phenomena in which we are interested. In general, missing data hinder our ability to explain and understand the phenomena that we study. We seek to explain and understand these phenomena by collecting observations. Research results hinge largely on the analyses of these observations or data. This empirical or data-driven approach finds its roots in Sir Francis Bacon's *Novum Organum* Book II (1620), in which he details the inductive method of scientific inquiry. Bacon argued that three Tables of Comparative Instances involving the presence, absence, and degrees of a phenomenon are the hallmarks for discovering the truth about nature. Observations of conditions where the phenomenon of interest is present, where it is absent, and where it is present in varying degrees define and remain hallmarks of the scientific method. When observations are missing for any reason, our ability to understand the nature of the phenomena is reduced, the extent to which is not often known. All three of Bacon's "Tables" may be affected by these missed observations, therefore affecting our ability to either infer or deduce the nature of the phenomenon of interest. We believe, therefore, that missing data in general pose a threat to the validity of scientific inquiry.

THE PREVALENCE OF MISSING DATA

If knowledge about the nature of particular phenomena is adversely affected by any missing data, then one would expect that researchers would attend to the problem of missing data. In other words, both prevention and remediation of missing data should be normative behavior for social scientists. Evidence, empirical and otherwise, suggests that this might not be the case. For example, the American Psychological Association (APA) Task Force on Statistical Inference (Wilkinson and APA Task Force on Statistical Inference, 1999) published recommendations for presenting empirical results in published manuscripts. Recommendations for analyzing and reporting missing data were included, which were:

> Before presenting results, report complications [including] missing data, attrition, and nonresponse. Discuss analytic techniques devised to ameliorate these problems. Describe nonrepresentativeness statistically by reporting pat-

> terns and distributions of missing data and contaminations. Document how the actual analysis differs from the analysis planned before complications arose. The use of techniques to ensure that the reported results are not produced by anomalies in the data (e.g., outliers, points of high influence, nonrandom missing data, selection bias, attrition problems) should be a standard component of all analyses. (p. 597)

Inspired by this report, three of the present authors gathered data on the prevalence, type, and treatment of missing data across 3 years of publications within a prominent psychological journal to assess both prevalence and treatment of missing data in the psychological literature. Estimates of amounts and types of missing data were recorded from over 300 articles across the 3-year period. The results were dramatic. Not only were missing data prevalent across studies (approximately 90% of the articles had missing data), but the average amount of missing data for studies in our sample well exceeded 30%. Additionally, few of the articles included explicit mention of missing data, and even fewer indicated that the authors attended to the missing data, either by performing statistical procedures or by making disclaimers regarding the studies in the results and conclusions. We suspected that there would be a fairly high rate of missing data, but we did not anticipate such lack of attention to missing data. The prevalence of missing data and the general lack of attention to it suggest a probable impact on the validity and interpretability of research results.

Our review of journal articles suggests that missing data are common and often not given adequate attention by social scientists; the problem is either ignored or finessed. That is, researchers are aware of the missing data and attend to it by rationalizing why it is irrelevant to the particular study. Sometimes this rationale involves a statistical sleight of hand in which statistics are used to convince us that missing data have no significant impact on study results.[1] Yet on closer inspection, the statistics are often used inappropriately and are therefore prone to misinterpretation.

Such a situation is not limited to social science or to science in general. Missing data are ubiquitous and often ignored or finessed in many disciplines, both within and outside science. For example, in softball, there exists a "mercy" rule to eliminate demoralization of the losing team. Teams that are behind the winning team by a specific number of runs at the conclusion of any inning are declared the loser. This rule has subtle consequences involving missing data. The losing team never gets the opportunity to attempt a comeback, which, although improbable, is possible. Thus, in softball, values for the missing data are inferred and few argue about those values or the consequences resulting from the conclusions drawn from incomplete data.

Other examples come from historical biographies and archaeology. In historical biographies, detailed information about a remarkable person's life quite often is undocumented and therefore must be extrapolated or imputed based on the norms of the time. For example, Thomas Jefferson's food preferences were not likely to have been recorded in any great detail, yet if that feature of his life were to become relevant in a biography or history, the author would likely infer that his preferences were similar to the norm of his day. Unless his habits were unusual and/or noteworthy, the contemporary normative behavior is likely to be imputed to replace the missing observations. Imputation of missing data can easily be justified. Richard Dawkins (1998) remarked that humans are designed to perceive stimuli that are novel in the environment. If Jefferson's dietary practices were notable in his day, his contemporaries would likely have noted these oddities. Otherwise, there is no compelling reason to think that the missing information would have been anything out of the ordinary.

Archaeologists and paleontologists almost always have more missing than complete data. They rely on logic, theory, and conjecture to piece together the bits of available data and produce a plausible and worthwhile story. Paleontologists piece together the skeletal remains of species long extinct. Rarely are there enough remains for the researcher to resurrect the entire bone structure, posture, or external features of the creature. However, museum curators impute that missing information and infer the physical structure when they build models of these creatures for public display. Sometimes these imputations are incorrect. A recent report noted that a major change in the inferred facial structure of a particular dinosaur was necessary to explain both new fossil discoveries as well as likely foraging habits of the animal. The change, as it turned out, was logical, but also revolutionary in the study of that type of dinosaur and of other dinosaurs from the same period.

These examples show the pervasiveness and ordinariness of missing data. There is no reason to consider missing data as a unique feature of social science. What makes missing data noteworthy is the influence, whether known or unknown, that it has on our conclusions and ultimately on our knowledge. Therefore, the fact that it is not unusual for social scientists to make little or no mention of the potential impact of missing data on research conclusions is worrisome. Scientists in fields where missing data are both common and obvious (e.g., paleontology) expect that future research will uncover the errors made because of incorrect imputations or extrapolations. Social science researchers, however, do not always have the luxury of these future corrections.

WHY DATA MIGHT BE MISSING

There are a variety of reasons data would be missing. We classify those into three broad categories related to (1) the study participants, (2) the study design, and (3) the interaction of the participants and the study design. For example, data might be missing because some participants were offended by certain questions on a survey (participant characteristics), or because a study required too much of the participants' time (design characteristics), or because those who were the sickest were unable to complete the more burdensome aspects of the study (participant and design characteristics). As we discuss in subsequent chapters, the reasons why data are missing can have important consequences on the amount and pattern of missing data, the selection of appropriate missing data handling techniques, and the interpretation of research results.

The stage of the study in which missing data occurs is also informative. Data can be lost at the study recruitment stage, the implementation stage, or the follow-up stage. Data missing from the recruitment stage could be due to exclusionary criteria for the study, dropout prior to assignment to experimental conditions (e.g., treatment groups), or participants losing interest in the study prior to signing a consent form. Data missing during the implementation stage might be due to skipped items on questionnaires, to absence during a data collection period, or to refusal to participate after being recruited. Data missing at follow-up is a familiar situation for longitudinal researchers: data could be missing due to participants dropping out of the study or to the inability to contact participants for follow-up data.

Another important aspect of missing data is the different units of analysis and different levels of measurement within the study. For example, a distinction is made in the missing data literature between "unit missing data," which refers to data for an entire unit of analysis (e.g., study participant) that is missing, and "missing values," which refers to scores on a particular variable (e.g., questionnaire item) that are missing. Moreover, in longitudinal studies, there can be "missing wave" data, that is, data that are missing at a particular occasion of measurement. However, even this seemingly fine-grained distinction does not convey a sufficient level of specificity. In multilevel studies (i.e., those in which participants are grouped into larger units), "unit missing data" can occur at the individual or participant level, at the group level (e.g., males or females), and/or at the organization or community level (e.g., clinics, hospitals, or schools). Similarly, "missing values" can occur for single items within a measure, for subscales, for entire test scores, or for multivariate latent variable scores.

Moreover, data can be missing cross-sectionally (for persons or variables observed at a single occasion) or across time in longitudinal studies (for persons, variables, and occasions of measurement). Noting all of these sources of missing data can assist researchers in determining the reasons for missing data and the amount and pattern of missing data. In turn, this information can help researchers as they develop methods of handling missing data and appropriately interpreting study results.

It is important to note that these different types of missing data exist for researchers collecting data directly from participants and for researchers collecting data from existing records such as police records or medical files. As with data collected directly from study participants, record data can be missing data for entire "cases" (e.g., individuals), for single items, for variables, for an occasion of measurement, and so on.

THE IMPACT OF MISSING DATA

The most pressing concern regarding missing data is the extent to which the missing information influences study results. For example, if the majority of study participants who fared poorly in an experimental intervention dropped out, the results would be based largely on the participants who responded positively. The missing information about the poorer outcomes would then lead to an overestimation of the benefits of the treatment. Yet because the data are missing, it is difficult to determine the impact of data that might have been present in the study. There are two aspects of missing data that can provide us with clues regarding the extent of the influence of the missing information on study results. First, the *amount* of missing data (see Chapter 5 for details) is related to its impact on research conclusions. In general, greater amounts of missing data are expected to have a large impact on study generalizability and statistical inference; however, as we will discuss later, these expectations are not always warranted. Under most conditions, data sets in which large amounts of data are missing result in smaller sample sizes and potentially unrepresentative samples of the population to which we wish to generalize. Further, the available data for the remaining sample might reflect a bias, thus resulting in biased parameter estimates and misleading statistical conclusions. Second, the actual process that causes missing data can affect the validity of the inferences made from the analyses. Depending on the causal origin, missing data can have dramatic influences on the validity of study findings. For example, in a study assessing the effects of two mathematics curricula on test performance, the students' current math abilities could be related to missing data; that is, if those likely to fail the test chose not to take it, then inferences based on study results about the effectiveness of the curricula would likely be misleading. Moreover, generalizability would be compromised because results would not include the poorer math students.

WHAT IS MISSING IN THE LITERATURE ON MISSING DATA?

The subject of missing data has been widely addressed in the statistical literature as well as in other relevant bodies of literature. Statisticians have attempted to assess and reconcile the problems associated with missing data theoretically and with practical solutions. In general, the statistical literature reflects an appreciation for the type and magnitude of problems associated with missing data, particularly with respect to how missing data affect statistical results. Much of the literature focuses on how to identify missing data and correct potential biases attributable to missing data. The collective effort has produced numerous working solutions to many missing data problems.

Unfortunately, the statistical literature appears to have had negligible impact on the research practices of social scientists when it comes to handling missing data. We offer several possible reasons for this lack of impact. One quite plausible reason is the fact that many social scientists lack the level of training and expertise in statistics or mathematics required to understand this highly technical literature, which includes proofs, theorems, and definitions expressed in mathematical notation. Another reason is the paucity of user-friendly tools available for handling missing data. Although most statistical programs now offer missing data handling procedures, these procedures are often difficult to use for a novice data analyst. Missing data "add-on" programs for statistical software packages often suffer from poor documentation or limited functionality. Stand-alone programs for handling missing data also exist (e.g., NORM; Schafer, 1997), but again, these programs are often complex and difficult to use. The tools are thus generally not easily adopted by most researchers.

A third reason that the statistical literature on missing data has had little impact on the practices of social scientists is that social scientists have not had much of a mandate to attend to the literature. Results from our previously mentioned analysis of missing data in journal articles suggest that such articles can be and are being published without their authors paying attention to the problem of missing data. This situation suggests that either reviewers and/or editors are not requiring investigators to address the issue of missing data. Our own direct experience with journal reviewers has led us to conclude that many reviewers who do comment on missing data tend to be misinformed about missing data issues, particularly with regard to statistical techniques for handling missing data. Our observations are consistent with those of other social scientists who are well informed about both the statistical literature and social science research in general. David Krantz, a renowned statistician and social scientist, remarked a while ago that most social scientists who consider themselves statistically sophisticated often are not (Krantz, 1999).

Prevention and Remediation

The contemporary and classical view of missing data is largely ensconced in statistics and primarily focused on prescribing remedies. While we subscribe to much of this work, we feel that the matter of missing data is far more complex than a remedial statistical conundrum. Missing data become a statistical consideration only after data have been collected and are ready to be analyzed. Prior to data collection, there are many available strategies that decrease the likelihood of missing data. For example, decreasing respondent burden or increasing benefits to participants tends to decrease the incidence of missing data. We believe that the problem of missing data is a larger issue that involves not only statistics but also logic and research methodology. Therefore, in this book we not only discuss statistical solutions for handling missing data, but we also address research design and measurement strategies for preventing the occurrence of missing data. Our goals are to combine the major findings of a technically daunting statistical literature with those of the research methodology literature, and to redirect the focus from solely remedial solutions for handling missing data to preventive ones as well. We thus provide a comprehensive view of solutions for handling missing data that cover the planning, implementation, and analysis phases of research.

Of course, we recognize that prevention of missing data is not always possible—for example, in the context of secondary data analysis, where the data have been collected by someone else and the goal is to analyze those data. Figueredo, Sales, Russell, Becker, and Kaplan (2000) conducted a study using data from male adolescent sex offenders (ages 13 to 18) who had been referred to an outpatient evaluation and treatment clinic for sexual offenders in New York City, for assessment and treatment, from 1985 to 1990. As a result of inconsistent data collection over the years by the clinicians, a large number of offenders had missing data. In such cases, only remediation of missing data remains an option, and it is necessary to carefully consider one's options for doing so.

A Structural versus Functional Approach

Much of the existing literature on missing data reflects an approach that is structural rather than functional. In other words, the traditional classification schemes for missing data emphasize what missing data are rather than what missing data do and, in turn, what one might do about them. The traditional terminology hails from the statistical literature and focuses on abstract mechanisms of missing data, for example, missing completely at random (MCAR), missing at random (MAR), and missing not at random (MNAR). As we discuss in detail in Chapter 3, these terms are defined by theoretical relationships between missing values and observed or unobserved variables, reflecting a focus on the structure of the missing data.

A functional approach would instead focus on how missing data functions with respect to research results and conclusions. For example, what are the implications for possible sampling bias of data being MCAR? Is the sample of nonmissing data that is available for analysis still representative of the original population? What are the implications of the data being MAR for the generalizability of our results? These are the types of questions that would be addressed by a functional approach as opposed to just describing the mathematical properties of the missing data. Our discussion will address both structural and functional approaches, with an emphasis on the functional approach (see Table 3.2 in Chapter 3 for an illustration of this integration).

A COST–BENEFIT APPROACH TO MISSING DATA

In emphasizing a functional approach, however, we do not provide a "cookbook" for handling the problem of missing data. Instead, throughout this book we advocate sensible and thoughtful attention to missing data. For two reasons we do not promote a "one-size-fits-all" method to solve the problem of missing data. First, there is no single method for handling missing data, and second, every researcher has his or her own priorities. As in any research study, there is no perfect design or method for handling missing data. The research goals and priorities ought to drive the selection of methods, not the reverse. In short, we discourage the tendency to allow tools or methods to drive decisions and to allow convention to dictate how we handle the problem of missing data. Although reliance on convention might be the most expedient means by which to handle missing data, it is often not the optimal choice.

What constitutes a thoughtful approach regarding the handling of missing data falls within the familiar framework of a cost–benefit analysis. Every decision has associated costs and benefits. We use this guiding principle to convey why no single solution is appropriate for handling missing data. As an illustration, consider a researcher who decides to gather a convenience sample by collecting data from participants who are easily recruited but not necessarily best suited for the research study. The researcher benefits by saving time and energy as well as possibly increasing the sample size. The costs of this sampling method may include one of many threats to validity, such as selection bias, maturation, and so on, which in turn call into question the study results. Thus, each researcher should consider the costs and benefits of study-related decisions in order to make more informed and potentially better decisions than would be made by conducting research in a standard manner with the same design methods and analysis. With respect to missing data, costs may come in the form of increased demands on resources such as time and money, threats to other aspects of the study such as statistical power, or opportunity costs (i.e., requiring resources that may be used more productively elsewhere). These costs may be associated with actions taken to prevent, treat, or diagnose missing data. Likewise, benefits may be expressed in the same forms and associations.

How Costs and Benefits Are Valued

Unfortunately, costs and benefits are often unknown to researchers. Common practice and research history or lore dictate decisions more often than researchers realize. Research fields often operate with an implicit valuing of inferential errors. For example, most formally trained biostatisticians are loath to make Type I errors, and thus guard against being too liberal in statistical testing by invoking the most stringent test. Conversely, clinical researchers are trained to guard against Type II errors by avoiding overly stringent statistical tests when evaluating treatments. Thus, the biostatistician would opt for more conservative methods while the clinical researcher opts for more liberal methods. These perspectives often lead to substantially different decisions and practices, though both groups are trained to recognize and deal with reliability and validity issues. We as researchers are often unaware of these implicit values, because we tend to follow convention in our field, doing what we were trained to do and being surrounded by people who do the same. Thus, biostatisticians are surrounded by others who maintain the same inferential risk values, as are clinical researchers. Neither perspective is necessarily wrong, but they do produce different decisions. One primary goal of this book is to make researchers aware of the implicit values behind the selection of various missing data strategies in order to facilitate informed decision making with respect to missing data. Treating missing data can be characterized by a series of decisions that are closely tied to both implicit and explicit values.

With missing data, a researcher ought to change the level of inferential risk based on these values. For example, if the main priority of a study is generalizability, it ought to have a different approach to missing data than a study whose main priority is high internal validity. In the first study, missing data that limit sample variability are detrimental, whereas in the second study, limiting sample variability would be optimal (not to suggest you should limit variability by tolerating missing data!). If researchers adhere to the process of explicitly stating the purpose or goals of a study, no single procedure will be a panacea for missing data. Rule-bound or practice-bound researchers will find little comfort in the pages ahead, since we stress that missing data situations are often unique. It behooves the researcher to carefully consider the costs and benefits of the missing data decisions.

The Facets of Costs and Benefits

The two facets of research that concern scientists are reliability and validity.[2] Reliability addresses the replicability or consistency of the observed findings and conclusions based on the data. If study findings fail to replicate, then the phenomena of interest are not well addressed by the methods, theory, and/or data used in the study. Similarly, if the findings are not consistent across all related outcomes, then the results may lack a suitable level of reliability. Validity—internal, external, and construct—concerns the issue of sound causal inference. Internal validity relates to the extent to which we can infer that the observed outcome is related to the independent or manipulated variable of interest. Internal validity is decreased when plausible rival hypotheses exist that the researcher has either failed to control for or failed to anticipate. External validity relates to the applicability of the findings to other observations or samples, settings, and constructs. The term *causal generalization* (e.g., Cook, 2004) refers to the broad notion of causal stability and external validity. Construct validity relates to the appropriateness of the measurements to yield accurate and worthy indicators of the constructs of interest. For example, whether an IQ test is a valid measure of intelligence is a question of construct validity. If measures are poor indicators of the theoretical constructs of interest, then information provided by statistical procedures may provide a poor test of the theory.

Regardless of the research content, researchers strive to maximize all three of these facets. Therefore, our discussion of costs and benefits with respect to addressing missing data will be constrained to these facets. There are other more worldly costs to these decisions, such as economic costs. If researchers considered the cost per unit analyzed, most investigators might be more motivated to carefully scrutinize lost data. Costs, however, we leave to economists and to the reader to address independently, since they are likely to be unique as well as quite variable between studies.

Missing data constitute threats to different forms of reliability, validity, and generalizability of study results. As detailed elsewhere in this volume, the application or nonapplication of different solutions to those problems can impact these threats directly. Therefore, handling of missing data is directly relevant to competing reliability, validity, and generalizability concerns. Because these concerns need to be considered relative to each other's competing demands, the judicious selection of treatment for missing data becomes likewise relative to this optimal tradeoff.

The Relationship between Costs and Benefits

Decisions that enhance one facet (e.g., external validity) may do so at the expense of another facet (e.g., internal validity). Simply put, costs and benefits may not be completely independent and may, in fact, be negatively correlated. Social science researchers have argued among themselves about the tradeoffs between experimental control and ecological validity. The argument provides insight into the mutual exclusivity of internal validity and generalizability. Researchers who value internal validity may operate at the expense of generalizability or, more importantly, at the expense of mundane realism.[3] Therefore, the valuing of each facet forms the basis for decision making when preventing, diagnosing, and treating missing data. Without knowledge of study priorities regarding these facets, the researcher is left to accept prescriptions from others who may not share the same priorities. For example, some critics appear to consider it akin to "cheating" to estimate missing data. We acknowledge that there is indeed an inferential risk in any method of estimating missing data. Nevertheless, this risk has to be considered in relation to the inferential risk of *not* estimating missing data and leaving unaddressed the possible errors in hypothesis testing and the invalid generalizations that may ensue from not imputing missing data. In these cases, it might emphatically *not* be the case that a bird in the hand (observed data) is worth two in the bush (imputed data). The available data, although seemingly more solid, might be less representative, generalizable, and valid than a reconstructed sample including some merely "estimated" data.

MISSING DATA—NOT JUST FOR STATISTICIANS ANYMORE

In addition to taking a cost–benefit approach, we view missing data from a comprehensive perspective. The majority of the extant missing data literature focuses almost exclusively on treatment. As a result, almost all discussions of missing data begin and end with statistical procedures. The following chapters detail our more comprehensive perspective, beginning with the formulation of the study and ending with the final step of disseminating the results. Each step along the way involves decisions that impact missing data. Carefully considering the potential influences of missing data in each step provides researchers with more information on which to base decisions. In addition, understanding the values placed on each facet (i.e., reliability, validity, and generalizability) will make the decision process easier to communicate to others. We hope that after reading this book readers will come see the presence of missing data as something that can be described, prevented, treated, and discussed without relying solely on statistical methods.

A Functional Emphasis

The functional approach taken in this book reflects a fourfold approach to missing data:

1. Explore the possibilities of where missing data originate so that their presence might be minimized by thoughtful prevention strategies;
2. Derive the implications missing data might have for the outcome of any analysis in terms of the reliability, validity, and generalizability of study conclusions;
3. Consider the various statistical options for dealing with missing data, including methods of data deletion, imputation, and model estimation;
4. Investigate the probable consequences of the options considered in the previous step on the study's results and conclusions.

We believe that this functional approach to handling missing data has the additional advantage of further enhancing the comprehensibility of scientific contributions. It is likely that many social scientists are not only confused by the technical vocabulary surrounding statistical descriptions of missing data but also befuddled by the lack of a pragmatic frame of reference for this technical information. By framing the problem in a functional rather than purely structural context, we hope to make the "bottom-line" relevance of missing data issues clearer to social science researchers. Our intention is to render the information understandable and thus highly usable.

PURPOSE OF THIS BOOK

The primary goal of this book is to eliminate at least some of the plausible reasons why social scientists fail to attend to missing data. We present the technical information on missing data accurately but with minimal reliance on statistical or mathematical notation. When information is presented in formalized mathematical ways, we provide explanatory information so that the reader can interpret the notation without needing to know advanced mathematics. We also provide practical examples that convey many of these abstract descriptions more concretely. In addition to making the information more available to a non-technically inclined audience, we present practical solutions for handling missing data. We include all information that is relevant to implementing these solutions, regardless of the research design or statistical package used. Our goal is to raise researchers' awareness of the importance of missing data by eliminating at least some of the obstacles to their understanding of this typically technical information and to their using all the available tools for handling missing data to ameliorate the problems posed by it.

Another purpose of this book is to dispel the implicit myth that missing data is just a statistical matter. We will discuss missing data as a threat to the internal validity of causal inference and to the external validity or generalizability of research results (see Chapter 2). We hope that this book will serve as an introduction to the conceptual and methodological issues involved with handling missing data as well as a reference for students, researchers, and reviewers.

Chapter 2 addresses the consequences of missing data. We describe the many possible consequences of missing data to emphasize that missing data is an important issue in the social sciences. In Chapter 3, we turn our attention to the classification of missing data. Since statisticians and other formally trained or knowledgeable data analysts discuss missing data using specific terminology, it is important that the reader become familiar with that terminology. The information is presented in a manner that requires little if any knowledge of statistics or statistical formulas. At the conclusion of our discussion of these topics, we direct the reader to our approach to missing data. In Chapter 4, we discuss how to prevent missing data by designing studies to decrease the likelihood of missing data. We also discuss the elimination of errors in data handling that often result in missing data. Chapter 5 presents diagnostic procedures that will enable the data analyst and researcher to better appreciate the extent, pattern, and nature of the missing data. Since a great amount of thought must go into choosing the methods for treating missing data, we cover the decision making process in great detail in the following chapter (Chapter 6). The next group of chapters (Chapters 7–10) discuss statistical methods for handling missing data. Broadly, these chapters address deletion procedures, augmentation methods, single imputation, and multiple imputation procedures. In each chapter, the methods are described and examples are given. Finally, we conclude the book in Chapter 11 with recommendations for how to report missing data.

NOTES

1. We discuss these statistical "sleights of hand" in subsequent chapters that address diagnosing (Chapter 5) and handling missing data (Chapter 6).

2. Information about these concepts is covered in greater detail by Cook and Campbell (1979) and Shadish, Cook, and Campbell (2002). The information provided in this text is cursory and ought to serve only as a review.

3. "Mundane realism" is a term used by Aronson and Carlsmith (1968) in a chapter on experimental research methods in social psychology. The term refers to the correspondence of the research situation to the situation most likely to be observed outside the research setting.

2

Consequences of Missing Data

The overarching message we wish to convey in this book is that missing data are prevalent and can lead to problems that affect the interpretation of research results, and ultimately our understanding and explanation of the phenomena we study. In this chapter, we focus on the consequences of missing data so as to highlight and underscore the importance of attending to this often overlooked issue in research design and study interpretation. We focus on when and how missing data can occur and how different types of missing data lead to different problems that compromise study interpretation. More specifically, we discuss the impact of missing data on three broad facets of the scientific process: measurement, understanding relationships between variables, and drawing scientific conclusions. At the conclusion of this chapter, the reader should be well aware that the impact of missing data goes far beyond reducing the available sample size.

Missing data problems arise from three broad sources: missing cases, missing variables, and missing occasions (e.g., follow-up data). Missing cases occur when study participants fail to provide data for a study, for example, due to illness or otherwise failing to show up for the study. Missing variables occur when participants fail to provide data for some but not all variables, for example, due to skipping test items. Missing occasions occur when participants are available for some but not all of the data collection periods in a longitudinal study, such as is often the case due to attrition or study dropout. From these three sources (cases, variables, and occasions), missing data can occur at different stages of the research process, including participant recruitment, assignment to conditions (in experimental studies), data collection and maintenance, data entry, data analysis, and reporting results.

Additionally, the pattern, amount, and mechanism of missing data are relevant to their impact on study results. These facets, along with the source of missing data and the stage at which missing data occur, can interact in a variety of ways and impact a study differentially. Therefore, consequences of missing data can be seemingly countless. However, most, if not all, consequences of missing data on the scientific process can be organized into three general consequences, which are the focus of this chapter. The emphasis of this chapter is on the impact missing data can have on the scientific process. As we better understand the impact of missing data, we realize the importance of preventive measures as well as strategies for dealing with its occurrence. The following discussion is not exhaustive; however, it portrays the range of potential effects of missing data on the scientific process.

THREE GENERAL CONSEQUENCES OF MISSING DATA

The scientific method involves making structured observations, drawing causal inferences based on those observations, and generalizing study results beyond the confines of the study. For example, in a study of the effects of counseling on drug abuse, a researcher would make systematic observations related to counseling, drug abuse, and other relevant factors such as treatment and drug abuse history. From the observations, the researcher would draw inferences regarding the effect of counseling and other factors on drug abuse. From the study results, the researcher as well as the scientific community would hope to be able to draw some conclusions about counseling and drug abuse beyond the confines of the study itself, such as what type of counseling is effective, and for whom.

Missing data can have consequences for each of these three broad activities associated with the scientific method. It can affect the quality (i.e., reliability and validity) of our systematic observations. When drawing inferences from our observations, missing data can affect the strength of the study design and the validity of our conclusions about relationships between variables. When we generalize study results, missing data can limit the representativeness of the study sample, the strength and fidelity of interventions, and other study facets such as time or place about which we wish to generalize. Thus, missing data can have a wide range of consequences for the scientific process.

To organize the broad range of consequences of missing data into some general domains within the scientific process, we offer the framework presented in Figure 2.1. The figure represents three general areas of the scientific process that can be adversely affected by missing data.

Addressing the task of making structured observations, the first area is *construct validity*, depicted in gray, where constructs *A* and *B* are inferred through the use of indicators *V*1 through *V*6. Next, we have *internal validity*, expressed as the arrow between constructs *A* and *B*, addressing the task of causal inference. Finally, the large box surrounding the entire model represents the *causal generalization* (Cook, 1990; Shadish, Cook, & Campbell, 2002). We now discuss these three broad categories and the influence missing data may have on each.

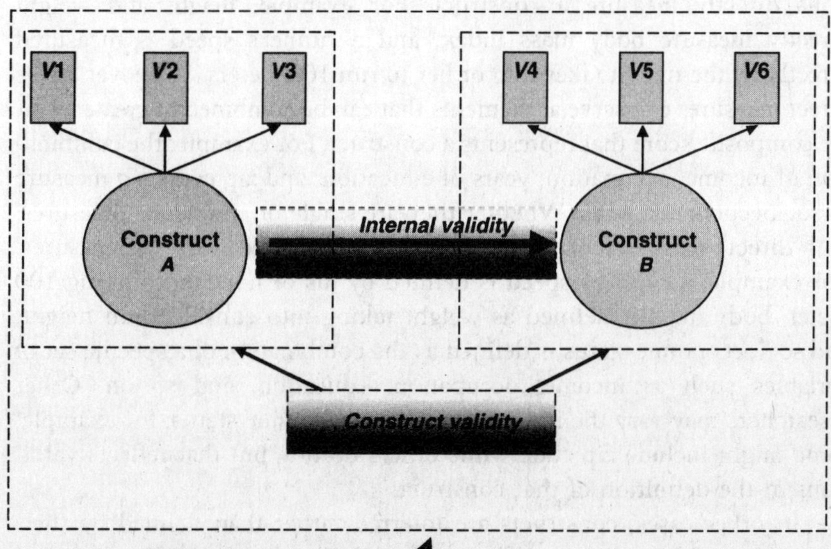

FIGURE 2.1. General areas of the scientific process.

CONSEQUENCES OF MISSING DATA ON CONSTRUCT VALIDITY

Missing data have the potential to influence the quality of the measurements we use to record our observations. In particular, missing data can affect the validity of our constructs. To avoid some of the problems with current and historical definitions of the term "construct validity," we adhere to the broad conception introduced by Cronbach and Meehl (1955), who noted, "the best construct is the one around which we can build the greatest number of inferences, in the most direct fashion" (p. 288). In essence, construct validity reflects how well our measures capture the constructs (or variables) we wish to observe and how well the scores on our measures predict other relevant variables. Regarding a measure of depression, for example, construct validity concerns include how well the measure captures the theoretical construct we call "depression" and the extent to which scores on this measure predict depressive behaviors. To assess construct validity, qualitative and quantitative methods of observation can be used from a variety of sources such as self-report and physiological or behavioral responses.

In the social and behavioral sciences, there are a variety of ways in which data are used to measure relevant variables. In some cases, observations directly measure a construct. For example, height and weight directly measure body mass index, and a runner's speed is measured directly by the time it takes him or her to run 100 meters. Moreover, these direct measures can serve as elements that can be combined to create a single composite score that represents a construct. For example, the combination of income, occupation, years of education, and zip code is a measure of socioeconomic status. Whether they are single or composite measures, with direct measurement the constructs are generated with the measures. For example, a runner's speed is defined by his or her time running 100 meter, body mass is defined as weight taking into consideration height, and socioeconomic status is defined as the combination of a specific set of variables such as income, occupation, education, and so on. Other researchers may vary the indicators of socioeconomic status; for example, some might include zip code while others do not, but that reflects variations in the definition of that construct.

In other cases, constructs are inferred rather than defined by their measures, much in the way a disease process is inferred by its symptoms. For example, we infer intelligence based on responses to items measuring various cognitive abilities, such as short-term memory and fund of knowledge. We infer self-esteem from responses to items assessing self-regard in areas as diverse as appearance and abilities. Constructs that are inferred are measured *indirectly* and are often called *latent* variables.

Regardless of these alternative measurement approaches, the goal is to represent the variables or constructs of interest as accurately as possible. Missing data can hinder researchers in meeting this objective, and the extent of the hindrance to some degree depends on whether the researcher uses a single measure (*mono-operations*) or multiple measures to capture the same construct. We discuss the impact of missing data on construct validity in mono-operations and in multiple measures situations.

Missing Data and Mono-operations

Researchers often use a single measure made up of either a single item or multiple items to represent a concept or construct. This approach to measurement is known as *mono-operations*. A researcher might measure income based solely on earned wages, or cigarette smoking based on a single item indicating the number of cigarettes smoked in the last 24 hours, for example. The most obvious problem of missing data for variables measured in this manner is that when an individual is missing data for that single item, all information regarding that construct for that individual is missing—that is, an entire variable is missing for that case. Unless there are other variables in the model that are related to the missing variable, the lost information may not be replaceable, which then becomes a problem for statistical inference, which we discuss in the following section.

In mono-operations where researchers employ a single measure consisting of multiple items to assess a variable, other problems can arise. When data for at least one of the items is missing, the ability of the measure to capture the variable of interest can be impaired. When items are highly correlated, missing item data might not be detrimental to construct validity, because data from the observed items can compensate for what is missing, depending on how the measure is scored. When items are highly correlated, missing values often can be justifiably replaced with observed values or the mean of the observed items, for example. However, when items are not highly correlated, missing items can be detrimental to the measure. In a measure of depression made up of items measuring symptoms, for example, missing values for some items like suicidality would result in an incomplete picture of depression and possibly an inaccurate representation of an important variable in the study.

One primary concern regarding the impact of missing data on construct validity is the effect of missing data on the reliability of measures. Since validity requires reliability, any threat to reliability will also have an adverse influence on validity. One consequence of missing data for mono-operations involving the use of single measures consisting of multiple items is a decrease in internal consistency, an index of reliability for multiple item measures. Attenuation of the internal consistency can occur due to either the decreased number of items or the elimination of information available for the analysis (e.g., no information about suicidality in a measure of depression). Lord and Novick (1968) noted that a measure's internal consistency reliability (ρ^2 in Equation 2.1) is defined as the degree of true-score variation relative to observed-score variation:

$$\rho^2 = \sigma^2_{true} / \sigma^2_{observed} = 1 - (\sigma^2_{error} / \sigma^2_{observed}) \qquad (2.1)$$

where ρ^2 is the reliability of the measure, σ^2_{true} is the true variability in the phenomena of interest, $\sigma^2_{observed}$ is the variation observed with our measure, and σ^2_{error} is the unexplained variability in the measure. Given its place in the equation, the reader should note that variance in the error term (σ^2_{error}) is important for the determination of reliability. As the error variance increases, reliability decreases. With respect to missing data, lost information can give rise to larger amounts of error variance.

According to classical test theory (see Lord & Novick, 1968, for details), a measure's internal consistency reliability is strongly related to the number of items. The Spearman-Brown prophecy formula dictates that as the number of items increases, reliability increases. In contrast, as the number of items decreases, reliability of the measure decreases. Because missing items in a measure result in even fewer items (and thus the possibility for more error variance), the likely result of this type of missing data is reduced measurement reliability.

Modern measurement theory (e.g., the Rasch model and Item Response Theory, IRT) holds that there is no definitive relationship between the number of items or indicators and the reliability of the measure. Instead, the actual performance of each item and the interrelationships among items dictate the measure's reliability. Therefore, the internal consistency of a measure is highly dependent on the item variances and covariances, and dependent to a lesser extent on the number of items. A short measure consisting of only a few highly reliable items would be more reliable than a measure with many poor items, according to modern measurement theory. Moreover, modern measurement theorists note that missing data can affect items differentially and therefore have unpredictable results for reliability. In sum, according to both classical test theory and modern measurement theory, measurement reliability is potentially threatened by missing data. Reduced reliability in turn reduces construct validity; that is, validity is called into question when a measure cannot consistently capture the construct it is intended to measure.

Measurement bias is another potential problem with missing data under mono-operations. For single measures composed of multiple items or indicators, construct validity can be affected by missing data, because the information obtained may reflect only a portion of the construct of interest (i.e., mono-operations bias). For example, if an index of socioeconomic status includes income, education, and occupation, and one or more of these indicators are missing, the construct is incomplete. The problem is compounded if the missing information is also the most critical component of the construct. For example, for a measure of quality of graduate schools, if job placement after graduation is the strongest indicator, missing data for that indicator can change the meaning of the measure due to the loss of information on that critical facet. In short, the construct coverage and therefore the construct validity are threatened. Mono-operations measurement with missing data leads to inconsistencies between the measured construct and its theoretical definition. As a consequence, the scores obtained provide an inaccurate as well as imprecise reflection of an individual's standing on the construct.

Missing Data and Multiple Measures

Researchers employ a method of critical multiplism (Shadish, 1994) by using multiple measures of the same construct. The goal is for these measures to converge (or *triangulate*) on the construct, thereby increasing the likelihood that it has been adequately captured by the measurement process. In many ways, the use of multiple measures protects researchers from problems stemming from missing data that occur when only a single measure is used. With multiple measures of the same construct, if data are missing for one or two measures, the others can still provide information about that construct, and therefore all is not lost. If a single measure was used and data were missing for that measure, information about that construct is generally much more difficult, and in some cases impossible, to recover.

Missing data problems can arise even when multiple measures of a single construct are used, however. When data are missing for the same variable across multiple measures, reliability and construct validity will suffer. For example, some study participants might object to providing personal information such as illegal substance use. If the study requires a reasonable assessment of substance use, and all relevant measures are missing this information for these participants, the use of multiple measures cannot provide alternative sources of information, as would be the case if only one or two measures were missing data.

As noted with regard to mono-operations, in classical test theory the number of items used to measure a construct is directly related to its reliability; more items increase reliability. The assumption is borne out in the Spearman-Brown prophecy formula (Crocker & Algina, 1986) whereby reliability is directly related to the number of items. Data that are systematically missing for a particular construct (e.g., illegal substance use) decrease the number of items, which in turn reduces reliability. Because the validity of measures is related to reliability, we should expect that less reliable instruments produce a less valid measure of the construct we intend to measure.[1] In the most dire measurement situation, all measures of a particular construct are missing (e.g., all measures of substance use). In Figure 2.1, this situation would occur if data for *V1*, *V2*, and *V3*, for example, were missing. In that case, construct A could not be measured.

Another problem relevant to multiple measures arises during the attempt to statistically recapture the missing information associated with missing data. Consider the case where illegal substance use data are missing for respondents who use drugs somewhat regularly. To recapture that lost information statistically, the data analyst must rely on the existing data provided by other respondents and perhaps observations from other variables related to substance use (we discuss these methods in detail in Chapters 7–10). Recapturing missing data that are completely missing for a construct for a subset of respondents tends to be problematic, because the observed data may not be terribly informative and therefore may lead to inappropriate estimates of the missing information. For example, the observed data may be misleading because those who provided the data are systematically different (e.g., non-drug users) from those who did not. Moreover, if respondents who failed to provide substance use data also failed to provide other data that may help estimate substance use (e.g., criminal, employment, or social history), the information recapture may be fruitless.

Despite these potential problems, multiple measures are almost always preferred to single measures, since there is less likelihood that the missing data will lead to uncorrectable problems. The use of multiple measures of a single construct can reduce the problems due to missing data because there are multiple sources of data and it is highly likely that not all of those sources will be missing. (But see Chapter 4 for a discussion on tradeoffs between the benefits of more measures and the costs in terms of respondent burden.)

CONSEQUENCES OF MISSING DATA ON INTERNAL VALIDITY

Beyond affecting the construct validity, missing data can affect both the reliability (i.e., stability, consistency, or reproducibility) and validity (i.e., accuracy, verisimilitude, or generalizability) of research findings. These facets are related to the internal validity of a study, which we define shortly. In Figure 2.1, internal validity is reflected by the ability to infer that *A* caused *B*. The reliability or reproducibility of study findings in this example would be shown if the relationship between *A* and *B* (illustrated with the arrow) could be reproduced in other studies. The validity of the relationship has to do with the true nature of the association between *A* and *B*. Both the reliability and validity of this relationship can be affected by missing data. If large portions of data are missing in any one study, for example, the data set used for analyses represents a smaller and potentially biased sample of participants, leading to inaccurate and unstable parameter estimates, respectively. In Figure 2.1, this means an inaccurate and unstable estimate of the relationship between *A* and *B*. Consequently, the reproducibility and validity of study findings is jeopardized. These two outcomes in turn lead to weaker causal inferences regarding the relationships between variables and thus lower internal validity.

Campbell and Stanley (1966), Cook and Campbell (1979), and Shadish et al. (2002) described in detail possible threats to internal validity for causal inference. "Internal validity," a term used with experimental and quasi-experimental studies, is often characterized as the extent to which a researcher can reasonably claim that a particular factor, usually an intervention of some sort, is responsible for the outcome(s) observed. The influence of other factors—confounds or alternative explanations for the outcome—weaken the inference that the experimental factor caused the outcome. These other factors are known as *threats to internal validity*, some of which are briefly addressed in Table 2.1. As shown in the table, missing data can contribute to different biases or threats to the validity of findings. In this section, we organize our discussion around elements of research

TABLE 2.1. Consequences of Missing Data

Type of consequence	Type of missing data	Aspect of study affected
Measurement (reliability, construct validity)	Measurement (items, single measures, multiple measures of the construct with data missing)	1. ↓ item pool → ↑ error variance → ↓ reliability of measure 2. ↓ information → incomplete representation of concepts → ↓ validity of measure
Reliability and validity of study results (internal validity)	Sample selection (differences between participants and nonparticipants, completers and noncompleters, participants with complete data vs. those with incomplete data)	Differences in characteristics of these groups → selection bias → unrepresentative sample → ↓ external validity
	Randomization 1. Nonparticipation 2. Data missing differentially	1. ↓ sample size → initial nonequivalence → ↓ internal validity 2. Initial nonequivalence → ↓ internal validity
	Participant attrition (differential)	1. Initial nonequivalence → ↓ internal validity 2. Unequal group size → violate statistical assumptions → ↓ statistical conclusion validity
	Data analysis (sample sizes)	↓ statistical power and violate distributional assumptions → ↓ statistical conclusion validity
Generalizability of results, policy implications	Any or all of the above	Any or all of the above problems → difficulty with statistical inference and interpretation of findings → inaccurate knowledge base → misinformed and possibly misleading policy recommendations

Note. Right arrows should be read as "leads to," and up and down arrows indicate a resulting increase or decrease.

design and analysis of study findings, both of which are components of internal validity. These elements include selection bias, failure of randomization, participant attrition, and issues associated with statistical inference (e.g., reduced statistical power).

Selection Bias

Generally speaking, *selection bias* refers to systematic differences on some characteristics between groups of individuals included in the study, such as those in the experimental and control groups (Shadish et al., 2002). Such between-group differences can influence study conclusions. When applied to the problem of missing data, broadly defined here as the lack of observations on subgroups of the target population, selection bias entails differences on some characteristics relevant to the study conclusion between (1) participants who completed the study (completers) versus those who did not (dropouts), (2) participants with complete data and those with incomplete data, and (3) individuals who consented to participate and those who refused to take part in the study. We discuss empirical studies assessing differences between the first two categories (study completers vs. dropouts and those with complete vs. incomplete data).

Completers versus Dropouts

Differences between participants who completed the study and those who did not have been reported in multiple studies. Sidani, McKnight, and McKnight (1997), for example, found differences between cases with complete and missing data in an experimental study with repeated measures. The study evaluated the effectiveness of an intervention to enhance women's adjustment to breast cancer and its treatment. Detailed analyses showed that cases with complete data across all occasions of measurement were on average younger than those with data missing on at least one posttest occasion. Conceivably, the difference in age, rather than the intervention, could explain differences in the outcome variables and therefore threaten the internal validity of the study.

Differences between completers and dropouts on various demographic and outcome variables have been reported in a variety of studies. Wade, Treat, and Stuart (1998) found that completers were older, with more years of education, reported "longer standing panic and agoraphobic symptoms, fewer depressive symptoms, and less antidepressant medication use at intake . . . and [were] less likely to have one or more comorbid conditions than those who dropped out" (pp. 235–236). Tix and Frazier (1998) reported that participants in a longitudinal study who completed only one of the two post-surgery follow-ups (i.e., dropouts) were less likely to be married, perceived less social support, and reported less life satisfaction than those who completed both follow-ups. Moser, Dracup, and Doering (2000) reported that participants who failed to complete a longitudinal trial were more frequently employed outside the home; had higher levels of depression, hostility, and general psychological distress; and held less optimistic views about the effectiveness of health care.

The examples illustrate that it is not always possible, or even accurate, to assume that completers and dropouts are equivalent on all measured and unmeasured variables. Systematic differences between the two groups may be responsible for the study outcome rather than the intervention itself, thus compromising internal validity. Furthermore, these differences may render the final sample unrepresentative of the target population. The study results, therefore, are applicable to only one portion of the population. Their generalizability is limited (Gibbons et al., 1993; Kaufman, 1988; Moser et al., 2000), a consequence we address in our discussion of causal generalization. Moreover, significant differences on demographic and baseline characteristics between completers and dropouts may produce a final sample that tends to be homogeneous relative to these variables. Increased sample homogeneity influences the magnitude of parameter estimates in correlation studies and may artificially inflate the observed treatment effects in experimental studies. Furthermore, these sample-specific parameters are not easily reproduced; thus the replicability of the findings is jeopardized.

Participants with Complete versus Incomplete Data

Differences between participants who provide complete data for all measures and those who do not have been examined less frequently. Tix and Frazier (1998) reported that 24% of patients and 20% of their significant others did not complete an instrument measuring religious coping. They found that patients who responded to the religious coping scale had higher scores on the Chance Control scale of the Health Locus of Control scale than those who did not. The nonresponders expressed having no religious preference. These empirical findings suggest that various personal characteristics of participants influence nonresponse to some items. If these characteristics occur differentially across study groups (e.g., Treatment A vs.

control), observed differences in outcome may not be due to the treatment, which may thus threaten internal validity.

Randomization

Randomization is used to counteract the influence of confounding variables on study results. By randomly assigning participants to different intervention groups, the researcher hopes to create groups that are equivalent on a variety of measured and unmeasured variables prior to intervention. Initial group equivalence helps to rule out confounding variables as the potential cause of the observed outcome.

Randomizing participants is often viewed as a guarantee for obtaining equivalent groups prior to intervention, which is critical for enhancing internal validity. If groups are equally distributed with respect to potential confounds such as age, severity of symptoms, willingness to participate, and so on, it is more plausible that the intervention is responsible for the outcome rather than a characteristic present in one group and not the other. However, when data are missing, two things can happen that threaten the ability to obtain initial group equivalence. First, missing data reduce the total sample size. Randomization relies on what statisticians refer to as the *law of large numbers*. To obtain initial group equivalence on participant characteristics that might serve as confounds to the study, it is important that the researcher has many participants to randomly assign to groups. When there are few to randomize, it is more likely that participant characteristics are not evenly distributed across groups. It is much more difficult to obtain an even distribution of age or gender, for example, in a sample of 10 versus a sample of 100. With smaller samples, randomization is more likely to fail to produce initial group equivalence.

Second, if data are missing differentially among the experimental groups, the likelihood that the groups differ on measured or unmeasured characteristics increases. Those differences may be at the baseline or pretreatment stages of the study. Therefore, initial group equivalence may not be attained, and these group differences may account for the observed differences after treatment, and again, they may pose a threat to internal validity. For example, if more individuals in the control group were missing data on depression symptoms at baseline, it would be difficult to conclude that decreased symptoms were the result of treatment and not of these initial and relevant differences that were present in the study groups to begin with.

Participant Attrition

Studies that involve multiple measures over time present many problems for researchers, especially when data are missing for some of those measurement occasions. Retention of participants in longitudinal studies may fail for varied reasons, and the failure to capture all data for all occasions presents serious threats to internal validity. When attrition or mortality affects treatment groups, the ability to attribute outcomes to the intervention is seriously jeopardized. Biases result when the dropout rates differ among the study groups.

Several factors can lead to differential attrition. Personal, psychosocial, and health-related variables have been found to affect an individual's decision to complete or leave a study. When a study group includes more participants with such characteristics than another group, the result may be more dropouts. The consequences of such differences are usually detrimental to the validity of study results. First, the final sample forms a subgroup that risks poorly representing the target population. Second, groups may have different attributes that serve as confounds, and thereby threaten the internal validity of the study. That is, differences in the outcomes demonstrated among the groups at posttest cannot be claimed, with confidence, to be caused only by the intervention, because they may be associated with these other factors. Finally, the number of cases included in the study groups is unequal. Unbalanced cell sizes may limit the use of some statistical tests (if deletion methods are used; see Chapter 7) and may reduce statistical power to detect significant treatment effects. Unequal cell sizes may result in the violation of two assumptions, normality and homogeneity of variance, that are the basis of the *t*-test and the *F*-test. Under these conditions, alternative formulas for these tests should be used to minimize the error of inference (Keppel & Wickens, 2004).

A mismatch between participants' preferences for treatment and their assignment to study groups could contribute to differential attrition bias as well. Participants may favor one intervention option over another. For example, when a new and promising intervention is being introduced, individuals often prefer that intervention to the control condition. Preference, however, is not taken into account with random assignment. In the presence of a strong preference for treatment, random assignment creates two subgroups within the sample: those who are satisfied and those who are not satisfied with the treatment allocated. The two groups may react differently throughout the study. Disappointed individuals may drop out of the study (Bradley, 1993; McPherson &

Britton, 2001). If groups are nonequivalent with respect to satisfaction with group assignment, that would result in differential attrition and might influence study outcomes.

Differential attrition also results in unequal group size. As noted previously, missing data reduce the sample size and thus the power to detect significant treatment effects. They also influence the magnitude of the effect size through either artificial inflation from uncontrolled extraneous factors or attenuation from increased within-group variance. Traditional statistical procedures employed in social science research are ill-suited for these conditions, yet researchers are often unaware of these problems.

Data Analysis

Although the effects of missing data are potential problems for reliability and validity of study findings, the adverse effects on statistical procedures are almost expected to be present. For example, statistical power (i.e., the probability that a null hypothesis will be rejected if the null hypothesis is false) is directly related to sample size. As the sample size decreases, statistical power decreases. Missing data often result in a smaller sample size and lower statistical power. Missing data might also have ramifications for certain statistical assumptions. Many statistical procedures assume a particular distribution for data or error (usually Gaussian normal), and missing data can affect these distributions in important ways. When missing data affect statistical conclusions, they pose a threat to internal validity by calling into question the accuracy of conclusions about the relationships between the study variables.

With respect to statistical power, missing data can have a variety of effects. Often, social scientists eliminate cases with missing data from data analyses (see Chapter 7 for data deletion methods), and frequently do so unwittingly. Whether the analysis is univariate or multivariate, missing data reduce the total number of cases when deletion methods are used. A smaller sample size reduces statistical power to detect significant parameters in correlation or comparative analyses. Low power is a threat to statistical conclusion validity, because it increases the likelihood of Type II error[2] (Ward & Clark, 1991).

When missing data are present in multivariate analyses, sample size and, therefore, statistical power are decreased drastically, particularly when different subgroups of cases have incomplete data for different subsets of variables. For example, if 10% of the cases in group *A* have missing values on variable *X*, and if another 10% of the cases in group *B* have missing data on variable *Y*, the total sample used to estimate the correlation between variables *X* and *Y* is reduced by 20% when missing values occur on several variables that are analyzed simultaneously. This is exacerbated when the initial sample size is small, a common problem in experimental studies that evaluate treatments. A small number of cases is often associated with increased within-group variance, small effect sizes, and consequently low power to detect significant treatment effects.

Statistical power is also related to the magnitude of the statistical effect, often referred to as the effect size (see Cohen, 1988, for a thorough discussion). In Figure 2.1, the magnitude of the relationship between *A* and *B* is measured by its effect size. Measurement reliability is an important component of effect size. As noted previously, missing data can reduce measurement reliability. As reliability decreases, effect sizes decrease and statistical power decreases. These interrelated factors all produce problems when analyzing data with missing values.

Missing data can also have dramatic effects on data analysis in how they distribute data and error. These effects can be better appreciated by understanding why distributional assumptions are important. Parametric tests, commonly used by social scientists, assume a specific underlying distribution. For example, the commonly used least squares analyses (e.g., analysis of variance, ANOVA; multiple regression) require errors (residuals) to be normally distributed. Failure to conform to these assumptions produces inaccuracies in the results that often dramatically affect significance tests and occasionally affect parameter estimates.

Missing data increase the likelihood that data do not conform to the assumed distribution when data are complete. In fact, analyses that require more stringent assumptions, such as multivariate normality, are almost guaranteed to be adversely affected by missing data (although Chapter 10 introduces statistical methods that can be quite useful for handling such data problems). Consider several hypothetical distributions in Figures 2.2–2.5. In the social and behavioral sciences, it is assumed that most observed data are either normally distributed or sampled from a true normal distribution of population values. Figure 2.2 represents the population distribution, Figure 2.3 represents the sample distribution, Figure 2.4 represents the analyzed sample distribution (with missing data), and Figure 2.5 displays the error distribution. The sample and population distributions are essentially equal; however, the sample available for analysis is distinctly different from the two previous distributions. The error distribution is important because significance tests rely on normally distributed

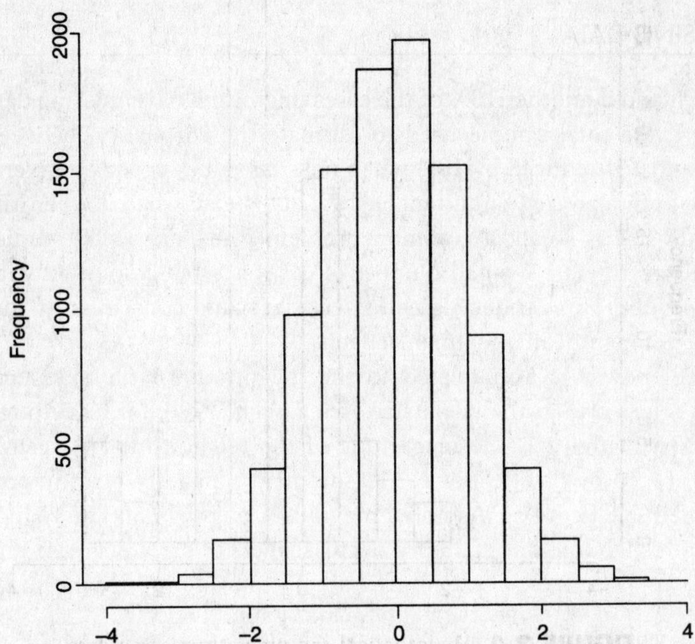

FIGURE 2.2. Hypothetical distribution of population data.

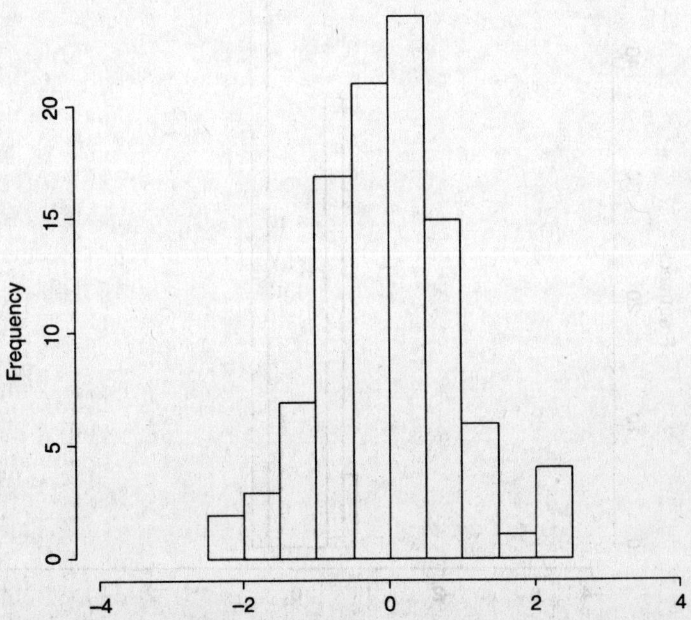

FIGURE 2.3. Hypothetical distribution of sample data.

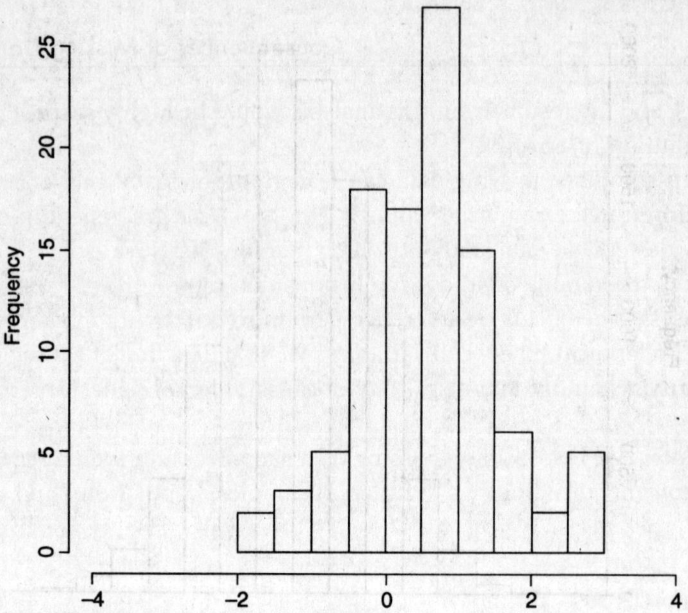

FIGURE 2.4. Hypothetical sample with missing data.

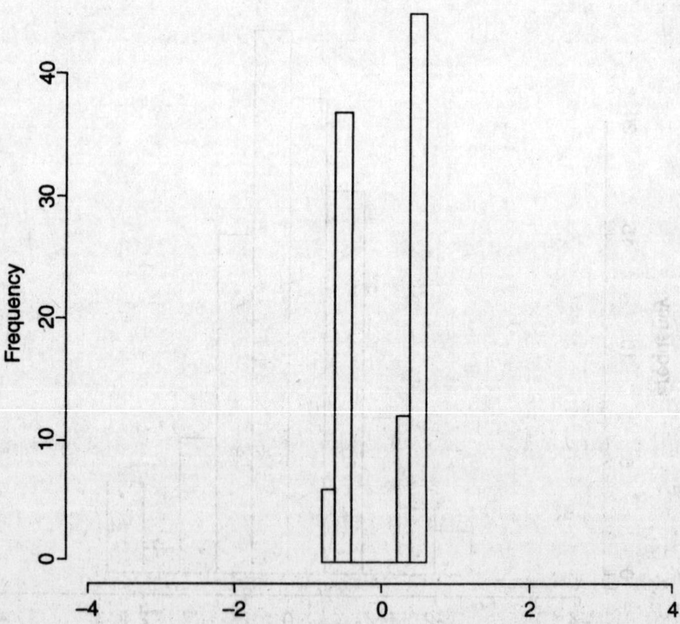

FIGURE 2.5. Hypothetical error distribution associated with missing data.

errors, and the results from this analysis would be highly suspect given the distribution of error.

In summary, missing data can lead to problems of inference and can therefore threaten internal validity. The problems are generally related to study design and data analysis, which includes statistical conclusion validity (i.e., the validity of study conclusions that can be drawn from statistical analyses). The effects on inference pertain to our ability to validly claim a causal relationship between variables. Missing data that affect the strength, integrity, reliability, and/or validity of causal inference affect internal validity.

Next, we discuss how missing data can affect how well researchers are able to generalize findings to different samples, populations, and measurement operations. We discuss these as threats to causal generalization.

CONSEQUENCES FOR CAUSAL GENERALIZATION

Missing data can influence the interpretation of findings in a single study, the synthesis of results across studies, and the process of building a sound knowledge base in a field. Most missing data discussions stop at the level of reliability and validity of single study findings. However, broader implications exist for results derived from samples with missing data, including implications for science and for policy. Global consequences of missing data are at the level of theory building and testing. Essentially, consequences include the effects of missing data on the pursuit of knowledge and understanding in a field, which in turn can influence policy decision making.

Science, as a human enterprise, is characterized as self-correcting. Over time, mistakes due to measurement, research design, data analysis, and conclusions are correctable by subsequent efforts in the same areas. Theories that fail to hold in repeated trials are often discarded in favor of more useful theories (Kuhn, 1970; Lakatos, 1978). Some debate exists as to whether theories are ever completely discarded in fields such as psychology, but the scientific ideal is to overthrow theories that have outlived their utility. Thus, the process of scientific inquiry maintains a self-corrective feedback loop.

Unfortunately, if the same errors continue to be propagated throughout all similar efforts (e.g., research programs), then the same biases are repeated and no correction can take place. For example, a great proportion of psychological research has been and continues to be derived from samples of college undergraduate psychology majors, sometimes called the "college sophomore problem" (e.g., Stanovich, 2004). Several researchers have criticized this practice (e.g., Dawes, 1994), yet it remains commonplace. The problem with deriving the majority of knowledge from a single population is the potential bias and limited generalizability of the findings. The phenomenon of interest may behave differently for college students than for the general population for a variety of reasons, including age, cognitive processing, familiarity with research and testing, and so on. Findings regarding alcohol abuse with undergraduates, for example, may not apply to the general public.

Likewise, if missing data are prevalent in all research areas and few researchers make an effort to either prevent or treat the problem in a sensible fashion, the same errors are likely to continue. In meta-analysis, for example, there is concern about publication bias resulting from the "file drawer problem," which is essentially a missing data problem. Meta-analysis is a quantitative approach to summarizing empirical findings in a particular area (e.g., treatments for adolescent depression). The meta-analyst obtains results from quantitative studies and combines them using specific statistical methods to get an overall estimate of effect size for a variety of parameters, including intervention effects or the magnitude of the relationship between two variables. Generally, the data used for meta-analyses come from published studies. Critics argue that published studies do not represent the entire domain of research in a particular area. Specifically, studies unable to produce statistically significant results are stored in the file drawer and therefore fail to contribute to the meta-analysis results. Some argue that this type of missing data has produced biased and therefore misleading meta-analytic results (e.g., Rosenthal, 1984), thus compromising what is regarded as scientific knowledge in a particular field.

Missing data present problems well beyond basic research that adversely affect social and public policy evaluation. A recent education policy evaluation illustrates the impact missing data may have on broader policy. In a *New York Times* article, "What Some Much-Noted Data Really Showed About Vouchers" (Winerip, May 7, 2003), the results of a widely cited study (Peterson, Myers, & Howell, 1998) were brought into question. The study, described as "the most ambitious randomized experiment on vouchers to date," claimed that school vouchers significantly improved test scores of African American children. The original study created quite a sensation and gained political backing for education policy regarding school vouchers. However, after the data were made public, Princeton economist Alan B. Krueger reanalyzed the data (Krueger & Zhu, 2004) and concluded that Peterson's results may be misleading due to missing data. The original study had failed to include 292 African American students' test scores, and after including them, Krueger's results suggested that vouchers made no difference for any group. Incomplete background data caused the elimination of 214 African American students from the results, because of incomplete background data, while the remainder had been incorrectly classified by race. Krueger's inclusion of these students expanded the total number of African American students from 519 to 811, and the differences detected in Peterson's analyses disappeared, thus calling into question the knowledge and policy built on a study rife with incomplete data.

The voucher study represents an excellent example of how missing data affect the generalizability of findings. In particular, the observed effects were likely attributable in part to the resulting sample that participated in the study. A related problem associated with missing data and resultant samples is the effect of nonparticipation on causal generalization. Social and behavioral scientists generally assume, whether wittingly or not, that study participants represent the population to which the scientists hope to generalize study findings. This assumption is reflected in the concept of *random selection*, which is assumed to mean that all members of the population of interest have an equal probability of being selected to participate in the study. That is, it is just as likely for one individual from that population to be selected as any other individual. Therefore, the sample of individuals who participate is representative of the larger population from which it came and to which the researcher hopes to generalize findings.

However, in social science research, study recruitment seldom employs a random selection process; more likely, those who are available and willing to participate are recruited. The resulting sample is often referred to as "convenience sample," for obvious reasons. Thus, in a sense, who participates or does not is a missing data problem. Those who would be eligible to participate but do not are essentially "missing data" on all study variables.

There is accumulating evidence that suggests that those who agree to participate in social science research differ systematically from those who do not. These differences involve characteristics that can have an effect on study interpretation. For instance, Schwartz and Fox (1995) found that clients who volunteer for psychosocial intervention studies tend to be female, Caucasian, unemployed, older, of lower socioeconomic status, and to have an internal orientation to locus of control and the motivation to improve their condition. Lack of interest in the research topic (Hox & de Leeuw, 1994) and logistical problems related to transportation are frequently reported reasons for refusal to participate in a study (e.g., Kotwall, Mahoney, Myers, & Decoste, 1992). In contrast, intellectual and emotional satisfaction, need for approval, desire to be altruistic, and compliance with authority are identified as reasons for participation in surveys (Barribal & While, 1999). Kaslow et al. (1998) conducted a descriptive correlational study on physical and nonphysical abuse and suicidal behavior in African American women, and found that women who refused to participate were older than those who volunteered, which may have produced a biased view of this topic.

In addition to individual participant characteristics, the design of the study may affect the decision to participate. Individuals may refuse to volunteer in a randomized clinical trial (RCT), for example, for two interrelated reasons: unwillingness to be randomized and a strong preference for one of the treatment options presented to them. When presented with two treatment options, individuals might decline enrollment in an RCT if they highly favor one of the two options and if they are aware that they may have only a 50% chance of receiving it (Awad, Shapiro, Lund, & Feine, 2000; Brewin & Bradley, 1989; McPherson & Britton, 2001). Llewellyn-Thomas, McGreal, Thiel, Fine, and Erlichman (1991) found that only 2 of 22 patients (9%) with a preference for the usual treatment agreed to participate in an RCT, while 22 of 36 patients (61%) with a preference for the experimental treatment agreed. If this pattern of patient preference is repeated across RCTs in general, the data that are missing from the individuals who have declined enrollment are likely biased and may produce misleading results about the interventions.

Similarly, in survey design, the research topic (e.g., interest in the research topic, sensitivity of the topic) and mode of administration (e.g., mailed out questionnaire, face-to-face or telephone interview) are considered key factors influencing an individual's decision to volunteer in a research study (Cooper & Groves, 1996). Therefore, individuals who participate in research differ in personal characteristics from those who are eligible but decline participation. They form a select subgroup and do not represent the full spectrum of the target population. Thus, the obtained sample likely does not adequately represent the various subgroups comprising the target population.

Lack of sample representativeness limits the external validity of a study's conclusions. That is, the results are not applicable to all subgroups of the population of interest, in which the subgroups are defined by the differences in the characteristics of participants and nonparticipants who met the eligibility criteria. When external validity is affected, decision making based on the results of such studies may not be wise, as is shown by the school voucher study.

SUMMARY

Missing data can have an effect on science at an immediate and direct level—a level on which the psychometric properties of measures might be affected (construct validity). Missing data can also have an effect on more indirect levels, in which the interpretation (internal validity) and generalizability (causal generalization) of study results and broader consequences involving theory testing/generation, decision making, and public policy are affected. Thus, prevention and correction for missing data can lead to dramatic changes from previous practice in the social and behavioral sciences. Improving research practice might have subtle effects in the short term, but it may have profound effects for changing the course of knowledge development and policy making based on that knowledge.

NOTES

1. There are three general uses of the term reliability: (1) internal consistency, (2) equivalence, and (3) stability (Wiggins, 1973, 1988). Each of these can refer to consistency or stability in different realms (e.g., across items, over time, across judges). See Wiggins (1973, 1988) for a detailed discussion.

2. Type I error refers to false rejection of the null hypothesis (Keppel & Wickens, 2004). Type II error refers to failing to reject the null hypothesis when it is false (Keppel & Wickens, 2004)

3

Classifying Missing Data

People develop classification systems for a variety of reasons. One reason is to facilitate communication. Psychologists and other mental health care professionals use the *Diagnostic and Statistical Manual of Mental Disorders*, 4th ed., text revision (DSM-IV-TR; American Psychiatric Association, 2000) to communicate with other mental health care professionals, patients, insurance companies, and so on, about an individual's complex of symptoms. Rather than providing an exhaustive description of each of the symptoms, the psychologist can use the classification system to give that complex of symptoms a name, thus facilitating communication. The name communicates features of these symptoms, etiology, treatment, and prognosis.

Classification systems also aid in recognition. A classification system lists the criteria for a particular type within the system, such as the criteria for obsessive–compulsive disorder (OCD). In many cases, we are interested in recognition of a type to inform us about action. If a pattern of symptoms were recognized and labeled OCD, the expected course of action would be quite different than if it were recognized to be schizophrenia. This form of recognition is more commonly known as diagnosis.

Statisticians have developed a classification system for missing data in order to facilitate communication, diagnose the problem, and identify the proper remedy. As we discuss in this chapter, different types of missing data are associated with different consequences that influence the course of action to remedy the problem. Thus, as in medicine, diagnosis informs treatment. Sometimes the diagnosis indicates that there is no remedy available, as in the case of a terminal illness. This can also be the case with the diagnosis of missing data.

In this chapter, we discuss the dominant classification system for missing data in the statistical literature. We discuss its limitations and suggest a more comprehensive approach that uses information about the reasons for and sources of missing data as well as the amount and pattern of what is missing. Our primary aim is to emphasize the relation between classifying missing data and selecting appropriate solutions for handling it. Individual solutions will be applicable only to certain conditions under which data are missing. If a solution is selected inappropriately, it can yield biased results—perhaps doing greater harm than the missing data problem itself.

The classification system we propose addresses missing data in a language consistent with research design. This language addresses the three goals of classification—communication, recognition (diagnosis), and treatment. The comprehensive system is an extension of Rubin's (1976) system, which is based on missing data mechanisms, and includes reasons, dimensions, amount, and pattern of missing data. Each of these facets is related to the impact missing data can have on parameter estimation, statistical hypothesis testing, and ultimately on the interpretation of study results. It is the impact of the missing data that should concern researchers.

"THE SILENCE THAT BETOKENS"

We start with a discussion of the various meanings that may be attributed to missing data. The primary concern is whether missing data are meaningfully and systematically missing. Although much has been written on the various possible causes of missing data, a historical illustration should help clarify the problem of distinguishing between meaningful and meaningless missing data. The award-winning motion picture *A Man for All Seasons* chronicled the political and ideological conflict between Sir Thomas More and King Henry VIII of England regarding the legitimacy of his second marriage, to Anne Boleyn, after his controversial divorce from

Catherine of Aragon. In 1535, as a test of loyalty to the English Crown in this political conflict, a document called the "Oath of Supremacy" was circulated among the Peers of the Realm asking them to endorse the legitimacy of the second marriage. This was a document that Sir Thomas refused to sign. Consequently, after much pressure to sign the document, he was arrested and put on trial for high treason. The prosecutor, Master Secretary Thomas Cromwell, made the case that refusal to sign the affidavit constituted evidence of disapproval of the marriage and thus opposition to the king.

Sir Thomas replied that an ancient Roman legal precept dictated that silence must be construed to imply consent rather than objection. Cromwell retorted that not all silences can be interpreted similarly, and that there is a difference between an innocent silence that signifies nothing in particular and what he called "a silence which betokens." Specifically, he charged that Sir Thomas's persistent refusal to sign the document was a silence that clearly "betokened" his opposition to the royal marriage. The rest, as they say, is history. Sir Thomas was convicted of treason and soon was beheaded. Four hundred years later he was canonized by the Roman Catholic Church (becoming St. Thomas More).

Missing data lie along a continuum between a "silence that betokens" and an "innocent" silence. Those that lie closer to the "silence that betokens" end of the continuum result in greater bias with respect to the validity of study conclusions than those that are "innocent." Variables within the same study can differ as to where they lie on this continuum. Some variables may have missing data with silent innocence while others might have missing data that betoken that something is amiss. Because missing data might be classified differently for each variable, or even for each individual within a data matrix, classification could become a needlessly complex process, which would thus defeat the purpose of easing communication. For the classification system to be most useful, the missing data within the entire data matrix of interest should be assessed along this continuum, thus maintaining some indication of the overall level of bias inherent in the missing data.

THE CURRENT CLASSIFICATION SYSTEM: MECHANISMS OF MISSING DATA

The most widely used missing data classification system evolved from the statistical literature and was introduced by Donald Rubin (1976). Rubin specified three distinct missing data types: missing completely at random (MCAR), missing at random (MAR), and missing not at random (MNAR). Each term refers to the *probability* of missing values, given information about (1) the variable(s) with the missing data, (2) associated variables (including covariates), and (3) a hypothetical mechanism underlying the missing data. Rubin's missing data types are related to the level of bias the missing data may exert on the statistical analyses, with MCAR having negligible potential impact and MNAR having the greatest potential impact. Rubin's classification system is pervasive in the statistics literature and has made its way into the less technical social and behavioral science literature as well (e.g., Allison, 2002). However, much of that literature is often confusing and/or misleading to nontechnical audiences.

The confusion is likely due at least in part to the abstract and relatively complex nature of the concepts that define this classification system. Rubin's classification scheme, once understood, has great value for assisting researchers in the selection of appropriate methods for handling missing data. In fact, many of the missing data handling techniques refer to Rubin's system for appropriate use. Therefore, researchers should be familiar with and understand this system.

Introduction of Statistical Terms

Prior to discussing Rubin's missing data mechanisms, we introduce the reader to the specialized terminology used in the missing data field. The language of missing data is often expressed in mathematical notation that employs statistical terminology. We refrain from this style of presentation as much as possible in order to allow readers without a strong mathematical and statistical background to understand the material. Our discussion begins with a hypothetical data set consisting of three variables: an independent variable, *Perceived Ability*, and two dependent variables, *Math Test 1* and *Math Test 2* (from here on referred to as *Test 1* and *Test 2*). These data are presented in Table 3.1 and identified by the heading "Original data."

There are 10 participants for whom data have been collected. Suppose these participants were asked to rate their arithmetic proficiency on a scale from 0 to 9 (*Perceived Ability*), and then administered a test of math ability twice, 1 week apart (*Test 1* and *Test 2*). Imagine three distinct situations where missing data appear at the second administration (*Test 2*). These three situations are marked by MCAR (missing completely at random), MAR (missing at random), and MNAR (missing not at random), and represent different mechanisms for why the data are missing. These are identi-

TABLE 3.1. Illustrative Data Set for Missing Data Mechanisms

	Original data			Mechanism on *Math Test 2*			Dummy codes[a]		
Case	*Perceived Ability*	*Math Test 1*	*Math Test 2*	MCAR	MAR	MNAR	D_{MCAR}	D_{MAR}	D_{MNAR}
1	3	25	28	■	28	28	1	0	0
2	2	22	19	19	19	19	0	0	0
3	4	23	26	26	26	26	0	0	0
4	5	27	32	32	32	■	0	0	1
5	1	15	16	16	■	16	0	1	0
6	3	16	20	20	■	20	0	1	0
7	7	22	25	25	25	25	0	0	0
8	8	28	26	■	26	26	1	0	0
9	9	30	35	35	35	■	0	0	1
10	5	26	31	31	31	31	0	0	0

Note. Black cells represent missing values for the variable *Math Test* 2. MCAR, missing completely at random; MAR, missing at random; MNAR, missing not at random; D_{MCAR}, dummy code for MCAR data; D_{MAR}, dummy code for MAR data; D_{MNAR}, dummy code for MNAR data.
[a]For the dummy codes, 1, missing data, 0, observed data.

fied in the center of the table as "Mechanism on *Math Test 2*" and will be discussed in detail later. Each of these three columns illustrates a different pattern of missing data for the variable *Math Test* 2.

A third set of variables called dummy variables are included in the rightmost columns of the table. These are binary variables that reflect the missing data status: when data are missing, the dummy variable is coded as 1. When data are not missing, the dummy variable is coded as 0. Use of the dummy variable helps to clarify patterns, if there are any to be seen, in what data are missing or the way they are missing. In our example, we create missing data from the original data set to illustrate the three mechanisms. In each case (MCAR, MAR, and MNAR), we create missing data for 2 of the 10 cases, indicated by the 1s in the "Dummy codes" columns.

In keeping with the statistical literature, we refer to the dummy variable as **R**. In the literature, **R** refers to an entire matrix of dummy coded variables, each representing a different variable in the original data set. For simplicity, the matrix **R** is a single vector (i.e., one column) in our example, representing the missing data for *Test* 2. Technically, **R** should be a matrix of three vectors: dummy variables for *Perceived Ability, Test 1*, and *Test* 2. When no data are missing, the dummy variable consists of all 0s.

To add another term, Y refers to the entire matrix of data (all variables and all cases), which in our example includes *Perceived Ability*, *Test 1*, and *Test 2*.[1] Y is divided into two subsets: $\mathbf{Y_o}$ refers to all the observed values in the Y matrix, and $\mathbf{Y_m}$ refers to all the missing values in the Y matrix. To avoid confusing the reader, we write $\mathbf{Y_o}$ as $\mathbf{Y_{obs}}$ and $\mathbf{Y_m}$ as $\mathbf{Y_{miss}}$. For example, in Table 3.1, there are three missing data situations for the variable *Math Test 2* that are illustrated in the central columns marked MCAR, MAR, and MNAR. $\mathbf{Y_{obs}}$ would represent a matrix of all the observed values for *Perceived Ability*, *Math Test 1*, and the observed values for *Math Test 2*. In the MCAR situation, for instance, $\mathbf{Y_{obs}}$ would include 8 observations for *Math Test 2*. $\mathbf{Y_{miss}}$, on the other hand, represents all missing values. Because they are missing, we do not really have access to them and therefore $\mathbf{Y_{miss}}$ is a hypothetical matrix that is invoked to help us understand these three different missing data mechanisms, MCAR, MAR, and MNAR, as we shall see.

For simplicity, our example data set in Table 3.1 includes missing data for only one variable, *Math Test 2*. This example illustrates a *univariate* pattern of missing data, where only one variable has missing data and the rest are fully observed. In this example, $\mathbf{Y_{miss}}$ refers to the missing values for *Math Test 2* only. If values were also missing for other variables, $\mathbf{Y_{miss}}$ would represent a matrix of all of those unobserved values. $\mathbf{Y_{obs}}$ represents all fully observed values, *Perceived Ability* and *Test 1* in the present example.

A final term to introduce is ϕ (phi), which is the relationship of the dummy-value matrix of **R** to the real-value matrices of $\mathbf{Y_{obs}}$ and $\mathbf{Y_{miss}}$. Suppose that in our example, only the lowest scores on *Test 2* are missing. In this situation, there is a reason that those particular values are missing on *Test 2*; specifically, there is a higher likelihood of missing data on *Test 2* for lower scores on that test. Thus, there is a relationship between **R** and the unobserved ($\mathbf{Y_{miss}}$) values in the data set. This relationship between **R** and $\mathbf{Y_{miss}}$ is phi (ϕ). The magnitude of ϕ is unknown because we would have to have the values for $\mathbf{Y_{miss}}$ to calculate ϕ, in other words to be able to confirm that they are indeed the lowest scores on *Test 2*. Yet we cannot know these values because they are missing! The difficulty of managing missing data is that we do not know the nature of ϕ because we do not know $\mathbf{Y_{miss}}$. Therefore, phi (ϕ) is a probabilistic, *theoretical* relationship, the exact nature of which cannot be directly assessed and therefore must be inferred.

Rubin's (1976) Missing Data Classification System

The two most important concepts in the classification of missing data mechanisms are **R** and ϕ. Again, **R** represents the matrix of 1s and 0s (dummy codes) for all missing and observed data in a data set. Phi (ϕ) represents the relationship between **R** and the observed (Y_{obs}) and missing (Y_{miss}) values in the data set. In the statistical literature, the relationship ϕ is known as the *mechanism* of missing data and serves as the basis for differentiating Rubin's three types of missing data: MCAR, MAR, and MNAR. It is important to note that the word "mechanism" is being used here in a specialized technical sense. It specifies the structural relationships between the condition of data that are missing and the observed and/or missing values of the other variables in the data without specifying the hypothetical underlying cause of these relationships. Use of the word mechanism, therefore, does not imply that we necessarily know anything about how the missing data came to be missing. We will, however, be discussing the possible causes of missing data elsewhere as a separate issue.

Thus far, we have addressed merely theoretical propositions regarding missing data mechanisms. To illustrate the use of these mechanisms for diagnosing missing data, we use an example data set. To define Rubin's (1976) classic mechanisms, MCAR, MAR, and MNAR, we refer the reader to the three middle columns of data in Table 3.1. The first of these three columns represents data that are missing completely at random (MCAR), the next refers to data that are missing at random (MAR), and the third column refers to data that are missing not at random (MNAR). To illustrate all three mechanisms, for simplicity and comprehensibility, we created missing data for a single variable only, that is, a univariate pattern in the way it is missing. We created Figure 3.1 to assist the reader in differentiating between the three mechanisms as we describe them in the following pages.

We created the MCAR data by randomly selecting values to omit from *Test* 2. Because the MCAR data were deleted randomly, there is no relationship between data that are missing and those that are observed. That is, scores on *Perceived Ability* and *Test 1* are not related to missing data for *Test* 2. When there are no systematic differences on fully observed variables between those that have missing data and those that do not, data are said to be "observed at random" (OAR). That is, there is no relationship between how they are missing (**R**) and the observed data (Y_{obs}). If, for example, only those with low scores on *Perceived Ability* had missing data for *Test* 2, there would be a systematic difference between those with and without missing data, and therefore the data would *not* be OAR.

Also, because values on *Test* 2 were deleted at random, some *Test* 2

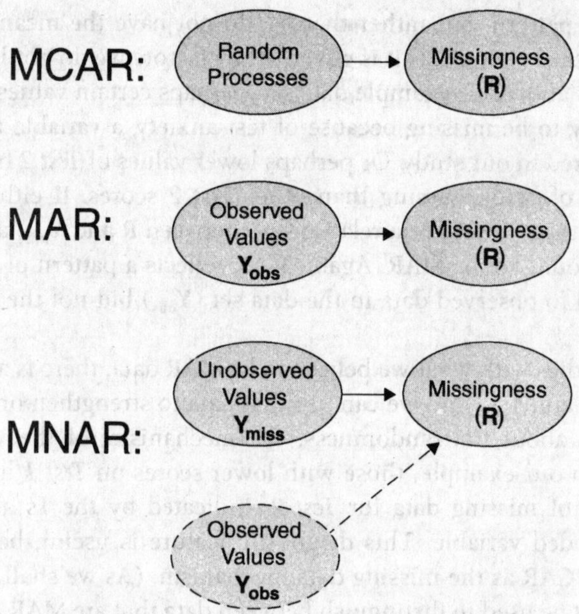

FIGURE 3.1. Rubin's categories of missing data.

scores are not more likely to be missing than other scores. That is, there is no systematic relationship between how scores are missing (**R**) and *Test 2* itself (Y_{miss}). Thus, for missing data that are MCAR, there is no systematic relationship between **R** and either Y_{obs} or Y_{miss}.[2] Using the example from Table 3.1, because the missing values for *Test 2* are unrelated to *Perceived Ability*, *Test 1*, and *Test 2*, there is no systematic process underlying the way data are missing on *Test 2*. As Figure 3.1 illustrates, randomness is the mechanism underlying data that are MCAR.

We produced the MAR missing data by systematically omitting two observations based on characteristics related to the observed data: We deleted two observations for *Test 2* where *Test 1* was <17. That is, respondents who scored low on the first test administration failed to attend the second administration. In this case, there is a systematic process underlying the way data are missing on *Test 2*: The lower the value of *Test 1*, the greater the likelihood that data will be missing for *Test 2*. Thus, there is a relationship between **R** and Y_{obs}.

However, for missing data that are MAR, there is no relationship between **R** and Y_{miss}. This does not mean the missing data do not have a systematic pattern, but rather that we do not have the means to see that pattern because if it exists it is governed by factors we do not have data for. If we think about our example data set, perhaps certain values of *Test* 2 are more likely to be missing because of test anxiety, a variable that we have not measured in our study. Or perhaps lower values of *Test* 2 have a greater likelihood of being missing than other *Test* 2 scores. If either condition were true, there would be a relationship between **R** and $\mathbf{Y}_{\mathbf{miss}}$ and the missing data would *not* be MAR. Again, MAR reflects a pattern of missing data (**R**) related to observed data in the data set ($\mathbf{Y}_{\mathbf{obs}}$) but not the missing data ($\mathbf{Y}_{\mathbf{miss}}$).

In studies with what we believe to be MAR data, there *is* a relationship between **R** and $\mathbf{Y}_{\mathbf{obs}}$, and we can use that data to strengthen or confirm our judgments about the randomness, the mechanism, of the way data are missing. In our example, those with lower scores on *Test 1* have a greater likelihood of missing data for *Test* 2, indicated by the 1s and 0s in the dummy coded variable. This diagnostic feature is useful, because it will rule out MCAR as the missing data mechanism. (As we shall see, this feature *cannot* be used to distinguish between data that are MAR and data that are MNAR.)

The term "missing at random" can be confusing. The distinction between MCAR and MAR can be seen in the following example: we created the MAR data by deleting values of *Test* 2 based on the fully observed variable *Test 1*—those who scored low on the first math test were more likely to be missing data on the second test. However, the missing values on *Test* 2 for those individuals are *not* related to *Test* 2 itself. So if we ignored *Test 1* and only examined *Test* 2 (and had access to the missing values), it could very well appear as if data were missing randomly from the distribution of scores on that variable. The missing values are not related to *Test* 2 itself, and the observed scores for *Test* 2 are considered to be a random subset of the population of possible scores for *Test* 2. Thus we use the designation "missing at random."[3] If it turned out to be true that the lower scores on *Test* 2 were more likely to be missing, the scores on *Test* 2 could not be considered a subset with only random values missing; the data would be considered missing *not* at random, or MNAR.

In fact, the MNAR variable was created by omitting the two highest values for *Test* 2. MNAR creates a missing data situation that is difficult to overcome. The way values are missing is *not* equally likely across the different scores of *Test* 2. The "missingness" of the values is related to the variable itself. When missing values are not equally likely across the different scores of a variable, **R** is said to be related to $\mathbf{Y}_{\mathbf{miss}}$. However, the relationship between **R** and $\mathbf{Y}_{miss}$ is unknown to the researcher because there is no access to the missing observations! This is the difficulty with data we classify as MNAR. Data that are MNAR have a relationship between **R** and $\mathbf{Y}_{miss}$, yet we cannot know that relationship because we have no access to $\mathbf{Y}_{miss}$. Moreover, a relationship between **R** and $\mathbf{Y}_{obs}$ may or may not exist for data that are MNAR. In our example, although missing values for *Test 2* are related to *Test* 2 (i.e., the highest scores), they may or may not also be related to the observed values of *Test 1*, depending on the correlation between *Tests 1* and 2. If higher values of *Test* 2 are related to higher values of *Test 1*, there would also be a relationship between missingness (**R**) and $\mathbf{Y}_{obs}$. Yet as long as there is a relationship between **R** and $\mathbf{Y}_{miss}$, the data are MNAR. Figure 3.1 illustrates this relationship, depicting the possibility of a relationship between missingness and observed values by the dotted line.

These features of MNAR are what make this classification system difficult in practice. To distinguish between MNAR and MAR, we need to know if there is a relationship between **R** and $\mathbf{Y}_{miss}$. Yet as noted, by definition we cannot know the actual nature of $\mathbf{Y}_{miss}$ because it is based on missing information. Thus the differentiating feature between MNAR and MAR is not available to us. The only information to which we have access is whether there is a relationship between **R** and $\mathbf{Y}_{obs}$. This information alone will not help us differentiate between data that are MAR versus MNAR, because data that are MNAR can also involve a relationship between **R** and $\mathbf{Y}_{obs}$. The only information a relationship between **R** and $\mathbf{Y}_{obs}$ can provide is that data cannot be MCAR. We discuss the implications of these difficulties for a missing data classification system later.

In sum, the relationship between missingness, represented by the dummy code matrix **R**, the observed values ($\mathbf{Y}_{obs}$), and missing data ($\mathbf{Y}_{miss}$) defines the three mechanisms of missing data that serve as the basis for Rubin's (1976) classification system. When there is no relationship between **R**, $\mathbf{Y}_{obs}$, and $\mathbf{Y}_{miss}$, the data are classified as missing completely at random or MCAR. Using our example data, the probability that data are missing on *Test* 2 for any given participant is unrelated to his or her own values on *Perceived Ability*, *Test 1* (both are $\mathbf{Y}_{obs}$), or *Test* 2 ($\mathbf{Y}_{miss}$). When there is a relationship between **R** and $\mathbf{Y}_{obs}$, but not between **R** and $\mathbf{Y}_{miss}$, the data are classified as MAR. Using our example, the probability that data are missing on *Test* 2 is related to a participant's scores on *Perceived Ability* or *Test 1*, but not on *Test* 2. Finally, when there is a relationship between **R** and $\mathbf{Y}_{miss}$, the data are said to be MNAR. Using our example, the probability that data are missing on *Test 2* is related to a participant's values on

Test 2. With data that are MNAR, there can be a relationship between R and Y_{obs}, but it is not necessary.

Ignorability

Another pertinent distinction in Rubin's missing data classification system is whether the missing data mechanism is ignorable. The term "ignorable" as it applies to missing data mechanisms does not mean that researchers can disregard missing data. In statistical usage, *ignorable* refers to whether the mechanism of missing data must be modeled as part of the parameter estimation process. When data are MAR and the parameters that govern the missing data process are unrelated to the parameters to be estimated, the mechanism is said to be ignorable (Allison, 2002). That is, the mechanism does not have to be modeled to produce good parameter estimates. Conversely, for MNAR data, the mechanism must be modeled to obtain good estimates of the parameters of interest.

An analogy might prove useful as an illustration of what is meant by "ignorable." Suppose we are interested in predicting a person's weight-lifting ability. If we exclude the person's biological sex, we might miss information that is relevant to our ability to predict. Sex, in this case, is not an ignorable variable. However, favorite color is an ignorable variable that easily could be omitted without any serious threat to prediction. If we do not have information about the biological sex of participants, we might be able to infer it based on other information we have collected from them, such as data regarding menstrual cycle or body mass index. In this circumstance, missing relevant data (i.e., biological sex), while imperative to the analysis, can be recaptured to some extent from the remaining information collected. This situation is similar to what occurs in data that are MAR, where the missing data mechanism is considered ignorable.

Another example lies in the area of survey research. If a person fails to respond to a survey because he or she is unwilling to share the requested information, failure to respond (i.e., missing data) is relevant and nonignorable. This is what occurs when data are MNAR: The likelihood of missing data is related to a person's status on the variable for which the data are missing. If, however, the person fails to respond because of a random occurrence, such as overlooking the survey with the rest of the mail, failure to respond is likely irrelevant to the variable for which data are missing and is therefore ignorable.

Ignorability becomes important when we need to assess the impact missing data have on data analyses and study conclusions. Mechanisms that are ignorable are considered to be easier to deal with because their effect on statistical models is available to the data analyst. Data that are MCAR should have no systematic effect on parameter estimation, because the way they are missing is random. When data are suspected of being MAR, there is a systematic process underlying the missingness, but it can be modeled with the observed data in the data matrix. The effect of nonignorable mechanisms, however, is unknown and therefore potentially dangerous. There is no information within the data set itself that allows us to model and understand the way data are missing, and therefore the impact on parameter estimation and statistical conclusions is unknown.

Discriminating between Missing Data Mechanisms

Having defined MCAR, MAR, and MNAR, it is important to discuss how their differences have implications for missing data detection, diagnosis, and handling. Recall from our earlier discussion that distinguishing between MCAR and the other two mechanisms is possible by assessing the relationship between **R** and $\mathbf{Y}_{\mathbf{obs}}$. If there is a relationship, the data cannot be MCAR. However, if there is a relationship between **R** and $\mathbf{Y}_{\mathbf{obs}}$, we cannot distinguish between MAR and MNAR, because that feature can be common to both (see Figure 3.1). The only distinguishing feature between MAR and MNAR is relationship between $\mathbf{Y}_{\mathbf{miss}}$ and **R**, and as noted repeatedly in this chapter, the nature of that relationship is not available to us because we do not have access to the missing data. The relationship could be established if we somehow knew that the way data are missing is *not* distributed equally across all potential values of the variable for which data are missing.

In our estimation, a classification system based on features that cannot be reliably detected has some practical limitations. It can be difficult, using such a system, to recognize and/or diagnose missing data. If diagnosis is made difficult, knowledge of useful remedies can be impeded as well. Although the system is useful as a heuristic by which to understand the importance and potential consequences of missing data, it often has less utility in its application. Because there are no practical ways (e.g., statistical tests) by which to differentiate MAR and MNAR, it must be done according to sound logic. Yet what is considered sound logic by one individual might be inadequate for another. Therefore, in light of these limitations, we introduce a process for classifying missing data, not as a replacement for Rubin's system, but as an expansion or supplement to that system.

EXPANDING THE CLASSIFICATION SYSTEM

Although useful in pursuing the goals of classification, classifying missing data solely on the basis of mechanism can lead to incomplete understanding, communication, and identification of missing data. First, Rubin's system focuses on the structure of missing data (i.e., relationships between R, Y_{obs}, and Y_{miss}) rather than their function, and therefore treatment recommendations are limited to statistical remedies. Second, missing data do not necessarily exist in three rigidly defined mechanistic categories (Graham, Hofer, & Piccinin, 1994; Schafer & Olsen, 1998). Instead, missing data are often likely to reflect all three mechanisms. In multivariate analyses, missing data may be MCAR for some components of the analysis, MAR and MNAR for others. An entire set of observations may be difficult to characterize by any single mechanism. The more likely situation is that missing data cannot be neatly classified using a single mechanism.

A more informative method of characterizing missing data would be to tie the mechanism with a functional description of the missing data. In Table 3.2, we offer an example of combining Rubin's mechanism with a more qualitative characterization of missing data, which simply describes the dimension for which data are missing. "Dimension" refers to the three facets of Cattell's (1966) data-box: variable or items, individuals or subjects, and occasions, all of which we will describe shortly. Cross-tabulating missing data between dimension and mechanism yields Table 3.2.

As Table 3.2 illustrates, by combining information about the dimension and mechanism, we gain a more thorough understanding of the missing data situation—one that will in turn better inform us about how to proceed with respect to handling the missing data. For example, the MAR × Individuals cell indicates that those missing data can be characterized by available demographic information. This suggests a missing data handling technique that uses demographic information in the statistical model to recapture the missing information. (As we note later, a real-world situation is far more complex than this example, because other information, including the amount of missing data, is also relevant.) The missing data solution just cited would be different from the solution for the MAR × Occasions cell, in which those who performed poorly on previous occasions failed to provide data. In such a situation, perhaps one could recapture missing values by imputing values based on expected trajectories for similar individuals. Although both situations reflect an MAR mechanism, they suggest quite different solutions due to the information gleaned from the dimensions (individuals vs. occasions) of missing data. Without infor-

TABLE 3.2. Merging Classification Systems for Missing Data

	MCAR	MAR	MNAR
Variable (Item)	Subjects randomly omit responses	Subjects omit responses that are traceable to other responses	Subject fails to respond to incriminating items
Individuals or Subjects	Subject data missing at random	Subject data missing but related to available demographic data	Subject data missing and related to unmeasured demographic data
Occasions	Subjects randomly fail to show up to data collection session	Subjects who perform poorly at previous session fail to show for subsequent session	Subjects who are doing poorly at the time of the session fail to show

Note. MCAR, missing completely at random; MAR, missing at random; MNAR, missing not at random.

mation about the dimension of missing data, we would know only that the mechanism is MAR.

There is nothing inherent in Rubin's (1976) classification system that would prevent the data analyst from going beyond identifying mechanisms and identifying other factors related to missing data. We are simply making the extension explicit and suggesting relevant factors to supplement missing data classification based on mechanisms. As noted in Chapter 1, our proposed extension adds a functional approach to the classification of missing data; that is, the focus is on what missing data do (how they impact results) rather than what they are. The combination of statistical and descriptive information provides a fuller, functional characterization of missing data that in turn ought to allow researchers to better understand, communicate, and treat missing data problems. The current system focused on missing data mechanisms communicates a limited amount of information: the extent to which missing information is retrievable. Because a functional approach is explicitly related to the reasons for missing data, it can help to differentiate mechanisms in difficult situations, for example, when we hope to rule out MNAR. We now elaborate on the functional extension of Rubin's classification method and begin with a brief discussion of the more common causes of missing data. Then we discuss the relevance of these causes to missing data classification.

Reasons for Missing Data

There are many reasons for missing data in research. We cannot cover them all, but it would be useful to consider some of the more common reasons for missing data in social and behavioral science research. Knowing the reasons for missing data helps in identifying and understanding the mechanism, which is key in deciding how to handle missing data. Chief among the reasons for missing data in this research realm are study design, participant characteristics, measurement characteristics, data collection and management conditions, and chance. It is critical to note that these reasons can occur individually or simultaneously within a particular study. A poorly designed study combined with poorly designed measures could lead to attrition as well as missing variables for those who complete the study, for example. Furthermore, data missing for several different reasons at once are additive. If 20 subjects dropped out of a study because of a burdensome intervention, and 20 others failed to complete all the measures, the resulting 40 missing observations might be enough to jeopardize validity.

Contrary to a common misconception, although reasons for missing data may help explain a missing data mechanism, knowing the reason does not automatically mean we can judge the ignorability of the missing data. Some reasons may provide a more likely situation for a particular mechanism, but the reader will soon realize that reasons and mechanisms can be conceptualized independently.

Data Missing Due to Study Design

One source of missing data is simply the study design. Campbell and Stanley (1966) stated that no research design is without flaws. Similarly, no research design eliminates missing data altogether. However, different designs yield different probabilities of missing data. Consider two fairly simple designs, the nonexperimental posttest-only design and the time-series design. In the former, only a single measurement occasion exists, while the latter design uses multiple repeated measurements. Although a study with the latter design would usually be a stronger study in ruling out plausible rival hypotheses, the posttest-only design is likely to result in less missing data. Making repeated observations, particularly over a long period of time, is more likely to result in missing data than making a single observation for an entire sample at one point in time. In general, the more burden a study design places on subjects, the more likely subjects will fail to respond to questions, comply with research protocols, or continue with the study. Some missing data, therefore, can be attributable to the burden imposed on participants as a result of the study design. This burden could include duration of the study, multiple repeated measures, long questionnaires, painful procedures, and so on. As the burden on participants increases, the probability of missing data increases.

Data Missing Due to Participant Characteristics

Rubin (1987) identified two general reasons for nonresponse to items: processing of information and refusal to provide information. These two reasons are associated with personal characteristics of the participants. Information processing may be related to reading and comprehension levels, proficiency in the survey language, or cognitive functioning. Nonresponse due to refusal may be associated with lack of interest in the subject matter, lack of motivation, and individual beliefs and attitudes toward the research topic and/or the content of particular items. Refusal to respond is reinforced by the right of self-determination that should be maintained to ensure ethical conduct of the study. Whatever the reason, the end result is a lack of complete information on the study variables for a subgroup of the sample. This, in turn, limits the generalizability of the findings to all subgroups of the target population.

Data Missing Due to Measurement Characteristics

Missing data can be due to the characteristics of the measures used in a study. By "measures," we mean tools or instruments used to quantify the concept of interest. There are a variety of ways that measurement characteristics can produce missing data. First, observations can be lost due to malfunctioning equipment (e.g., electroencephalogram, or EEG, equipment). Second, data can be missing due to the burden on the respondents, caused by the length, invasiveness, tediousness, or complexity of measures. Invasiveness can be physical (e.g., painful procedures such as blood draws) or emotional (e.g., asking personal or sensitive questions). Third, measurement characteristics may produce missing data at different rates for subgroups within the same population. For example, those unaccustomed to the rigors of testing may be more likely to drop out of a study, which in turn may adversely affect generalizability or statistical inference.

Data Missing Due to Data Collection Conditions

In some instances, the conditions under which observations are made can increase the probability of missing data. Traveling long distances to participate or unpleasant conditions (e.g., noisy, dirty, hectic, dangerous) can lead to participants dropping out of a study. Additionally, timing of observations (e.g., early in the morning, summer vacation) could increase the likelihood of missing data. Also, participants who feel rushed or pressed to respond by an interviewer may decide to withdraw or not respond to items. These are all examples of obstacles for the participants, many of whom are participating voluntarily and often for little to no compensation. Removing as many obstacles as possible to participation in a study is likely to both guarantee greater participation and decrease missing data.

Data Missing Due to Data Management

Despite efforts to obtain complete data from all participants, investigators can lose data due to poor data management. Many investigators rely on transferring data into different formats (e.g., entering paper-and-pencil questionnaires into a computer database). Data can be lost in the transfer process. For example, data entry personnel might systematically delete observations due to unclear writing or unconventional responses, or they may inadvertently skip survey items. Poor data storage can also result in missing data (e.g., faulty or nonexistent computer file back-up plans). Disorganized data storage could also result in loss of data. A research colleague once reported the case of a what was effectively a *triple*-blinded study design in which the researcher, the participants, and the data analyst were blinded to the intervention conditions because the data manager failed to document them! The lost codes resulted in completely missing data and therefore the existing data were meaningless.

Data Missing Due to Chance

Despite an investigator's efforts to design the study well and measures taken to reduce the likelihood of missing data, missing data still occur by chance. That is, there is no systematic reason for missing data but rather a variety of odd circumstances that lead to missing data for completely unrelated reasons. For instance, participants inadvertently skip items, some do not realize that a questionnaire is double-sided, investigators miss appointments, participants become ill or move to another location and fail to show up for the study, or data managers misplace surveys.

Unlike the previously mentioned reasons for missing data, chance, by definition, does not produce a bias on statistical conclusions or causal generalization. However, the role of chance on missing data is not always harmless. It may produce large amounts of missing data because of the occurrence of multiple chance events. Recall Simpson's paradox (Simpson, 1951), where single insignificant events when added up produce a troublesome situation. Large amounts of missing data produce their own sets of problems (e.g., decreased statistical power), which we discuss in more detail in Chapter 5.

The following sections address how we classify missing data, for the purposes of improving understanding, diagnosis, and treatment. Classifying missing data according to dimensions is appropriate because the dimensions are related to the aforementioned reasons for missing data.

Dimensions of Missing Data

Cattell (1966) formulated data in terms of dimensions of a "data box." Each of the three dimensions of the box represents a different facet of data: individuals, variables, and occasions. Figure 3.2 illustrates these three dimensions of data. As Nesselroade (1991) notes, the design and measurements that produce a set of data can be described in terms of these three facets of the data box in order to obtain a set of observations for analysis and interpretation. Thus, Cattell's data box is a useful heuristic by which to discuss missing data and their consequences.

Data can be missing for one, two, or all three facets. A questionnaire might be missing data for a few items (variables facet), an individual might fail to show up for a study (individuals facet), and/or follow-up data might

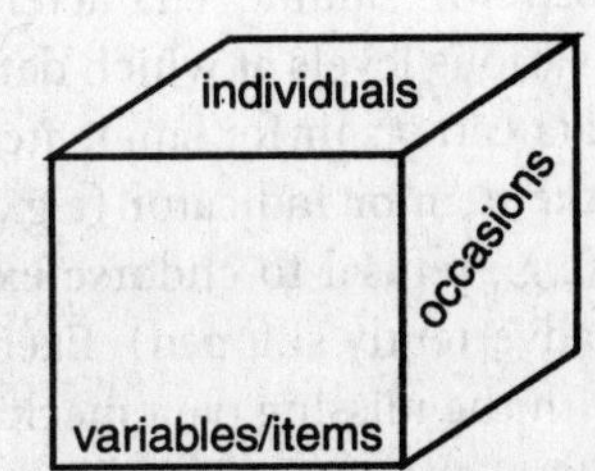

FIGURE 3.2. Cattell's (1966) data box.

be missing for the experimental group (occasions facet). Survey methodologists have traditionally distinguished these three sources of missing data as *unit nonresponse* (when an individual fails to respond), *item nonresponse* (the individual participates but fails to respond to some items), and *wave nonresponse* (in longitudinal studies, individuals may be present for some occasions of data collection and not others) (Schafer & Graham, 2002).

Often, missing data are evident in all three dimensions of the data box. In a longitudinal study, for example, data might be missing at particular measurement occasions, as well as for items or entire measures, and because individuals could drop out of the study. In this example, there are multiple dimensions of missing data, all of which have different implications regarding bias, generalizability, and the ability to draw conclusions from study results.

Within each of these dimensions are hierarchies or levels at which data can be missing. Within the variables/items facet, data can be missing for single items or aggregates of items (e.g., factor scores or scale scores). Within the individuals facet, data can be missing for single individuals or groups, such as a classroom or clinic. For the occasions facet, data can be missing at a single time point or across multiple time points.

The following addresses a variety of types of missing data based on the three facets of Cattell's data cube and the hierarchies or levels within those facets. The discussion is not exhaustive, but it should illustrate the complexities of missing data that can go undetected when the focus is solely on missing data mechanisms.

Missing Data on the Variables Dimension

With respect to the variables dimension, data can be missing on dependent variables, independent variables, covariates, and even demographic or classification variables used for sample characterization. Furthermore, within this facet there are various levels at which data could be missing. At the micro level, missing data can occur for single items and could be associated with the nature of the item or indicator (e.g., sensitive or offensive items), response options (e.g., refusal to endorse extreme positions), and chance (e.g., an item is inadvertently skipped). Each one of these circumstances, in combination with the missing data mechanism, presents different problems for data analysis and interpretation.

At a more macro level, missing data can occur for latent versus manifest variables. *Latent* variables are those that represent theoretical constructs that cannot be directly observed but are presumed to underlie particular observed measures (Byrne, 1994). Latent variables are commonly referred to as factors. Because they are unobservable, latent variables are measured indirectly by two or more correlated indicators (e.g., measuring intelligence with IQ tests). In contrast, *manifest* variables are measured directly (e.g., height, income). Missing data for manifest versus latent variables can have different consequences. When data are missing for some but not all of the indicators of a latent variable, missing data might be reconstructed from observed data for the remaining indicators, because they are correlated. However, when data are missing for a manifest variable, the data are difficult to reconstruct if there are no other variables with which the manifest variable is correlated.

The different levels at which data are missing have different implications for understanding, diagnosing, and treating the missing data. For example, data missing at the item level for a factor are likely to have a lesser impact on generalizability and interpretation of results than data missing at the latent variable (factor) level. In combination with the amount and pattern of missing data, data missing at different levels can have completely different impact. In situations where there are many missing items or a systematic pattern in how they are missing (e.g., all items for a particular subscale), the resultant bias may be greater than the bias associated with data missing inadvertently at the factor level, for example, due to faulty equipment or a skipped page on a survey.

On the variables dimension, missing data have different effects if they are missing from dependent versus independent variables. For example, if there are multiple independent variables, a variety of methods could be used to replace missing data, based on information from correlated independent variables, as in multiple imputation (see Chapter 10). The same methods can be used for data missing for a dependent variable in multivariate analyses with correlated dependent variables. However, if analyses are univariate (i.e., a single dependent variable) or dependent variables are uncorrelated, these methods do not apply.

Missing Data on the Occasions Dimension

The occasion of measurement is the time point at which data collection occurs. Missing data can occur both *within occasion*, that is, at only one time point, or *between occasions*, that is, over time. Within occasion, missing data include nonresponse, subject omission, inappropriate skip pattern, and refusal to answer. Missing data between occasions includes dropout, attrition, subject unavailability, and failed follow-up. Data that occur at one time point are referred to as cross-sectional, while data resulting from repeated observations over a time sequence are referred to as longitudinal. Missing data in cross-sectional studies biases results in quite a different way than data missing longitudinally do. In longitudinal studies, data missing at baseline might have different implications than data missing in the middle of a study or at follow-up. For example, at baseline, missing data cannot be the result of the intervention, whereas after baseline, they can. Both scenarios influence generalizability of study results differentially. In the first instance, those who drop out at baseline after consenting to participate might be systematically different from those who remain, while in the second scenario, those who complete an intervention study might be quite different from those who do not. In either case, generalizability might be compromised.

Data missing at various time points can also have consequences for the measurement of change. For example, the impact of missing data may vary depending on the underlying change trajectory of the phenomena of interest. If the trajectory is assumed to be linear (i.e., change occurs at a consistent rate), then data missing at baseline, the middle, or at follow-up can be imputed readily from other values along the trajectory. However, if the "true" trajectory is a more complex function, perhaps changing direction several times, it may be more difficult to impute valid missing values because the exact nature of that trajectory is less understood. Moreover, the impact of missing data is likely related to the number of occasions of measurement. Data missing from a study in which only two or three repeated measures are taken are likely more problematic than data missing from a study in which multiple repeated measures are made, particularly with more complex change functions.

Missing Data on the Individuals Dimension

The third and final dimension of the box refers to missing data associated with study participants. The levels within this dimension are more obvious. The micro level refers to individual subjects, while the macro levels refer to groups of individuals. Studies could be missing data from single individuals or from groups, such as subgroups within a study, entire classrooms, clinics, or sites within a multisite study. As with the other dimensions, missing data give greater or lesser cause for concern on the individuals dimension, depending on what level data are missing (e.g., if data are missing for individuals or for whole subgroups). Moreover, the mechanism for missing data on this dimension can either be ignorable or nonignorable, and can vary in amount and pattern. Nonignorable missing data at the individual level can be more detrimental to statistical conclusions and generalizability than ignorable missing data at the group level.

Amount and Pattern of Missing Data

Two other considerations in analyzing missing data are the amount (quantity) and the pattern of how they are missing. Because we cover these topics in greater detail in Chapter 5, we attend to them only briefly here, as they relate to classification.

As noted in Chapter 5, *amount* is a concept used ambiguously in the missing data literature. Most often it refers to the number of subjects for whom data are missing, but it can also refer to the total number of missing observations from a particular variable or set of variables or to the total number of missing observations from a data set. The amount of missing data becomes particularly important when deciding on statistical techniques for handling missing data. Although there does not appear to be a heuristic by which to classify amounts of missing data as small, medium, or large, it is generally understood that less missing data is better. However, we are cautioned to focus not only on the *quantity* but on the *quality* of missing data. If a large proportion of data are missing completely at random (MCAR)—that is, if there is no systematic reason for the missing data—such a situation might be better for parameter estimation than smaller amounts of missing data that are nonignorable (i.e., MNAR). Although a large amount of data might be missing, when the mechanism is MCAR, the observed data may be sufficient to produce valid (i.e., unbiased) parameter estimates. Smaller amounts of nonignorable missing data, on the other hand, can produce biased estimates. Moreover, if the statistical goal is hypothesis testing, sufficient statistical power is required, and large amounts of missing data, regardless of the underlying mechanism, are never a good thing. Thus the amount of missing data, in combination with the reason, dimension, mechanism, and pattern, can be informative diagnostically and thus inform treatment of missing data.

The *pattern* of missing data has to do with whether there is consistency in the way data are missing. For example, a study in which all participants are missing values for the same variable has a consistent, unique, and detectable pattern. In a situation in which participants are missing data for different variables, the missing data are inconsistent and do not produce a detectable pattern. As noted earlier in this chapter, a univariate pattern occurs when data are missing for only one variable and the rest of the variables in the data set are fully observed (see Table 3.1). This pattern can occur at the item level as well, in which a group of items is either entirely observed or entirely missing for each person. A *monotonic* pattern in the way data are missing occurs when missing items or groups of items are dependent or conditional on missing data for other items or groups of items. For example, if individuals drop out of a study, subsequent measurement occasions will be missing data.

As we discuss in Chapter 5, how clearly the pattern shows itself suggests how systematic the process is that is producing the missing data. Chapter 5 differentiates between the patterns of missing data and how they are related to decision making with respect to missing data handling techniques.

SUMMARY

Classification systems are for the purpose of facilitating communication and providing guidance for action. The goals of a useful classification system for missing data should be to improve communication and understanding, and to inform the proper treatment of missing data. The current classification system, with its focus on mechanisms of missing data, can be limiting in its utility. First, it limits our understanding of missing data. Because Rubin's (1976) system is conceptually complex and technically oriented, those who are not trained as statisticians find the system difficult to understand. A system that is difficult to understand fails to meet the goal of easing communication. Second, the current system is limited in its ability to inform recognition or diagnosis. As noted throughout this chapter, there are practical difficulties with diagnosis using this system, due at least in part to the use of diagnostic criteria that are unavailable to the diagnostician (e.g., the inability to determine a relationship between **R** and $\mathbf{Y}_{\mathbf{miss}}$). Third, because missing data mechanisms fail to communicate to the researcher the underlying processes responsible for missing data, they offer a limited approach to remedying the problems associated with missing data. In general, the remedies are statistical in nature and do not promote an understanding of the potential extent of bias or impact on statistical and study conclusions.

We attempt to extend the current classification system with further criteria for characterizing missing data. By adding more facets to the classification system, including the three dimensions of Cattell's data cube, the hierarchies or levels within those dimensions, the amount and pattern of missing data, and assessing potential reasons for the missing data, we hope to increase the utility of the classification of missing data for social and behavioral scientists. The more comprehensive approach to classification offers several advantages over the focus on missing data mechanisms: (1) it decreases the technical language, thus clarifying what can be an obtuse literature, (2) it adds diagnostic criteria in a language that is clear and familiar to researchers, and (3) it adds relevant features to the diagnosis that enhance our ability to make informed decisions about the treatment of missing data. The nontechnical, familiar language ought to improve the classification system with respect to our understanding of the phenomenon. Similarly, added features that are readily available to the diagnostician (e.g., variables, individuals, and measurement occasions) ought to improve the diagnostic utility of the system. By improving the understanding and diagnostic capabilities of the system, we hope to improve its utility for informing the treatment of missing data. With the extended system, the researcher has more options for handling missing data, including prevention—an option that is not part of the current system based on mechanisms. Because the extended classification system includes dimensions such as study design and measurement, researchers can better understand and therefore anticipate where missing data might occur a priori and thus engage in prevention efforts such as reducing the burden on participants. Combining the dominant statistical approach with our extended functional approach can yield a classification system that improves our understanding and handling of missing data.

Finally, it is critical to reiterate a point made earlier in this chapter: it is likely that the missing data produced within a single study will not be neatly classified into a single type or category of missing data. As this chapter has emphasized, there are many reasons for and dimensions of missing data, many of which can occur in a single study. Therefore, we hope to introduce a more thorough approach to missing data diagnosis. Better diagnosis should inform more appropriate methods for handling missing data and ultimately improve our understanding and interpretation of study results.

NOTES

1. In the statistical literature, Rubin's (1976) classification system is almost always discussed in terms of missing data for the dependent variable(s), noted as Y.

2. Additionally, for missing data that are MCAR, a sample of cases with no missing data will constitute a random subset of the full set of cases.

3. Schafer and Graham (2002) note that most misunderstandings of MCAR, MAR, and MNAR come from the use of the term "random." They attribute it to the fact that statisticians are talking about randomness in probabilistic terms, degrees of randomness or the likelihood that data approach true randomness. By contrast, what people think of as randomness probably applies mainly to MCAR.

4

Preventing Missing Data by Design

The maxim "an ounce of prevention is worth a pound of cure" generally applies to health problems, but it also pertains to missing data. Reducing the likelihood of missing data by design is probably more productive than remedying the problem after it has already occurred. Prevention minimizes the need for the statistical strategies we discuss in subsequent chapters. The missing data prevention discussed in this chapter decreases the probability of missing data and may prove to be a researcher's best treatment for missing data.

We strongly recommend that researchers carefully review the study plan for factors that might lead to missing data and devise strategies to address these factors effectively; the aim should be to prevent or at least reduce the probability of incomplete data. In this chapter, we discuss five aspects of a study that can be associated with missing data: (1) overall study design, (2) characteristics of the target population and the sample, (3) data collection and measurement, (4) treatment implementation, and (5) data entry. For each aspect, we identify factors that may contribute to missing data and we briefly present possible solutions that can minimize the problem. Our coverage of these factors and solutions is intended to be illustrative, not exhaustive. We stress in this chapter that using study design to prevent missing data is optimal and should decrease the need for statistical solutions that are usually problematic.

OVERALL STUDY DESIGN

The overall design of a study refers to a clearly defined structure within which the study is implemented. Of particular interest here is the number of measurement occasions, the timing for collecting data, the number of variables included in the study, and the assignment of participants to the study groups (when applicable). In this section, we discuss how these aspects of a study could contribute to the missing data problem, and we offer suggestions for how to decrease the likelihood of missing data. We also present strategies for reducing attrition, which is the most salient form of missing data in longitudinal or repeated measure designs.

Measurement Occasions and the Timing of Data Collection

Experience has shown that longitudinal designs are prone to missing data for persons, variables, and occasions—all three facets of Cattell's data cube (presented in Chapter 3). As studies carry on over longer periods of time, participants are more likely to drop out, neglect to complete measures, and/or skip data collection periods. Yet longitudinal designs are the most appropriate for detecting change in variables over time. Therefore, attention ought to be given to ways in which the demands on participants and research staff can be reduced to decrease the likelihood of missing data.

One facet of study design that can have a great influence on the likelihood of missing data is the number of measurement occasions and the time interval between them. Frequent data collection and short intervals can put a substantial burden on study participants and research staff, increasing the likelihood of participants dropping out (attrition), skipping study sessions, and neglecting to complete study measures. Yet, all too often, researchers persist with overly involved study designs and burdensome schedules, perhaps underestimating or even disregarding the risk of negative impact from these conditions, because they believe that frequent measurements enhance the likelihood of detecting change in the outcome of interest.

Frequent, short-interval measurement is justifiable in certain situations (e.g., when the knowledge of the pattern of change is limited). In such cases, it does make sense to measure frequently to avoid missing critical change periods. However, this practice occurs far too often in fields in which knowledge of change patterns is not as undeveloped. Where theoretical, empirical, and/or clinical information exists about expected patterns of change, such information can be used to determine the most appropriate data collection schedule for capturing change rather than a design based on convenience or convention.

Existing information can help determine if the data collection should be event- or time-based, for example. In the event-based approach, assessments are made in reference to a particular event (e.g., treatment onset, testing during the school year, onset of puberty, and so on). In the time-based approach, assessments are done at prespecified times, such as 3 or 6 months following baseline measurement. Whether data collection should be event- or time-based ought to be determined by the study question and existing information about change in the phenomenon of interest. Determination of the frequency and spacing of data collection should not be an afterthought based on convenience.

For example, we might expect a substance abuse treatment to produce dramatic positive changes early on, followed by more subtle change, and then dramatic decay. A pattern of frequent data collection might be chosen to capture the rapid change, but data collection might become less frequent as changes become slower and steadier. Frequency would increase again to capture the rapid decay that is expected to ensue. In comparison, a change process expected to be slow and steady throughout would dictate less frequent and perhaps evenly spaced measurement.

Determining a data collection schedule based on the expected pattern of change makes sense not only from a design standpoint but also with respect to missing data. Short and frequent data collection intervals increase the likelihood of missing data, for reasons previously stated. If frequent data collection is not required based on the expected change trajectory, there is little reason to justify this practice. Instead, reducing data collection to occur only at key phases of change reduces the response burden on participants and allows research staff to be more vigilant at each occasion. Moreover, for the processes that social and behavioral sciences tend to study with longitudinal designs, reducing the occasions also maximizes the variance between occasions and thus yields the best "bang for your buck" in data collection. That is, because these processes generally do not fluctuate rapidly—if they did, a longitudinal design would not be appropriate—frequent measurement is not likely to pick up much change. In short, using existing knowledge based on theory, data, and/or experience to determine the number and spacing of measurement occasions is vital to minimizing missing data.

Number of Variables

The number of variables in a study can also have an influence on missing data. Measuring a large number of variables puts a burden on the participants, data collector, and data entry staff and increases the likelihood of missing data. Multiple items or measures to complete can lead to boredom or frustration for respondents, more data to enter can lead to more mistakes in data entry, and long data collection sessions can make research staff less vigilant about rigorous data collection methods. All of these things can increase the probability of missing data. Therefore, careful attention to the inclusion and exclusion of variables in a study is warranted. Many social scientists have fallen into the habit of including additional items or measures "just in case" the data might be useful. This step is often taken with no particular theoretical rationale as to why the data are needed and how they will be used in either a conceptual or statistical model. The situation is akin to rounding up the "usual suspects." A humorous example of thoughtless data collection occurs in the movie *Ghostbusters*, when Bill Murray's character, while gathering data on a woman's recent paranormal encounter, asks the irrelevant question about her last menstrual cycle. When a bystander questions the need for such information, Murray replies, "Back off, I'm a scientist!"

Unfortunately, most study participants do not share the same unquestioning awe of scientists. Study participants can and do question the need for including items that appear to be irrelevant, and are known to leave the items blank or, even worse, respond carelessly. These outcomes lead to either bias (i.e., systematic error) or noise (i.e., random error), but the researcher has no idea which condition occurs. For example, in a study by one of the authors of this book, of women recovering from rape, anonymous reviewers of the grant application insisted on the inclusion of a measure of social desirability to assess for response bias to study questions. Koss, Figueredo, Bell, Tharan, and Tromp (1996) examined characteristics of memories formed in response to rape and other intense unpleasant and pleasant experiences. To address concerns that responses may have been motivated by a desire to appear socially appropriate on this mailed survey,

11 items from the Marlowe-Crowne Social Desirability Scale (Crowne & Marlowe, 1960) were included. Unfortunately, the intent of these items was completely transparent to any reasonably intelligent respondent. Because women who have been raped have already had numerous adverse experiences with having their credibility doubted or impugned, a large proportion merely refused to answer these items but responded to the remainder of the questionnaire, in which their report of their experiences was treated with greater respect. We conclude from such experiences that "just in case" is often a poor justification, and a stronger rationale is needed to justify the inclusion of additional measures that might be perceived as extraneous (at best) by respondents.

Including additional variables, if they are judiciously selected, does not always have an adverse effect, in terms of missing data problems. Additional measures of the same construct may enhance the reliability and validity of measurement and may provide the raw material needed for some techniques for imputing missing data. It may happen that a study participant omits responding to a single measure of a construct but does respond to other measures of the same construct that overlap with the omitted response. This circumstance would facilitate imputation of the missing value, depending on the technique being used. Using multiple measures of any latent construct, aside from being advisable for other methodological reasons, is thus a prudent safeguard against the likelihood that there will be a certain amount of missing data. Though there are costs for increased measurement, it is likely the most appropriate safeguard against missing data.

Assignment to Intervention Groups

Assignment of consenting participants to intervention groups is a study stage in experiment designs that can lead to attrition and missing data. Generally, attrition occurs in two situations. First, when participants perceive the available alternative treatment to be more favorable than the treatment to which they are assigned, they may experience "resentful demoralization," a threat to the internal validity of the study (Shadish et al., 2002). Disappointment with the treatment allocated can result in the decision to withdraw from the study. One strategy is to offer each intervention at different but comparable sites. In doing so, those at the comparison site are less likely to be aware of the alternative and therefore less likely to be resentful. Another method is to "market" the potential interventions as equally effective or at least of equal potential. Either through blinding participants to other treatment options or marketing, resentful demoralization can be addressed and likely reduced.

Assignment to groups contributes to attrition when it generates a mismatch between the treatment assignment and treatment preference. Bradley (1993) and McPherson and Britton (2001) proposed an alternative research design (the *partial randomized controlled trial*) that accounts for participants' preference to enhance satisfaction and researchers' intent to minimize attrition. Participants who indicate no treatment preference are randomly assigned to treatment options, while those with a preference are assigned to the preferred option. This design seems beneficial for reducing attrition; however, it may increase the likelihood of selection bias and/or threaten validity in terms of expectancy or placebo effects. The scientific utility of this method has yet to be fully studied, but from a missing data perspective, it appears to offer an advantage over traditional randomized controlled designs.

Another potentially useful strategy is to maintain random assignment but offer the preferred option after a certain period of time. For example, in a treatment study, those assigned to the control group could be offered the treatment after posttest data collection—a situation similar to wait list control designs. Offering sham or pseudo-treatments (also called minimal treatments) is another alternative. These treatments mimic the intervention of interest in every way with the exception of the active ingredients that characterize the experimental intervention. A clever example is sham surgery, in which the participant's preparation for surgery mimics all activities except the actual surgery itself. Randomized controlled trials evaluating the efficacy of knee surgery have used sham treatments such as needle injections of saline placebo with the control group (Felson & Buckwalter, 2002). The sham surgery reduced missing data in a most subtle way — most participants believed they were randomized to the treatment group and therefore had faith that the treatment was appropriate.

Second, perceptions of efficacy while undergoing an intervention may contribute to attrition. When participants perceive improvement it can lead to the decision to terminate participation in the study. Likewise, lack of improvement or experience of adverse effects can lead to withdrawal from the study. Dropout is associated with treatments that create stress or hardship on participants. The end result is data missing at follow-up periods and a sample of completers who might not be representative of the target population. Strategies to prevent missing data in these situations include offering incentives for continued involvement in research (and increasing those incentives as the study progresses), carefully selecting the control condition (e.g., minimal treatments or placebos), and using a wait-list control design where participants assigned initially to the control condition receive treatment at a later point in time.

Attrition and Retention Strategies

In longitudinal designs, researchers should incorporate strategies to reduce attrition. As noted in Chapter 2, attrition compromises internal and external validity. Reducing the likelihood of attrition, therefore, is necessary in order to enhance the validity of the study conclusions. By understanding the factors contributing to attrition, investigators are better able to design appropriate strategies to minimize loss of participants. Obviously, no single strategy is appropriate for all circumstances.

There is accumulating evidence that attrition does not occur at random; instead, participants with complete data on all occasions of measurement tend to differ from those with missing data at data collection points. Moser et al. (2000) categorized the factors influencing dropout into sociodemographic and clinical characteristics of participants, as well as characteristics of the study design (as discussed earlier). Several characteristics have been consistently found to be associated with attrition. It is more likely that participants will miss follow-up assessments if they are young or retired, if they are male or are members of minority groups, if they have low income or are of low socioeconomic status, if their level of education is low or they have less residential stability and therefore greater geographic mobility, or if they are in poor health (Aylward, Hatcher, Stripp, Gustafson, & Leavitt, 1985; Boyd, Cousins, & Kriukov, 1992; Constantine, Haynes, Spiker, Kendall-Tackett, & Constantine, 1993; Moser et al., 2000). This evidence suggests that attrition is not random; therefore, missing data of this type are likely to result in biases with unknown effects.

Investigators who are aware of the characteristics that tend to be associated with attrition can use appropriate strategies to target similar participants and make efforts to retain them in the study. Multiple retention strategies have been proposed, but they have not been systematically evaluated for their effectiveness. They include

- Establishing a detailed record of the participants' current and alternative addresses (including contact information for friends or relatives).

- Establishing formal and informal relationships with staff at agencies providing services to participants.
- Creating a project identity by selecting a study logo.
- Using incentives for participation (e.g., money, pens, educational material, entry in a lottery). It is recommended to offer the incentive after completing the data collection, at each occasion of measurement, and increasing the incentives as the study continues.
- Maintaining frequent contact with participants (e.g., postcards, telephone calls, visits) between measurement occasions.
- Making study protocols convenient for participants (e.g., scheduling interviews at a convenient place and time, and making data collection convenient, such as with telephone interviews, providing postage, transportation, or even child care during data collection).
- Developing a screening measure to identify individuals likely to drop out of the study. The measure can be administered at the initial contact to select those least prone to drop out. (Although useful for minimizing attrition, it can lead to the selection of a biased sample.)
- Making sure, through training and monitoring, that research staff understand the importance of tracking participants, being available to participants, and handling refusal to continue participation.

This list of strategies is not exhaustive; it merely serves to illustrate a variety of tactics that could be used to decrease the likelihood of attrition. It is important to note that incorporating multiple strategies into the research design may be more effective in promoting retention than single strategies used alone.

CHARACTERISTICS OF THE TARGET POPULATION AND THE SAMPLE

Participant recruitment is another design element associated with missing data. Target group identification and recruitment are two stages in which missing data can be prevented. Because individuals or groups from the targeted population differ on their probability of producing missing data, efforts to identify a sample that is easiest to contact and more likely to comply with study protocols is critical. For example, homeless individuals, physicians, and migrant farmworkers are more difficult to recruit and to locate for follow-up data collection. Studies often use "captive" groups like prison inmates, college undergraduates, and patients admitted to in-hospital units.

Another consideration for sample identification and recruitment is the likely perception of the study topic. Participants differ in their level of interest in and/or familiarity with the research topic. Salience of the research topic has been consistently found to increase response rate in surveys (Hox & de Leeuw, 1994). Those who perceive the topic to be of interest tend to participate and provide complete data. Similarly, the intrusive nature of information sought may deter some participants from responding. Anticipating what might be viewed as intrusive by a targeted sample can reduce the likelihood of missing data. For example, questions about sexual behaviors are known to be viewed as intrusive by those for whom it is unacceptable to discuss these issues with strangers. Information about illegal activities (e.g., stealing, drug use) and antisocial behavior (e.g., lying, cheating) is also known to be thought of as intrusive. Sometimes, it is difficult to anticipate what might be viewed as intrusive by a particular group. For example, one of us recently had the experience of collecting data from a group of Native Americans who found questions about dropping out of school to be intrusive. It was suggested that the wording be changed, from "dropped out" to "did not finish" high school, to make the question less objectionable. Fortunately, this issue was discovered during the questionnaire development stage rather than during the data collection stage, where such a question might have resulted in missing data. Needless to say, in order to decrease the likelihood of nonresponse, it is important for investigators to be knowledgeable about potentially sensitive subject areas for the target group.

Certain sociodemographic characteristics of target groups are known to be more likely to produce missing data. For example, older persons tend to have a higher rate of nonresponse (Bradburn, 1992) and incomplete data. Several factors could contribute to nonresponse, including illness, mobility problems, fatigue, memory deficits, impaired hearing, language barriers (Wilson & Roe, 1998), visual impairment, difficulty concentrating, transportation problems, and seasonal migration. Those with little formal education and people with low English proficiency also tend to have high nonresponse rates in surveys (Bradburn, 1992). They may not adequately understand instructions or item content. This situation may increase frustration or affect confidence, which can lead to omission of items or refusal to participate.

A number of strategies exist that can reduce missing data due to characteristics of the target sample. As noted, understanding these characteristics in advance allows for planning appropriate prevention strategies. Conducting pilot studies of test instruments and response patterns helps investigators to identify potential difficulties with target samples. Response tendencies and measure characteristics such as comprehensibility, length, ease of use, and relevance of content can be assessed through focus group sessions with individuals representing the target population. Items likely to be viewed as intrusive can also be identified this way. Revisions of the instruments prior to data collection can reduce missing data during the study implementation phase.

If it could be anticipated that individuals would be difficult to locate in the future, the incentive and other methods described earlier for decreasing attrition would apply. For those who may be unfamiliar with the research topic, the researcher could (1) clearly delineate the target population and use nonprobabilistic strategies (i.e., intentional) to sample knowledgeable participants or (2) systematically eliminate high-dropout-risk individuals by conducting an initial, brief screening to determine their level of familiarity.

For subjects likely to view data collection as intrusive, along with the strategy of using pilot testing, as mentioned above, a good idea would be to provide confidentiality assurances about responses to questions that are sensitive or intrusive. Singer, van Thurn, and Miller's (1995) meta-analysis of studies testing the relationship between confidentiality assurance and survey response showed that assurance of confidentiality slightly improved response rates and that the improvement was greatest with surveys that addressed sensitive topics.

For elderly participants, researchers might take special pains to schedule data collection at a convenient place and time, provide breaks for the respondents when they are completing questionnaires, conduct face-to-face interviews in which interviewers assist the participants as needed to reduce the burden and ensure complete data, and use large print to make reading easier.

For subjects with a low educational level and/or low English proficiency, here are some suggestions for extra efforts to make: test the measure's readability level (e.g., grade level, Rigby Literacy Level) and ensure that items and their responses are at an appropriate reading level for the intended sample. Again, pilot testing with a smaller sample that is representative of the target group is helpful. Translate questionnaires into the dominant language of the target sample (and check the accuracy of the translation in a pilot test). Face-to-face interviews are also useful, in which the meaning of responses can be double-checked.

A standard practice is to "pad" a study with more participants than would be required for a valid result (determined by a power analysis). This is to compensate for nonresponses and attrition. An additional 15% to 25% of the required sample size is commonly recommended. This strategy does not correct for biases that may be causing the nonresponses and attrition, but at least it protects against underpowered studies.

DATA COLLECTION METHODS

There are various approaches to gathering pertinent information. They include monitoring physiological indices, observing behavior, conducting interviews, obtaining filled-out questionnaires from participants, and reviewing preexisting materials such as hospital records. Each method has the potential for data loss and can require different strategies for reducing missing data. When data collection involves a combination of these methods, the likelihood of missing data is increased. For instance, when clinical observations are abstracted, in the form of chart reviews, say, there are two potential sources of missing data: missing clinical observations and oversight during the chart review. The following sections provide descriptions of missing-data risks for each method and suggestions for reducing that risk.

Physiological Indices

Physiological data can be obtained through laboratory tests performed on samples of body fluids or tissue, or through electronic means such as an electroencephalograph (EEG). In both methods, missing data can result from preventable human error or unavoidable equipment failure. For example, improper handling of blood samples (e.g., delay in transferring the sample to the laboratory) can result in missing data, often necessitating the collection of new samples. Yet the procedure for obtaining the samples is often invasive, which may preclude replacement and ultimately result in missing data. Samples collected during a specific time frame, such as immediately after an intervention, cannot be replaced without repeating the entire process. To avoid human error, investigators should have detailed protocols, train research assistants in these protocols, conduct random checks on adherence to these protocols, anticipate problems and develop solutions prior to data collection, and hire skilled persons with experience in obtaining and handling the samples. Similarly, missing data associated with equipment failure can be prevented—if such failures are anticipated. Precautions include regular equipment checks prior to the data collection and ensuring backup plans are in place if equipment fails (e.g., alternative power sources, extra equipment). A trial run to make sure everything works as expected might be worthwhile too.

Observation of Behavior

This data collection method involves a trained person observing a target situation (e.g., person, event, setting) and recording relevant information. The design and implementation of observations, as well as observers' knowledge and skills, contribute to missing data. Some observation protocols may require observers to record many events within a restricted period of time, thus increasing the likelihood of missing data. Poorly trained and/or unmotivated observers often miss relevant cues and fail to record information when, in fact, the target phenomenon was present, resulting in missing data. Comprehensive and complex observation methods that require observers to attend to multiple aspects of the target or make observations in short, frequent time intervals or on a continuous basis are not only burdensome and hard to implement but are also prone to loss of information. However, complex observation methods may be unavoidable for certain research questions. Therefore, strategies to lower the probability of missing data should be followed. It is important that investigators consider the target to be observed as well as the conditions of observation, decreasing the complexity of observational methods whenever possible. If an observer's ability is somehow compromised (e.g., if he or she is at the back of a classroom), this increases the likelihood of missing data. Similarly, a poorly defined target such as "obnoxious behavior" can contribute to loss of data because vagueness makes appropriate cues difficult to monitor. Defining the target in as clear and objective terms as possible should decrease this type of missing data. For example, "obnoxious" could be defined as speaking in an unusually loud voice, using vulgar language, pushing, and so on.

The observation setting should be considered a priority as well, with the target in mind. For example, if facial expressions are the target, the observer should be situated close enough to see those expressions and where there are few obstacles. Consideration must be given to the reactivity of the observation setting as well, in order to reduce the potential for bias associated with a change in behavior due to the subject's awareness of being observed. Those who observe teachers, for example, generally avoid sitting at the front of the classroom and taking notes.

Other situations likely to result in missing data include requiring constant and/or continuous observations of a target. This is particularly difficult when observers are recording observations by writing or typing, which can distract them. Ongoing observation also results in fatigue, which can decrease diligence in recording data and lead to missing observations. A contemporary example is the continuous data gathering at airport security gates. Security personnel make decisions based on continuous data, and fatigue causes many of them to miss relevant cues. Fatigue from this type of observation could be lessened by videotaping and having observers review videotapes at their own pace. In fact, the FAA does use videotape review as part of security.

Using multiple observers to record different facets of the same targets reduces the burden on individual observers and thus decreases the likelihood of missing data. When observing Coach John Wooden during the UCLA basketball season, two investigators—Ron Gallimore and Roland Tharp—sat in different sections of the bleachers and recorded their observations separately. Afterward, they compiled and compared their notes, to generate a more complete picture of Wooden's coaching style. The investigators noted that having two observers greatly reduced the likelihood of missing targets of interest (Roland Tharp and Ron Gallimore, personal communication, October 20, 2002).

Interviews

Interviews involve verbal communication between the interviewer and the participant during which the interviewer records responses. Interviews can be done face-to-face, over the telephone, or through other means such as videoconferencing. Various aspects of interviews can result in missing data. Whether the interview is conducted in a convenient setting, and with enough time given, are relevant concerns. Participants might fail to show up, or, if they are inhibited by the setting, their responses might be less than candid, and so on. Informing participants in advance about the conditions and duration of interviews should reduce the likelihood of missing data in such cases.

Interviewer characteristics can increase the likelihood of missing data as well. While there are no systematic studies of the influence of interviewers' characteristics on participants' responses, the following issues have been derived from our experience and from relevant literature.

- Participants feel uncomfortable and thus are reluctant to respond to items with sensitive content in the presence of interviewers who are not perceived as similar (e.g., by gender, sexual orientation, race, and ethnicity; Julion, Gross, & Barclay-McClaughlin, 2000). For example, one of the authors found that Native Americans generally respond more willingly and openly to Native American interviewers than Caucasian interviewers during the collection of personal information such as income, educational attainment, and so on.
- Participants may feel uneasy in the presence of an interviewer perceived as being more knowledgeable or skillful in the area being assessed. When the assessment clearly shows the respondent is failing, he or she might become demoralized and either decrease effort or simply stop responding. To avoid either situation, interview items can be sorted from easiest to most difficult, and after the respondent fails several questions in a row, the interviewer can skip to a new domain of items or terminate the interview. This technique is often used in IQ tests and in computer adaptive testing (CAT; see Wainer, 2000, for a more comprehensive discussion).
- Participants may not be willing to respond in the presence of interviewers who appear to be unfriendly, disrespectful, hurried, disinterested, or judgmental. Thus, careful selection of interviewers and training in interviewer deportment, including communication skills, are important. Random monitoring of interviews and providing feedback as needed can help to maintain high-quality data collection.

Whether interviews are conducted by telephone, face-to-face, or in other ways also has considerations which should be kept in mind. Dillman (1978, 2000) provides a number of suggestions for improving telephone interviews in order to obtain quality information, and notes that "many interviewers have a tendency to underestimate the difficulty of the respondent's task." He offers the suggestion that interviewer training should include having interviewers take the role of the respondent in order to better understand the difficulty of the task. If the respondent has a copy of the questions and any multiple choice-style answers to refer to during the interview, that should help in reducing missing data caused by respondents' forgetting response options (Wilson & Roe, 1998).

Interviews by their very nature have some advantages over other data collection in reducing item nonresponse. Interviewers can check that all questions are completed before ending the interview, participants can ask for clarification if they do not understand a question, and interviewers can use alternate wording or probes, which can enhance comprehension and completeness of responses while leaving the meaning unchanged. Face-to-face interviews provide an opportunity to check for missing data at the time of completion and to remedy missing information immediately. The response rate to interviews has been reported to be higher than that of self-administered, mailed questionnaires, particularly for older adults and participants with low educational level, inadequate language skills, visual impairment, or difficulty writing (Barriball & While, 1999).

Interviews can also be systematized, which can reduce the incidence of missing data. One method of systematizing is to implement a computer-assisted interview (CAI). Computer assistance requires the interviewer to enter responses into a computer program, which then directs him or her to the next relevant question, thus eliminating the potential for error and missing data. CAIs may be used for both telephone (computer-assisted telephone interviews, or CATI) and person-to-person (computer-assisted personal interviews, or CAPI) interviews.[1] Although making interviews systematic is useful for preventing missing data, there is a potential cost to not having the interviewer build rapport with the respondent. The investigator should weigh the likely benefits of CAIs against this potential cost.

Filled-out Questionnaires/Scales from Participants

Self-administered forms are the most common method for collecting data in the social sciences. Participants receive a copy of the measures and are asked to read the items carefully and to respond appropriately. Self-administration is accomplished through different means, such as paper-and-pencil (PAP), computer assisted (including web-based testing), and voice or touch-tone telephone. The latter two were recently introduced in research and are new ways of handling the difficulties of classical PAP methods. The present discussion focuses on PAP exclusively since it is the most prevalent means for self-administered data collection.

PAP measures can be given directly to participants or mailed. The former presents substantial advantages over the latter for several reasons. Clarification of meaning and checking for incomplete responses can be done immediately, thereby minimizing the likelihood of missing data. In addition, "captive" respondents (e.g., patients in a clinic waiting room) tend to be more responsive to measures when sufficient incentive and information are provided (Hox & de Leeuw, 1994), thus reducing the incidence of missing data.

Self-administered, mailed questionnaires produce higher amounts of nonresponse than most other data collection methods (Hox & de Leeuw, 1994). The missing data occur at all dimensions (i.e., occasions, individuals, and variables/items). At the occasions dimension, nonresponse is associated with the mailing process itself (e.g., incorrect addresses). At the individuals dimension, nonresponse is related to respondent characteristics such as comprehension or level of interest in the research topic (Rubin, 1987). At the variables/items dimension, nonresponse is associated with the characteristics of the participants, of the questionnaire, and of the situation under which the questionnaire is completed.

With self-administered scales, investigators assume that the respondents will understand the questions and instructions as intended, an assumption that is often unjustified (Schwartz & Sudman, 1996). Relying on respondents to accurately interpret instructions and the content of scales places a burden on them that can result in nonresponse or withdrawal from the study. If instructions and questions are unclear, the result may be invalid responses or missing data.

Missing data with PAP measurement may be reduced prior to the study by clearly wording items, by providing clear and concise instructions, and by offering cost-effective incentives. After administration, researchers may spot missing responses when the instruments are returned. A quick follow-up on review may remedy the situation as long as the responses are not anonymously returned or returned in bulk.

Reviewing Preexisting Materials/Records

This approach gathers information that has not been acquired by the researchers themselves; rather it relies on official or personal documents such as medical charts, police records, and so on. The unique feature of this mode of data collection is that it involves making data not collected for the purpose of the current study conform to the needs of the current study. Thus, there are two sources of missing information in record-review studies: data that are missing from the original records and data that are missing due to an oversight in the review process. The data of interest to researchers may be missing for some measures, for some persons, and/or at some occasion of measurement.

Data abstraction requires important safeguards. Careful training of data abstraction staff is necessary to ensure quality data collection. Available records often contain data that are difficult to interpret (illegible handwriting in clinical records). Organization-specific acronyms and/or terminology might be difficult to decipher. If reviewers are unfamiliar with terminology, they might inadvertently skip recording relevant information. If the review process becomes tedious, they might skip relevant information to move the process along. Efforts to provide coding manuals and training in record interpretation are valuable strategies for reducing the likelihood of missing data due to reviewer error. Similarly, efforts to emphasize the importance of thorough and accurate record reviews and random checks of reviewers' data collection can be useful for ensuring data quality.

It is important to try to develop rapport with staff members who are familiar with the records in order to elicit their cooperation in locating data missing from records, if possible. For example, birth dates, diagnoses, and dates of previous visits can often be retrieved by a quick search of other records. Never assume that missing data are not retrievable unless told otherwise by the records staff. Multiple sources and the search for those sources, therefore, are the remedies to missing data in record review.

Characteristics of the Measure, or Instrument

The measure (or instrument) used is another study design factor associated with missing data. The following measure characteristics are associated with the likelihood of missing data: length, content, and layout. The length and content of measures are often to blame in research with a lot of missing data.

Length of Measures

Long measures with many items to fill out require more time to complete, are burdensome, and lead to fatigue or boredom. They are therefore more likely to produce missing data.

Test or questionnaire developers often include large numbers of items in order to capture a breadth of information and to enhance the reliability of the instrument. The Spearman-Brown prophecy formula says that longer tests are considered to be more reliable, since as the number of items increases the reliability of a measure increases. Thus, some important, well-known instruments are quite long and take a long time to complete. For example, the Minnesota Multiphasic Personality Inventory-2 (MMPI-2) is a 567-item questionnaire frequently used by researchers to measure psychopathology and takes 60–90 minutes to complete (Butcher, Dahlstrom, Graham, Tellegen, & Kaemmer, 1989). Respondent fatigue is a realistic concern for such a measure. Respondents are likely to hurry to complete the measure, with diminishing regard for accuracy, and those who find the experience too burdensome may simply quit. The length of a questionnaire has been found to affect response rate in surveys. Yammarino, Skinner, and Childers (1991) did a meta-analysis of 115 studies that assessed the effects of several factors on response rate. Surveys longer than four pages showed a statistically significant and consistent negative effect on response rate. From a practical point of view, the latter finding implies that survey length greater than four pages would reduce response rate by 7.8%.

Lee Cronbach (e.g., Cronbach & Gleser, 1957) has made the distinction between measurement *bandwidth* and *fidelity*. Bandwidth is the breadth of information acquired with the instrument, and fidelity is the amount of information acquired about a particular area of inquiry. The point of optimal measurement return lies somewhere between the two extremes of high bandwidth and high fidelity. If researchers favor a breadth of information, then the depth must suffer or missing data will result from overly burdening respondents. The difficulty for researchers is to make the decision about which to maximize, bandwidth or fidelity. Maximizing both has a high respondent burden and therefore increases the probability of missing data. This is just one of the tradeoffs to be considered when deciding how to prevent missing data due to measurement.

One obvious solution is to use shorter versions of the instrument of interest. Many measurement developers recognize the problem of response burden and have done extensive work to validate shorter versions. The Medical Outcome Study—SF 36, which measures functional status, initially included 36 items; it has been shortened into 20-item, 12-item, and even 8-item versions.[2] The Geriatric Depression Scale (GDS; Yesavage & Sheikh, 1986), which initially contained 30 items, has been reduced to 15-item and 4-item versions. The short versions, taking less time and effort to complete, produce more complete data than the original version. It would be useful to consider how much of a decrease in the time it takes to complete a measure would be required by respondents in order to appreciably decrease the probability of missing data. We want to emphasize, however, that an instrument should not be shortened solely to minimize missing data potential.

Content of Measures

As noted earlier, the content of an instrument can also lead to missing data. Respondents' perceptions—of how interesting an instrument is, how salient the topic is to their concerns, whether they perceive the questions as intrusive, and so on—influence response and completion rates. Since it may not be scientifically valid to alter the questions enough to avoid these problems (e.g., by making questions unintrusive) researchers must carefully plan how the data will be collected and train the data collectors. The following actions can enhance willingness to provide complete data: (1) explain the significance of the research topic to participants; (2) inform respondents that some items inquire about personal affairs, which may create some discomfort, and acknowledge that the discomfort is a common and acceptable response while pointing to the importance of the responses; and (3) assure privacy and confidentiality and show respondents the methods used.

Another content-related concern is clarity. If respondents have to tease out the meaning of questions, this increases their burden (Dillman, 1978, 2000). Strategies to enhance clarity include simplifying the language, avoiding ambiguous or unfamiliar terms, and/or providing definitions of terms that are likely to be misinterpreted. Piloting the questions for clarity is generally a useful strategy.

Response options can contribute to missing data as well. Some measures provide preworded, multiple-choice, "all of the above" checkboxes, true/false responses, Likert-scale responses, or written-out answers. Response options that are unfamiliar, complex, or confusing can lead to missing data (Dillman, 2000; Schwartz & Sudman, 1996; Sudman, Bradburn, & Schwartz, 1996). Providing an example of how to use response options is usually a good idea.

Layout of Measures

Even something as mundane as the layout of a questionnaire can lead to missing data (Dillman, 1978, 2000). If the type is too small, if the measure has been photocopied over and over, if the page is crowded, or if there is not enough space between items, this can result in unintentional skipping of items. Some suggestions to prevent these problems include

- Ensure good print quality (e.g., so that print is dark, clear).
- Use large print to make reading easier, especially for older persons and those with visual impairment.

- Have enough space between items to avoid crowding. Separate the items and their corresponding response options.
- Maintain accurate alignment of items and response options.
- Put a reminder at the bottom of each page to go to the next page or the other side of the questionnaire, if it is printed double-sided.
- Edit the questionnaire for omissions and misspellings.

TREATMENT IMPLEMENTATION

Treatment implementation refers to the operationalization of the independent variable in experimental studies and may be related to the incidence of missing data. The relationship between treatment implementation and missing data is mediated by three treatment factors: reactivity, burden, and method of administration. The discussion of these factors is based on our experience because relevant literature is almost nonexistent.

Treatment reactivity refers to the situation in which the mere assignment to a particular treatment condition elicits a negative reaction from the study participant. Problems related to this situation have already been addressed in the section "Assignment to Intervention Groups." *Treatment burden* refers to the demands the treatment implementation imposes on the participants. Treatments that require a great deal of time and/or effort on the part of the participant or that impose pain or suffering are more burdensome and thus are more likely to cause failure to complete the treatment, or worse, drop out. Treatment burden can be increased by frequency, duration, and/or intensity of sessions. For example, short-term but intense interventions (i.e., multiple sessions with short intervals between them) might be more burdensome than long-term interventions that are less frequent and spaced across longer intervals. When possible, researchers should design interventions to facilitate adherence and prevent attrition.

Two aspects of treatment administration need to be considered by researchers: treatment providers and the context of treatment delivery. Characteristics of providers can influence how participants react to the intervention, including whether they comply with study protocols and complete the study. If providers are viewed negatively (e.g., as unskilled or unfriendly) it is more likely that participants will not comply and/or will drop out of the study. Attrition might also be due to odd circumstances that researchers might fail to consider, such as a parking lot that is far from the study site.

DATA ENTRY PROCESS

Assuming that all relevant data have been gathered, getting the data into a suitable form for analysis is yet another step at which data can be lost, and its potential for data loss has received little attention. Data entry can be a tedious job, perhaps done by research assistants less invested in the accuracy of the final outcome than the lead researchers themselves would be, and the importance of data entry being done well may be overlooked unless obvious mistakes are discovered. Simple, dull, and repetitive tasks are likely to produce careless errors. The burden is increased if there are multiple pages per measure to enter.

Researchers should consider whether they can improve the accuracy of data entry by adding incentives and feedback to reduce the amount of careless work that may occur. Data entry personnel who have an incentive to be careful *and* expedient rather than simply expedient should save time and money in the long run. Processes by which entry can be validated and cross-checked should be considered and tested. There is data entry software that reduces invalid entries by setting validity parameters outside of which the program alerts the user to change the value. Double-entry methods, in which two different individuals enter the same data, with inconsistencies flagged and changed to reflect the accurate value, are also useful. An additional individual can also serve as a verification check by checking entries for randomly selected cases (e.g., every tenth one). Thoughtful application of multiple safeguards can virtually eliminate this often ignored source of missing data.

SUMMARY

Of course, the best solution to missing data is for there not to be any. Why not simply prevent the problem in the first place, or at least minimize it? Unfortunately, the extant literature on missing data does not emphasize prevention; the literature focuses on statistical remedies, after the data are missing. In other words, using terminology from medicine, the missing data literature focuses primarily on tertiary care rather than prevention.

In this chapter, we discussed the importance of minimizing missing data and offered broad suggestions regarding research design strategies that reduce the probability of missing data. Many of these suggestions are based on empirical findings, while others are based on common sense. Most have to do with reducing the burden of participating in studies. The greater the burden, the greater the likelihood that participants will fail to comply with study protocols, including not completing measures or not completing the study. The end result is more missing data.

Although the suggested research design strategies are important for reducing missing data, each strategy comes at a cost, and some solutions may be impossible given the study context. The investigator should consider the costs of a prevention strategy prior to implementation. For example, targeting samples that are easily recruited, likely to comply with treatments, or likely to respond to all questions in order to reduce the likelihood of missing data might not result in a generalizable sample of the intended population. In such a case, the benefit of less missing data should be balanced with the cost of less generalizability. Similarly, shortening measures to increase the likelihood of completion may compromise the breadth or depth of items and therefore threaten construct validity. The costs may be too great and may therefore render these missing data prevention strategies less than optimal.

Some missing data prevention strategies are not available in certain situations. For example, researchers conducting secondary data analyses cannot remedy missing data problems by changing the design of the study, which has already been completed. Thus feasibility must also be taken into consideration, along with the costs and benefits, when selecting prevention strategies. The benefits of a prevention effort might be great, but when that cost outweighs the problems posed by the missing data, another method, such as a statistical treatment, must be considered.

Although the strategies suggested in this chapter can be useful for reducing missing data, investigators should always heed Murphy's Law: "If something can go wrong, it will" (Tenner, 1996). Things happen that were unforeseen during the study design and outside the researcher's control that can lead to missing data. To illustrate with an extreme example, the species of hunting wasp on which Niko Tinbergen conducted his famous ethological investigations of landmark learning became completely extinct in Northern Europe between successive study seasons, resulting in a serious case of missing data and making it impossible to continue the experiments. Had researchers in the last few decades of the 20th century been interested in investigating individuals' responses to smallpox, they would have faced a similar missing data situation, because smallpox was eradicated worldwide in the 1980s.

Although cases of missing data in the social sciences are not usually that extreme, missing data can be a major problem.

NOTES

1. See *http://www.qualitymetric.com/innohome/insf36.shtml* for a description.

2. Both methods are discussed in detail in the following document made available to the general public by the American Statistical Association: *http://www.stat.ncsu.edu/info/srms/survcoll.html*

5

Diagnostic Procedures

The aim of this chapter is to provide the reader with a detailed presentation of the statistical procedures available for diagnosing the type and extent of missing data using the most popular statistical software packages. The chapter provides an important link between the theoretical classification system discussed in Chapter 3 and the subsequent treatment of missing data discussed in the following chapters. In this chapter, we emphasize the importance of diagnosis as part of the decision-making process in selecting the appropriate missing data handling technique, and the implications that diagnostics have for the validity of study results. This chapter provides the basis for choosing and implementing the methods presented in Chapters 6–10 concerning the selection of missing data handling procedures, because proper diagnosis should always occur prior to the identification of the appropriate solutions.

Assuming that the investigator's prior efforts successfully minimized but did not altogether eliminate missing data, the next task is to diagnose the missing data (e.g., the type, extent, mechanism, and pattern). Diagnostic procedures are not an end in themselves. The information gained from diagnostics is helpful in directing the selection of the most appropriate missing data handling techniques in a particular situation. As noted in Chapter 6, selection of procedures is dictated by the amount and pattern, dimension (variables vs. individuals vs. occasions), and mechanism of missing data. Also, proper diagnostics inform the researcher about the inferential limitations from the observed data and the proper level of caution to exercise when interpreting results. For example, if diagnostics indicate that missing data likely do not threaten internal validity but do pose a threat to external validity, caution should be exercised when discussing the generalizability of statistical results. Missing data diagnostics are an indispensable step in the process of data analysis. Not only do they guide us in determining the most appropriate methods for handling the missing data, but they also inform us about inferential limitations of our data.

TRADITIONAL DIAGNOSTICS

Essentially, missing data diagnosis involves understanding and appropriately characterizing missing data, as we discussed in Chapter 3. Diagnostics can be used to determine the mechanism, dimension, level, pattern, and amount of missing data. Traditionally, formal diagnostic procedures focus primarily on determining the mechanism of missing data, that is, deciding if the missing data are MCAR, MAR, or MNAR (detailed in Chapter 3). Often, these diagnostic procedures involve testing for differences and correlational analyses to test for biases in missing data. For example, researchers test for differences between participants who complete and those who fail to complete studies on a variety of demographic variables (e.g., sex, race, age).

We contend that the traditional approach to missing data diagnosis is incomplete and that it can be misleading as well. First, the traditional methods rarely, if ever, test the missing data mechanism explicitly. Noting differences between those with and without missing data on demographic variables—or other theoretically relevant or irrelevant variables—does not provide sufficient information by which to differentiate between data that are MCAR, MAR, or MNAR. Second, the traditional methods fail to provide sufficient information by which to assess the impact of missing data on study conclusions. For example, means testing of demographic variables might inform us as to potential limitations on generalizability due to missing data, but it fails to provide information about the potential biases on parameter estimation. Third, the traditional approach fails to address other important facets of missing data, such as amount and pattern, in any formal, rigorous manner. In total, in our view, traditional missing data diagnostics are limited in the information they can provide.

There are a variety of approaches to the diagnosis of missing data that focus beyond the mechanism of missing data and address other missing data characteristics as well. These characteristics were discussed in Chapter 3 and include not only the mechanism but also the amount, pattern, dimension (i.e., variables, observations, and occasions from Cattell's data cube), and the levels within those dimensions (e.g., item versus scale scores, individuals versus groups) of missing data. Moreover, diagnostic procedures ought to make use of numerical and graphical methods, and we divide our discussion accordingly.

DUMMY CODING MISSING DATA

Before introducing diagnostic procedures, we first present a simple data set used throughout this chapter for demonstration. Consider a research project where 10 participants are measured on two demographic variables (age and sex), two predictor variables (*IV*1 and *IV*2), and one dependent variable (*DV*)—five variables in all. The data matrix is presented in Table 5.1. Values in each of the columns represent observed data for each variable, while empty cells represent missing observations. For example, subject 9 is missing age data but has no other missing observations. There are 2 of 10 participants missing data for the dependent variable (*DV*).

TABLE 5.1. Illustrative Data Set for Diagnostics

Subject	*Age*	*Sex*	*IV*1	*IV*2	*DV*
01	25	M	3		25
02	29	F	2	3	22
03	20	M	4	8	23
04	21	M	5	9	
05	20	F	1	1	15
06	24		3	2	16
07	26	F	7	3	22
08	29	F	8	5	
09		M	9	7	30
10	30	M		9	26

*Note. IV*1, independent variable 1; *IV*2, independent variable 2; *DV*, dependent variable.

All diagnostic procedures start with one fundamental step—dummy coding missing values. The process is simple. If a value is missing in the data matrix, a dummy code corresponding to that variable is coded as 1; otherwise, the variable is coded as 0. The process is repeated for every variable in the matrix.The dummy coded matrix is similar to Rubin's (1987) **R** matrix (discussed in Chapter 3), with one minor difference: Rubin's system of labeling dummy codes was opposite: 0s were assigned to missing values and 1s indicated nonmissing values. Because this system seems confusing and less intuitive compared to common dummy coding practices, we assign 1s to missing values. An example of dummy coding is illustrated in Table 5.2.

As illustrated in Table 5.2, missing observations for the variable *Age* are coded 1 for the dummy code *DAge* and the observations with nonmissing values are coded 0. From Table 5.1, one can see that Participant 9 was the only person missing age data. As a result, a single 1 was assigned in the dummy code matrix (the column for the variable *DAge*), and the rest of the codes are zeros (0). This process is repeated for every variable. In Table 5.2, we have five variables—*Age, Sex, IV*1, *IV*2, and *DV*—and five dummy codes, one for each of the variables—*DAge, DSex, DIV*1, *DIV*2, and *DDV.*

Dummy coding serves as the basis for numerical diagnostic ap-

TABLE 5.2. Illustrative Data Set with Dummy Codes Added

						Dummy codes				
Subject	*Age*	*Sex*	*IV*1	*IV*2	*DV*	*DAge*	*DSex*	*DIV*1	*DIV*2	*DDV*
01	25	M	3		25	0	0	0	1	0
02	29	F	2	3	22	0	0	0	0	0
03	20	M	4	8	23	0	0	0	0	0
04	21	M	5	9		0	0	0	0	1
05	20	F	1	1	15	0	0	0	0	0
06	24		3	2	16	0	1	0	0	0
07	26	F	7	3	22	0	0	0	0	0
08	29	F	8	5		0	0	0	0	1
09		M	9	7	30	1	0	0	0	0
10	30	M		9	26	0	0	1	0	0

Note. DAge, dummy code for missing data for the *Age* variable; *DSex*, dummy code for missing data for the *Sex* variable; *DIV*1, dummy code for missing data for the first independent variable; *DIV*2, dummy code for missing data for the second independent variable; *DDV*, dummy code for missing data for the dependent variable.

proaches, in which the dummy codes are analyzed for patterns and correlations among themselves and with other variables, and for graphical approaches. We turn our focus on these two different and complementary approaches to the diagnosis of missing data.

NUMERICAL DIAGNOSTIC PROCEDURES

Numerical procedures produce diagnostic information in the form of quantitative indices. Interpreting those values is the most important—yet most difficult—step in the process. Although there are likely multiple quantitative indices that could be useful in diagnosing missing data, we focus on several that we have found to be helpful in our own research. Our general approach is to identify useful indices of missing data that allow us to determine the extent and nature of missing data. We present quantitative indices that can be used to assess the facets of missing data discussed in Chapter 3: mechanism, amount and pattern, dimension, and level of missing data.

Diagnosing the Missing Data Mechanism

First, we briefly review Rubin's (1976) three missing data mechanisms, missing completely at random (MCAR), missing at random (MAR), and missing not at random (MNAR), discussed in detail in Chapter 3. The reader will recall that MCAR is the situation in which there is no systematic relation between how data are missing (**R**). That is, if we had a data set such as that in Table 5.1 and randomly deleted values for a given variable or variables, the mechanism for that missing data would be MCAR. The probability of particular values being missing for any variable is not related to other variables in the data set nor to the variable itself.

MAR, on the other hand, is present when the way values are missing from the data set (**R**) is influenced by other variables in the data set—observed data (Y_{obs})—but the fact that there is a missing-data relationship at work in the data set is not presumed to have a meaningful effect on missing data in the variable of interest. If we took our data set and deleted data for *IV*1 based on *Age* (e.g., <25 years) but not on where one stands in the distribution of *IV*1, the mechanism would be MAR. That is, those with missing data on *IV*1 are younger, but their missing values on *IV*1 are no more likely to fall in one area of the distribution than any other.

Finally, MNAR is present when there is a systematic relation between the causes for data being missing (**R**) and the missing data ($\mathbf{Y}_{\mathbf{mis}}$). For example, if we deleted values for *IV*1 based on where they fell on *IV*1—say, if we deleted higher scores—then the mechanism for missing data would be MNAR. The reader will recall that using values that are not present in the data set to detect this systematic pattern of how data are missing is impossible; the pattern can be detected only logically, not through a statistical test.

MCAR Diagnostics

As mentioned in Chapter 3, only the absence of the missing completely at random (MCAR) mechanism can be reliably detected. More specifically, *failure to confirm* MCAR using statistical tests leads to a rejection of MCAR as the missing data mechanism. We accept MCAR as the missing data mechanism if we cannot rule it out. However, if we rule out MCAR, then we accept *either* MAR or MNAR as the plausible missing data mechanism. Yet the reader will recall from Chapter 3 that it is impossible to differentiate between MAR and MNAR in any reliable fashion. Therefore, *both* MAR and MNAR must be considered as a possible missing data mechanism when MCAR has been ruled out.

There is only one known formal method for diagnosing MCAR—a procedure proposed by Little (1988). Prior to Little's method, data analysts used *t*-tests to assess whether missing data were, in fact, MCAR. The *t*-test method was usually limited to situations where only one or very few variables were missing data. The analyst would create dummy codes for all of the missing variables and, based on those dummy codes, create two groups for each variable of interest: those missing and those with complete data. From Table 5.1, there would be two participants in the group without observations for the *DV* (participants 4 and 8), and eight in the group with observations for the *DV*. The analyst would then conduct *t*-tests by comparing the means for each of these two groups on some or all of the remaining variables in the data set in order to detect if there was a difference between those with and without missing data. A significant difference between the two groups was taken as evidence against MCAR (Little, 1988). Going back to our example from Table 5.1, we could compare the two groups with and without missing data for the *DV* on mean *Age*, mean scores on *IV*1, and so on.

It should become clear that this means-comparison method becomes quite cumbersome when the data set contains many variables that are not fully observed. The maximum number of *t*-tests conducted is equal to the number of variables in the data set (p) minus the one with the missing data on which the two groups are based, or (p – 1) *t*-tests. Using our example data set, there are five variables (p) and t-tests could be conducted for four of them ($p - 1$) to compare those missing and not missing data for the *DV*. In other words, we could compare these two groups on mean *Age*, mean *Sex* (which is interpreted as the proportion of males or females as long as one group is coded as 0 and the other as 1), and mean *IV1* and *IV2* scores. If we looked at all the variables with missing values, a total of 20 t-tests are necessary to use the means-comparison method. The 20 t-tests come from the ($p - 1$) t-tests for each variable, and so the five variables with missing data result in $5 \times p - 1$, or 5×4 variables. The number of t-tests results in dramatic alpha inflation and an increased likelihood of Type I errors or incorrectly rejecting the null or claiming that the variables differ when, in fact, they do not.

Little's (1988) MCAR test avoids the problem of alpha inflation associated with multiple significance tests and results in a less cumbersome process having only one statistic to interpret: a chi-square distributed value. The MCAR test compares the observed variable means for each pattern of missing data with the expected population means (i.e., maximum likelihood estimates) and computes an overall, weighted squared deviation—almost like a sums of squares weighted by the covariances between variables. The rationale is that if data are truly MCAR, each subsample conforming to a specific pattern of missing data ought to produce the same means for each variable as those computed for the entire data set using a robust method of parameter estimation. If there are many patterns of missing data and each tends to produce a different mean for each variable in the data set, the likelihood that the data are MCAR is remote. Little (1988) describes the method of taking these weighted sums of squared deviations from the maximum likelihood estimates and testing the null-model (i.e., there is no difference between the subgroup means and the estimated population mean) by comparing the sum with the chi-square table—assuming degrees of freedom equals the sum of the number of variables for each pattern minus the total number of variables.[1] The chi-square is an omnibus or "all possible" test comparing what would appear to be randomly missing with what is observed. If the data deviate from the completely random process (i.e., there are differences between missing and nonmissing cases for all observed data), then the chi-square test would be significant and the data analyst would conclude that the data are not MCAR.

MAR and MNAR Diagnostics

The distinction between MAR and MNAR lies in the special case known as "ignorable" missing data. As discussed in Chapter 3, the missing data mechanism is considered to be ignorable if the mechanism that created the missing data is related to information that is known. Both MAR and MCAR are considered ignorable missing data mechanisms. Hence, to distinguish between MAR and MNAR, one must establish whether the missing data mechanism is, in fact, ignorable. Unfortunately, there is no diagnostic procedure, numeric or graphic, that validly differentiates between MAR and MNAR. Instead, we must rely on logic and a sound understanding of the study design and domain. Thus we return to our earlier emphasis (Chapter 3) on how properly characterizing and understanding the sources of missing data are not only relevant—but critical for handling missing data statistically. Schafer (1997) provides guidance for cases in which ignorability is known to be plausible and when it is not. The following summarizes those guidelines.

According to Schafer (1997), there are four situations where ignorability may be safely assumed. First, *double sampling* (e.g., Cochran, 1977)—a situation whereby some information is collected for all participants and additional information is collected for only a subset of the original sample—can be safely assumed to produce ignorable missing data (MAR) if the subsample is selected by a mechanism related only to the information collected from the complete sample. For example, in a clinical trial, the researcher would randomly select a set of participants from all of those who are missing data on study variables. This subset would be contacted to provide more in-depth information about the study variables of interest for which data are missing. They might also be asked to provide additional information that is informative regarding the missing data. For example, they might be asked whether the study questionnaires were understandable, whether the clinical procedures were bearable, and so on, in order to uncover consistent reasons for the missing data, if they exist.

A second situation applies to survey research, in which researchers have no information about nonrespondents. Unlike the clinical trial in which all participants, by definition, must be enrolled in the study, survey researchers do not have access to information about those who received the survey but failed to respond. However, if the survey researcher is able to randomly select nonrespondents for intensive follow-up in large surveys, the missing data produced by nonresponses may be considered MAR or ignorable. For example, if we conduct a survey by zip code and find that the majority of nonrespondents live in one particular zip code area, we could randomly select individuals from that area to answer questions that would give insight into the reasons why data are missing (e.g., nonapplicable or intrusive questions). Because they are randomly selected from the set of nonrespondents, we assume that these individuals are representative of the other nonrespondents in that zip code area. We then ask this subset of individuals to provide either more in-depth information related to study variables or additional information pertinent to the study. This allows the researcher to either reduce the missing data or to understand why data are missing.

The third case is more applicable to randomized controlled trials, in which the number of participants in the different interventions (or treatment "arms") is unequal or unbalanced. In cases where this unbalance is due to chance, the missing data mechanism can be assumed to be MAR, because the reason for the unbalanced data is not due to a systematic process, such as participant dropout.[2] Unbalance can be due to chance in studies in which participants are assigned to treatment arms based on a randomly generated number (e.g., odd numbers to the experimental treatment and even numbers to the control group). In smaller studies, there could be an unequal number of odd numbers generated just by chance, resulting in an unbalanced number of individuals in the experimental versus control group.

Schafer (1997) proposes to balance out these types of studies by adding *balancing cases* with completely missing data. That is, if just by chance, more odd than even numbers were randomly generated and 10 individuals were assigned to the experimental group while 14 were assigned to the control group, the experimental group would be assigned 4 balancing cases. Those 4 cases would have completely missing data. By adding these balancing cases, one changes the sample size from 24 to 28, despite the fact that 4 of the 28 have completely missing data. The advantages of this procedure are statistical. The balancing cases improve statistical power due to increased sample size (reflected in degrees of freedom for statistical tests). Also, by creating a situation in which missing data are MAR, a wide variety of solutions for handling missing data (e.g., multiple imputation) becomes tenable.

The fourth situation in which it is plausible that missing data are ignorable occurs in circumstances similar to those in double sampling. Specifically, if measures are administered to a complete sample and then additional measures are administered to either a randomly selected subsample or a selected subsample based on information gained from the initial administration, missing data for the additional measures are considered MAR. Additionally, the random administration of forms or sections of measures produces missing data that can be considered MAR.

In all of these circumstances in which missing data can be plausibly regarded as ignorable, the missing data are either randomly missing or the missing information is related to available data. As discussed in Chapter 3, the missing data mechanism is regarded as ignorable if the mechanism that created the missing data is either random (as in the case of unbalanced cases due to a random process) or it is related to information that is present (as in the case of double sampling). The following is a summary of circumstances in which missing data are *not* likely to be ignorable.

It is implausible that missing data are ignorable when the missing data are not missing randomly and when the information that would explain why they are missing is unavailable. Schafer (1997) suggests three situations where the plausibility of MAR is either unknown or unlikely. First, sample surveys without intensive follow-up of nonrespondents are unlikely to provide strong support for MAR or ignorability. Without following up with nonrespondents to understand the nature of the missing data, it is indefensible to assume the missing data are ignorable. Second, planned experiments (i.e., random assignment is used) where observations are missing unintentionally produce missing data that, again, may not be ignorable. One of the defining features of experimental design is the random assignment of individuals to different conditions. If data are missing differentially, that is, if the number of participants with missing data is greater in one condition than the other, researchers ought not to assume that the missing data mechanism is random or ignorable. For example, experiments in which one condition creates a greater burden on participants than another can produce differential missing data due to dropout, low morale, fatigue, and so on. In such cases, the missing data mechanism is not ignorable.

A third condition that likely results in nonignorable missing data occurs in observational studies when it is beyond the control of the researcher to prevent relevant data from being missing. For example, a researcher might be interested in developmental trajectories of delinquency. The sample for the study should include the full range of delinquent activity. However, it is not uncommon that the most severe cases are unavailable for study due to suspension or expulsion from school, imprisonment, and so on. Thus the missing data are relevant to the study question and therefore nonignorable.

Ignorability is implausible in these three situations because only information we do not have on hand would explain why the data are missing. Since we do not have full knowledge of the situation, only logic can guide the decision as to whether the data are appropriate for missing data handling techniques that require ignorability as a missing data mechanism. According to Schafer (1997),

> When data are missing beyond the investigator's control, one can never be certain whether MAR holds. The MAR hypothesis in such data sets cannot be formally tested unless the missing values, or at least a sample of them, are available from an external source. When such an external source is unavailable, deciding whether or not MAR is plausible will necessarily involve some guesswork, and will require careful consideration of conditions specific to the problem at hand. (p. 22)

In other words, investigators must look to sources of data outside their study, such as previous findings (e.g., parameter estimates from previous studies), normative data, intensive follow-up with nonrespondents, and so on, to determine whether data are likely to be MAR or ignorable. When external data are used to supplement research findings to eliminate threats to validity, such as those produced by missing data, methodologists sometimes refer to such study designs as "patched up" (see Campbell & Stanley, 1966, for an early discussion of these designs). Diagnostic procedures that help the researcher to better understand and appreciate the extent and pattern of missing data should aid in the careful consideration of specific conditions that is necessary for determining whether missing data are likely to be ignorable.

We now turn our focus from the diagnosis of missing data mechanisms to procedures that focus on the extent and pattern of missing data.

Diagnosing the Amount of Missing Data

The word *amount* in the phrase "amount of missing data" is frequently ambiguous in the missing data literature. Most often, amount refers to the number of incomplete cases (i.e., those participants who are missing data in a given data set). In Table 5.1, there are 6 participants (1, 4, 6, 8, 9, and 10) missing data for at least one variable (60% of the participants). Yet *amount of missing data* can also refer to the total number of missing observations for a particular variable or set of variables, although use of the term in this sense is less common. There are two cases (20%) that are missing data for the *DV* in Table 5.1. *Amount* of missing data can also refer to the total number of missing observations out of an entire data set. In Table 5.1, there are 6 cells missing data out of a total of 50 cells (10 participants × 5 variables), or 12% of cases missing data.

Although it might seem a trivial difference, these three meanings of amount each provide unique information about the missing data in a study. The number of incomplete cases, for example, provides information by which to assess statistical power for statistical procedures intended for *complete case* analysis (when only those participants without missing data are included in statistical analyses, detailed in the following section). If complete case analyses were used for the data in Table 5.1, only the data for participants 2, 3, 5, and 7 would be used, which would decrease statistical power substantially. Similarly, we might compute missing data as a function of variable rather than case—a method we call the *complete variable* method. The analysis might therefore be restricted to only those variables fully observed. Amount of missing observations for a variable or set of variables provides information for statistical procedures that allow *available case* analysis, when all available observations are included in statistical analyses. When amount of missing data is defined in this manner, we can assess differential rates of missing data between variables to evaluate their potential influence on data aggregation or on interpretation of results. If we wanted to correlate *Age* with the *DV* from our example data set, there would be 9 values for age and only 8 for the *DV*. Three participants (4, 8, and 9) would have data for one variable but not the other, which would affect the calculation of a correlation coefficient such as Pearson's *r*. Although some statistical procedures allow for available case analysis, large discrepancies between the number of available cases for each of the variables in the analysis often produce interpretation problems that are insurmountable.

Given the three different notions of the amount of missing data, there are different methods for assessing the extent to which data are missing. We discuss the *listwise* or *complete case* method, the complete variable method, the *available case* method, and the *sparse matrix* method and its related *ratio* method.

Listwise or Complete Case Method

When the amount of missing data is viewed as the number of cases with missing data for at least one variable, the listwise or complete case method is used. This method entails counting the number of participants or "cases" with complete (or no missing) data. Many statistical software packages default to listwise deletion for some or all inferential statistics procedures as a means for handling missing data and report amount of missing data as the number of missing cases. Yet relying on complete case accounts of missing data tells only part of the story. For example, it is quite possible that a large portion of the study sample is missing data on a single variable. In Table 5.1, six participants are missing data for a single variable.

Using the listwise method to estimate the amount of missing data indicates that 60% of the sample was missing! The result would be exactly the same if 60% of the sample were missing data on all study measures. Obviously, these two missing data circumstances are substantially different in their implications for handling missing values as well as for interpreting statistical results. In the former case, estimating a value for the single missing variable might be relatively simple and result in less biased results than would the procedures for replacing missing values and/or interpreting statistical results when data for all five variables were missing. Complete case analysis can be, and often is, a problematic solution to missing data problems.

Computing the amount of missing data using the complete case method involves checking across all rows of the dummy coded matrix for the presence of missing values. Rows represent each case or study participant, and rows that have at least one missing value are considered incomplete.

Complete Variable Method

Similar to the complete case method, the complete variable method provides an estimate of the proportion of variables (rather than cases) that contain missing values. Knowing how many variables have complete data is also helpful for getting complete data estimates. The proportion of the total number of variables with missing data to the total number of variables in the data set provides the data analyst with an index of the extent of missing data. Higher values mean fewer completely observed variables. It is rare that researchers report or even compute the missing data estimate according to complete variables, but we see no reason to focus attention on missing cases and ignore missing variables. Therefore, we offer this proportion as equivalent to that of the complete case method.

Available Case Method

When amount of missing data is defined as the number of missing values for each variable, then the available case method is used. This method is sometimes referred to as *pairwise* deletion. In contrast to the complete case method, the available case method requires computing the amount of missing data for each variable. Unfortunately, this procedure creates a large amount of data for the researcher to peruse. However, the available case method yields useful information that is unavailable when using the complete case method. Specifically, the information provided is pertinent to understanding patterns of missing data. If all six participants in our example data set were missing values for only *DV*, only one variable will have missing values while the remaining variables would be regarded as completely observed. Such a pattern should caution the researcher that there may be a potential bias in the data, possibly due to the measurement or participant characteristics related to the *DV*. Another scenario, as Table 5.1 illustrates, is one in which multiple variables have missing data. In this example, each variable has only one missing value, except the *DV*, which has two. The pattern in the way data are missing is not uniform: for each variable, a different participant is missing a value. If those six participants were missing data for the same variables, such as *IV*1 and *DV*, there would be a uniform pattern in the way they are missing. Thus, available case methods inform us about the pattern of missing data, as well as the amount. Because of this, available cases are complementary to the complete case approach in diagnosing the amount of missing data.

Sparse Matrix Method

An alternative to the complete case and available case methods is computing the amount of missing values in the total matrix of data, a method we refer to as the *sparse matrix* method. For example, a maximum of 50 observations is possible in our data set in Table 5.1 (10 participants × 5 variables). Of those 50, six cells are missing. This is illustrated as well in Table 5.2, in which the data set with the dummy codes for missing data is presented. There are 44 items coded as 0 and 6 coded as 1 in the dummy coded data matrix; thus 6/50 or 12% of the entire matrix is missing.

This procedure provides different information from that of the two previous methods. According to the complete case method, 60% of the data are missing because 6 of 10 participants are missing data on at least one variable. Yet according to the sparse matrix method, only 12% of the data are missing. According to the available case method, the proportion of missing data is computed only for the variables used in a particular statistical analysis (e.g., bivariate correlations) as opposed to the entire matrix of data.

Taken alone, the sparse matrix method provides only limited information. However, as we discuss shortly, it serves an important role for other diagnostics.

The Ratio Method

A useful index that makes use of the information garnered from a sparse data matrix diagnosis is the ratio of sparse matrix amount missing to complete case amount missing. The sparse-matrix-to-complete-case ratio provides information about the amount of missing data for each case or individual who is missing data. The higher the ratio, the more missing data are present for each case. For example, a ratio of .90 versus .40 suggests that on average there are more missing data per case in the former than in the latter. The ratio is asymptotically bounded by 0 and 1 and offers an average proportion of missing variables per case with missing data. A value of .90 would mean that on average 90% of the variables were missing.

From our example data in Table 5.1, the sparse matrix amount of missing data is 12% and the complete case amount is 60%. The sparse-matrix-to-complete-case ratio is .12/.60 or .20, indicating that the average amount of missing data per incomplete case (i.e., those who are missing data) is about 20%.

The average amount of missing data per variable serves as an alternative to the ratio of amount missing per observation. To compute this value, we compute the ratio between the sparse matrix and proportion of incomplete variables (rather than cases). That quotient represents the proportion of missing cases per variable with missing values. Both proportions provide us with some estimate of the density of missing values at either the case or variable level.

The combination of the five diagnostic procedures—complete case, complete variable, available case, sparse matrix, and ratio of sparse matrix to complete case or complete variable—allows for a more thorough investigation into what constitutes the amount of missing data. Each method provides a different perspective on the same set of missing data, providing different and complementary information to use in evaluating the potential effects of missing data, and points to the appropriate solutions to use in handling the missing observations. The amount of missing data can refer to different dimensions that have differential import depending on the chosen analytic strategy for the study. As Schafer (1997) notes, it is important to have a thorough understanding of missing data prior to selection of missing data handling techniques. These five approaches provide a better foundation for assessing amount of missing data than the traditional complete case methods commonly reported in the literature.

Diagnosing Levels and Pattern of Missing Data

The *level* or *unit of analysis* often dictates whether missing data will have meaningful effects. In education, we might wish to focus on students rather than on schools. Thus we analyze the data using student-level information, whereas if we wanted to focus on schools, we would use school-level information. Multilevel models (Bryk & Raudenbush, 1992) allow us to look at both levels. Similarly, in a study that uses questionnaires with likert scale measures, we might wish to focus on items within a scale rather than on factors made up of multiple items and/or scales. Here, item-level information would be the unit of analysis rather than scale scores or factor scores.

In Chapter 3 we used Cattell's data box (Cattell, 1966) as a heuristic for discussing the different dimensions of data (i.e., variables/items, individuals, or occasion). As noted in that chapter, these dimensions all have distinct levels. For the individuals dimension, data can be missing at the level of individuals or of groups. If an analysis is focused on the group level, as in ANOVA, data missing at the individual level have different effects than if the analysis focuses on individuals, as in multiple regression. Similarly, for the variables/items dimension, if the focus is on factors rather than on items, missing item data would have different effects on the analytic results. Diagnosing missing data often involves evaluating a combination of the dimension of the missing data and the unit of analysis (level).

The level at which data are missing can be assessed after the amount of missing data is determined. Diagnosing the level of missing data involves analyzing the *pattern* of missing data from the dummy code matrix. In the data set in Table 5.1, two of the three dimensions of the data cube are included: individuals and variables/items. Because data were collected at a single occasion (i.e., cross-sectional data), the occasions dimension does not apply. The individuals dimension is characterized by 60% of the participants missing data, while for variables/items, each of the variables (100%) has at least one instance of missing data.

The pattern of missing data can be calculated by a simple, straightforward procedure whose purpose is to create a unique code for each pattern. After a dummy code matrix for the missing data is created for the data set (see Table 5.2) each study variable is represented numerically as a binary exponent. Specifically, 2—the binary number—is raised to the power equal to the number of the column represented by that variable in the data set. So the first study variable in the data set (ignoring the Subject variable) will take the value $2^1 = 2$, the second variable (found in the second column) assumes the value of $2^2 = 4$, and so on.[3] In Table 5.1, *Age* is the first study variable and therefore is coded as 2^1 or 2, and *Sex* is the second study variable and is coded as 2^2 or 4. Each variable is therefore represented by a different number. In the next step, the binary exponent associated with a particular variable is substituted in the dummy code matrix for the 1 that represents missing data. Thus, for every missing value (coded as 1) for the first variable, we substitute 2, and for every missing value for the second variable, we substitute 4, and so on. In Table 5.2, the 1 indicating the missing value for subject 9 in *DAge* is changed to 2, while the 1 for the missing value of subject 10 for *DIV*1 (the third variable) is changed to 2^3, or 8.

The next step involves summing these new values in our dummy matrix for each participant. Thus, each variable and participant is represented by a total that is used to indicate the pattern of missing data. Table 5.3 illustrates this final step. The "Value" row indicates the binary exponent associated with each variable (e.g., *DAge* = 2, *DSex* = 4, *DIV*1 = 8, and so on). The "Total" column indicates the sum for each row of all the values within that row. Because Subject 2 has no missing data, her total equals 0, while Subject 4 has a total of 32 because he is missing data only for the fifth variable ($2^5 = 32$ and $0 + 0 + 0 + 0 + 32 = 32$). Other than the value of 0 shared by those who are not missing data, two subjects have the pattern of 32, but the other patterns vary quite a bit. A varied group of patterns like this is also known as *arbitrary* missing data (Schafer & Graham,

TABLE 5.3. Dummy Code Matrix for Table 5.1 with Missing Data Pattern Information

	Dummy codes					
Subject	*DAge*	*DSex*	*DIV*1	*DIV*2	*DDV*	Total
Value	2	4	8	16	32	
01	0	0	0	16	0	16
02	0	0	0	0	0	0
03	0	0	0	0	0	0
04	0	0	0	0	32	32
05	0	0	0	0	0	0
06	0	4	0	0	0	4
07	0	0	0	0	0	0
08	0	0	0	0	32	32
09	2	0	0	0	0	2
10	0	0	8	0	0	8

Note. DAge, dummy code for missing data for the *Age* variable; *DSex*, dummy code for missing data for the *Sex* variable; *DIV*1, dummy code for missing data for the first independent variable; *DIV*2, dummy code for missing data for the second independent variable; *DDV*, dummy code for missing data for the dependent variable. The "Value" row denotes the binary codes discussed in the text. The "Total" column is a sum of values in each column for each subject.

2002). Note that higher values do not necessarily indicate more missing values overall. In Table 5.3, those with higher values are merely missing data for variables that are further to the right in the data matrix.

The final step in this method for diagnosing the pattern of missing data is to sort the summed values (in the "Total" column) in ascending order so as to facilitate direct observation of the missing data patterns. This process is particularly useful as data sets become larger. For our example in Table 5.3, we would sort the participants by first combining all of those with a total of 0, followed by Subject 9 with a total of 2, followed by Subjects 6, 10, 1, and 4 with totals of 4, 8, 16, and 32, respectively.

Common values in the "Total" column can be analyzed to test the degree of similarity of missing data patterns. For example, one might search to find out whether all cases with a total of 4 are similar with respect to a particular variable, such as age or standing on the dependent variable. These analyses are conducted using more formal statistical procedures (see Schafer, 1997). Missing data patterns known as *monotonic* missing data can be detected in this manner. A monotonic pattern is one in which data are missing for one variable; the likelihood of missing data increases for subsequent variables (e.g., in the case of attrition in a longitudinal study).

Another important task in the diagnosis of missing data patterns is to code the levels of each dimension of Cattell's box (i.e., observations, variables, and occasions) prior to the analysis. For example, if an investigator is interested in comparing patient outcomes from different clinics, it is important to code each of the different clinics prior to performing missing data diagnostics in order to assess whether patterns in the ways data are missing are related to the different clinics. The coding process is the same as when creating a categorical variable in which each number represents a different level of a factor in an ANOVA model (e.g., control group = 1; intervention *A* = 2; and intervention *B* = 3). Coding the different factor levels allows for easier examination and interpretation of missing data patterns. If, for example, missing values occur only for males, and sex was not coded prior to the missing data diagnostics, this fact would be lost to the data analyst. The fact that missing data are restricted to males may not only be a strong indication of an actual missing data mechanism, but may also be evidence of the limited generalizability of statistical results.

Diagnosing patterns of missing data is important because patterns may emerge that have statistical and scientific implications. Statistically, different patterns present somewhat different problems when treating missing data. For example, randomized controlled trials with longitudinal data often result in monotonic missing data patterns. These patterns are characterized by missing values that follow other missing values in time. If a participant failed to provide data at the second data collection period in a five-period trial and all subsequent time periods were missing as well, we would classify that pattern as monotonic. Monotonic missing data patterns have a certain predictability to them. Unfortunately, they also generate large proportions of missing data at the variable and occasion levels. Monotonic patterns are far easier to detect with graphical methods than with numerical methods.

An alternative to the monotonic pattern is the completely random or arbitrary pattern. If each participant's pattern of missing values is different, the reasons for the missing data might be truly random. This pattern suggests a different statistical approach for handling missing data than would be used for the monotonic pattern. Because arbitrary missing values suggest an MCAR mechanism, statistical procedures appropriate for MCAR data may be appropriate. Similar to the monotonic pattern, we find that arbitrary patterns of missing values lend themselves well to detection using graphical procedures, such as the pattern plot. Plotting supplements the numeric approach of summing missing data scores to detect patterns.

Diagnosing Data Missing by Occasion

In our previous example, we used a cross-sectional data set to look at patterns of missing data relevant to individuals and variables/items. In repeated measures and/or longitudinal studies, we have another facet to consider: occasions of measurement. Repeated measures and/or longitudinal study designs often produce missing data, frequently for an entire occasion; that is, persons are missing data for *all* variables (rather than an item here or there) on that particular occasion of measurement. Participants often drop out of longitudinal studies, thus failing to show for follow-up measures, which results in missing data for each of those occasions. Diagnosing missing data patterns that involve more than one occasion of measurement calls for a different procedure than the one outlined earlier. For multiple-occasions data sets, we need a diagnostic test to assess the similarity of missing data patterns across all occasions. The degree of similarity between missing data patterns can be assessed using statistical tests of homogeneity for contingency tables, such as chi-square. We illustrate this type of procedure by expanding our data set from Table 5.1 to include an additional occasion of measurement, as illustrated in

Tables 5.4 and 5.5. These two tables include the same data, but they are presented in two different data structures commonly used with longitudinal data: multiple-variable format (as in Table 5.4) and multiple-record format (as in Table 5.5). Both data structures provide the same information but in different ways.[4] When diagnosing missing data patterns by occasion, the patterns to be compared are those for the variable blocks for the multiple-variable format (Table 5.4) and for the time variable in the multiple-record format (Table 5.5). The coding system for diagnosing missing data patterns (as discussed in the previous section) can be applied to both the multiple-variable or multiple-record data formats.

The totals (see the "Total" columns in Tables 5.4 and 5.5) indicate the location and pattern type of missing data; however, the totals offer somewhat different information for each data structure. The multiple-variable format contains a wider range of possible values for the missing data codes due to the increase in number of columns, and missing data occurring at later occasions result in substantially larger total values. In contrast, totals are not influenced by missing data at different occasions in the multiple-record format because the repeated measures data are recorded in rows, not columns. Therefore, in order to understand the differences in missing data patterns between occasions in the multiple-record format, the patterns need to be explicitly compared; that information is readily available in the multiple-variable formatted data. Interactions between occasion and measurement level, however, are best appreciated by an explicit contrast

TABLE 5.4. Illustrative Dataset for Diagnosing Missing Data Patterns across Occasions (Multiple-Variable Format)

			Occasion 1			Occasion 2			
Subject	*Age*	*Sex*	*IV1_1*	*IV2_1*	*DV1*	*IV1_2*	*IV2_2*	*DV2*	Total
Values	2	4	8	*16*	*32*	*64*	*128*	*256*	
01	25	M	3		25	2	5	28	16
02	29	F	2	3	22				448
03	20	M	4	8	23	5		26	128
04	21	M	5	9		6	4	32	32
05	20	F	1	1	15				448
06	24		3	2	16	4	4	20	4
07	26	F	7	3	22	10	5	25	0
08	29	F	8	5			8	26	96
09		M	9	7	30	12		35	130
10	30	M		9	26	5	7	31	8

TABLE 5.5. Illustrative Data Set for Diagnosing Missing Data Patterns across Occasions (Multiple-Record Format)

Subject	*Age*	*Sex*	Time	*IV1*	*IV2*	*DV*	Total
Values	*2*	*4*	*8*	*16*	*32*	*64*	
01	25	M	1	3		25	32
01	25	M	2	2	5	28	0
02	29	F	1	2	3	22	0
02	29	F	2				112
03	20	M	1	4	8	23	0
03	20	M	2	5		26	32
04	21	M	1	5	9		64
04	21	M	2	6	4	32	0
05	20	F	1	1	1	15	0
05	20	F	2				112
06	24		1	3	2	16	4
06	24		2	4	4	20	4
07	26	F	1	7	3	22	0
07	26	F	2	10	5	25	0
08	29	F	1	8	5		64
08	29	F	2		8	26	16
09		M	1	9	7	30	2
09		M	2	12		35	34
10	30	M	1		9	26	16
10	30	M	2	5	7	31	0

available to the multiple-record formatted data. Specifically, if data were likely to be missing on a particular variable—but only at the last measurement occasion—then the multiple-record format would show a similar missing data pattern total for only the last occasion. Information regarding both measurement levels and occasion levels can be obscured by the multiple-variable format in larger data sets with missing data. Regardless of these differences, this process of coding in order to assess missing data patterns is informative for cross-sectional as well as longitudinal data, in both multiple-record and multiple-variable data formats.

Diagnosing "Messy" Missing Data

The number and types of patterns of missing data within a particular data set are important sources of information in the missing data diagnosis process. When there are multiple patterns of missing data, missing data are referred to as *messy*. The level of messiness is relevant when selecting appropriate solutions for addressing missing data. For example, multiple patterns of (or messy) missing data can pose problems for statistical procedures that replace missing values based on observed values, such as regression imputation methods. These procedures are detailed in Chapters 9 and 10, but it is sufficient to note that many of the statistical procedures for treating missing data have requirements that depend on the number of patterns of missing data, making the use of certain procedures untenable when missing data are messy.

The level of messiness of missing data can be viewed along a continuum: at the lesser extreme, only one missing data pattern for all participants, and, at the other extreme, different patterns of missing data for each participant. Missing data are referred to as *clean* when there are not many missing data patterns. For example, a pre- and posttest design with missing data for only a single outcome variable at posttest has one missing data pattern, and thus it has clean missing data. Conversely, situations with many participants missing data for different variables on different occasions have messy missing data. As another example, in a 30-item survey of adolescent substance use practices, a subset of individuals might skip two items about hard drug use (e.g., crack, heroin) but respond to all other items. This systematic skipping results in one to two patterns of missing data and is regarded as clean. Conversely, when different individuals are missing data for different sets of survey items, the pattern is less systematic.

We have developed our own index of messiness to aid in missing data diagnosis. We suggest that the ratio of missing data patterns to the number of participants with missing data serve as a reasonable indicator of messiness. Messy missing data will yield higher ratios than clean missing data. If every participant has his or her own unique pattern of missing data, the messiness ratio would equal 1, because the number of patterns would equal the number of cases. In contrast, the ratio indicating clean missing data is bounded by 1 divided by the number of participants with missing data (there must be at least one pattern of missing data if missing data exist). For a data set with 100 participants, the cleanest missing data index would equal 1/100, representing only 1 pattern of missing data. Applying our messiness index to the data set in Table 5.3, we have six participants, each of whom is missing data on one variable; therefore, our messiness index equals 1, which indicates messy missing data.

Messy missing data may be more likely to be missing completely at random (MCAR) than clean missing data, although that need not be the case. Recall that clean missing data are those that reflect only one or very few patterns of missing data. When missing data are concentrated on a single variable or occasion, this suggests a systematic missing data mechanism (i.e., one that is not random and that is possibly nonignorable). For example, data missing on a single occasion, such as at study follow-up, suggests a systematic missing data mechanism like study dropout. Conversely, sporadic missing data on more variables and multiple occasions are less indicative of a systematic reason for data being missing. Participants might be missing data for different items, different variables, and/or different occasions due to many unrelated reasons, which suggests mechanisms that might be ignorable.

Unfortunately, messy missing data complicate some techniques for handling missing data, particularly procedures for recovering lost information. Researchers use multiple variables to impute missing values for a predictor variable, but there may be values missing for those variables as well. Imputation under these circumstance is very difficult. Because the missing data are messy, variables to be used in the imputation might have more observations than others.

Clean missing data present unique problems as well. As noted previously, if a single pattern of missing data is present for many subjects, it may be indicative of a nonignorable missing data mechanism. Individuals who engage in certain behaviors, such as sexual practices at risk for HIV transmission, would probably be less likely to answer questions about their behavior than those who do not. Missing data of this kind would be considered nonignorable and problematic for almost any of the available missing data handling techniques. Properly diagnosing missing data on the clean–messy continuum provides the data analyst with a more detailed perspective on what obstacles to overcome when handling missing data. In addition, the diagnostics provide information about whether a particular approach would be suitable for a given situation.

DIAGNOSTIC PROCEDURES USING GRAPHING

Many software packages that include or are devoted to missing data handling techniques come with graphical methods for diagnosing missing data. For example, the statistical package SPSS (SPSS, Inc.) has special graphical output that helps the data analyst to better understand the missing data patterns, potential mechanisms, and the amount of missing data. In addition, these graphical techniques convey the amount of missing data in a more qualitative fashion. Although some researchers may be more predisposed to numerical methods, the graphical methods can reveal patterns that are not so obvious by examining quantitative output. The qualitative information does not replace the numerical information but, rather, complements it. Also, for less quantitatively oriented researchers, the graphical methods may be a good starting place for diagnosing missing data. Once the researcher understands the graphical output, he or she can refer to the numerical output for a more thorough understanding of the missing data problem.

The first and most effective graphical procedure for understanding the nature and extent of missing data is the data matrix plot. The data matrix, after being dummy coded for missing data, is plotted in two colors (usually black and white) to represent missing and nonmissing values. The dummy-coded data from Table 5.3 are sorted by missing data pattern and then plotted in Figure 5.1. The figure shows that a small proportion of the total number of observations is missing, and there does not appear to be a systematic pattern of missing data, given that each individual with missing data is missing values for a different variable.

These graphical procedures offer little information beyond the numerical procedures detailed earlier; however, for large data sets, they may be more efficient for a quick visual scan and an assessment of the proportion or amount of missing data as well as the pattern(s) of missing data. Again, this is not unique information unavailable to numerical procedures—it is merely the same information presented in a visual way. For those who ben-

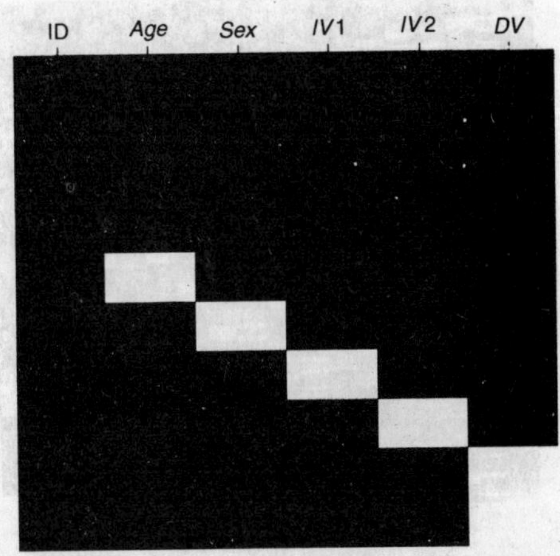

FIGURE 5.1. Missing data matrix.

efit from visualizing their data, this method is useful and quick. Moreover, with data sets that include many participants and variables, a graphical display can be almost necessary for summarizing a large amount of information in an efficient manner. Figure 5.2 uses the same graphical data matrix technique as Figure 5.1 does, but for a large, longitudinal data set with many cases and variables. As the figure illustrates, there are numerous patterns to be seen in the missing values, with larger amounts for the variables further to the right. Because variables further to the right in this longitudinal data set indicate later occasions of measurement, it appears that attrition is an issue—not an unusual problem for longitudinal studies.

An alternative to the matrix plot is the dot chart, popularized by Cleveland (1993). The dot chart is a graphical depiction of the missing data patterns sorted by a specified grouping variable. Suppose we were interested in looking at the differences between men and women for missing data. The dot chart shown in Figure 5.3 is produced when we specify sex as the grouping variable. The *Y* axis of the plot in Figure 5.3 represents the pattern of missing data, indexed by the sum of the exponential values, which are summed in the "Total" column. One pattern is 0 (where there are no missing data); other patterns are 2, 4, 8, and so on. The *X* axis represents the number of individuals exhibiting the particular pattern of missing data. No individuals are missing values for the pattern 4 (males) nor for the patterns 2, 4, 8, and 16 (females). One individual has no missing

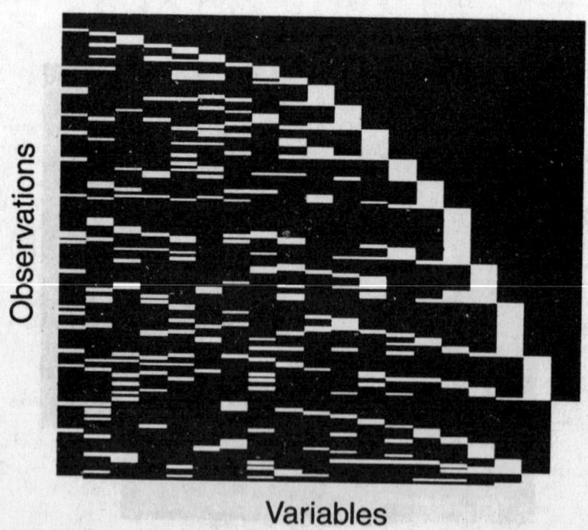

FIGURE 5.2. Missing data matrix for a large data set.

values, pattern 0, and one individual each is missing data with the patterns 2, 8, 16, and 32 (males), and pattern 32 (females). Three females exhibit pattern 0 (i.e., no missing data). The dot chart in Figure 5.3 shows that missing data are "messy" in that there are numerous patterns and they do not appear to be systematic. If there were no missing data whatsoever, all cases as indicated on Axis *X* would have values of 0 indicated on Axis *Y*.

Graphical diagnostic tools are not limited to any particular facet (i.e., mechanism, amount, or level) of the missing data. Some plots are better at communicating information regarding a particular facet than others, but overall they can be informative about all three facets. The matrix plot can be instrumental in adding to the diagnosis of mechanism, level, and amount of missing data. The dot chart, in contrast, may be more helpful in

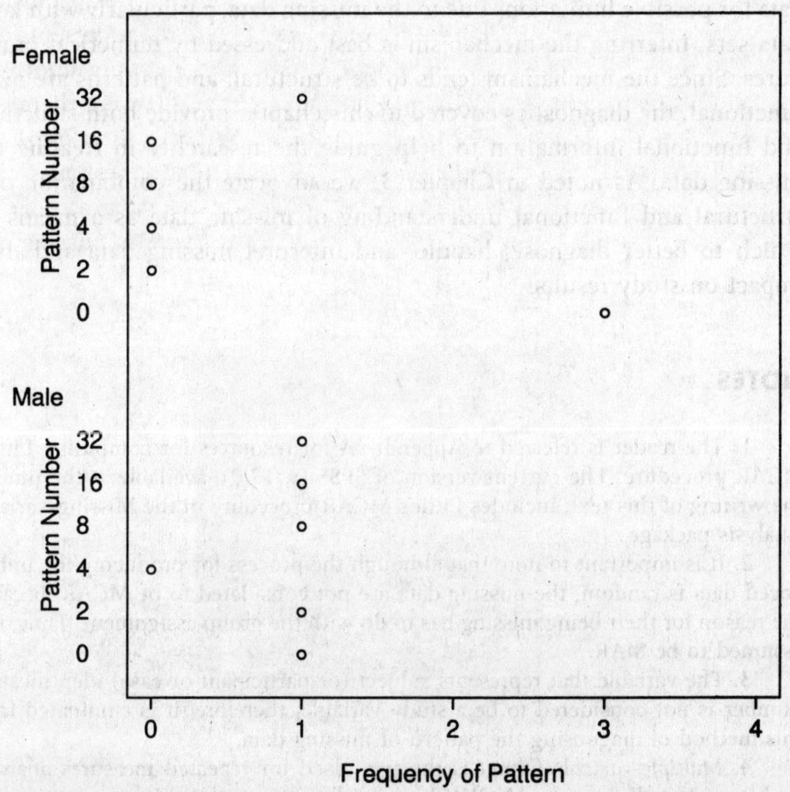

FIGURE 5.3. Dot chart of missing data for a grouping variable.

understanding information about missing data on specific variables, particularly regarding different occasions, provided that time is specified as the grouping factor.

SUMMARY

Diagnostic procedures yield rich information about the nature of missing data and potential biases attributable to missing data. Both numerical and graphical diagnostic procedures help us to characterize missing data. Numerical procedures tend to provide information pertaining to mechanism, amount, and patterns while graphical procedures are likely to provide qualitative information about amount and pattern only. Graphical procedures, while limited, may offer an easier method for perusing the data for possible limitations due to the missing data, particularly with large data sets. Inferring the mechanism is best addressed by numerical procedures. Since the mechanism tends to be structural, and patterns are more functional, the diagnostics covered in this chapter provide both structural and functional information to help guide the researcher in treating the missing data. As noted in Chapter 3, we advocate the combination of a structural and functional understanding of missing data as a means by which to better diagnose, handle, and interpret missing data and their impact on study results.

NOTES

1. The reader is referred to Appendix A for resources for computing Little's MCAR procedure. The current version of SPSS (v. 12.0), available at the time of the writing of this text, includes Little's MCAR procedure in the Missing Variable Analysis package.

2. It is important to note that although the process for producing the unbalanced data is random, the missing data are not considered to be MCAR, because the reason for their being missing has to do with the group assignment. Thus, it is assumed to be MAR.

3. The variable that represents subject (or participant or case) identification number is not considered to be a study variable; therefore, it is eliminated from this method of diagnosing the pattern of missing data.

4. *Multiple-variable format* is the type used for repeated measures analyses such as repeated measures ANOVA. In these data sets, each subject occupies a separate row and the repeated measures occupy different columns. In Table 5.4, *IV1*

and *IV2* are each measured on two separate occasions, each represented by a different variable name occupying a separate column. *Multiple-record format*, on the other hand, is the type used for individual growth curve analyses such as hierarchical linear models or latent growth models. It is also used in event history analyses (e.g., survival analysis). In these data sets, each subject occupies the same number of rows as the number of repeated measures, and a variable is created to code the measurement occasion at which each measure was taken. Thus, in Table 5.5, all observations taken at the first occasion are coded as 1 in the time variable, while the repeated observations are coded as 2. Note that *IV1* and *IV2* form a single column, and the values for the repeated observations for each subject fall within those two columns.

6

The Selection of Data Analytic Procedures

Missing data are pervasive in most research studies and, despite all efforts, are virtually guaranteed in the social and behavioral sciences. Moreover, a large number of researchers are unfamiliar with how to handle missing data. In a preliminary review of journal research articles, we found that even in top-quality journals, scientists appear to be unfamiliar with how to handle missing data and how to report them. By far, convenience seemed to guide which approaches to missing data were chosen, rather than a sound rationale based on a thorough understanding of the missing data. In fact, in many cases, missing data were simply ignored. Authors frequently failed to address the potential effect of missing data on study results—even when studies were missing 50% or more of the data! It is likely that this failure is at least partly related to the fact that many researchers are unaware of both the consequences of missing data and how to determine the best method for handling them. The purpose of this chapter is to provide a decision-making guide to assist researchers in the selection of the optimal methods for addressing missing data, in specific ciircumstances. The proper application of missing data techniques should help the researcher avoid the types of biases associated with missing data that were detailed in previous chapters.

This chapter is focused on guiding the decision-making process for handling missing data, which inherently deals with uncertainty. Therefore, we follow the steps recommended by experts in optimizing outcomes for those making decisions under conditions of uncertainty (e.g., Hammond, Keeney, & Raiffa, 1999). These steps include (1) identifying the problem, (2) specifying clear objectives, (3) maximizing the number of alternative solutions, (4) developing an awareness of the consequences of each alternative, (5) compromising between tradeoffs to meet objectives, and (6) avoiding common traps that can lead to poor decisions. Regarding the first step, the nature and consequences of the problem of missing data have been explicated in detail in previous chapters. Regarding step 2, the objective is to minimize the bias resulting from failing to address the problem of missing data appropriately. This chapter focuses on steps 3 and 4, which guide researchers in maximizing the number of choices for how to proceed and selecting one based on understanding its consequences.

We start with a focus on important preliminary steps the researcher should take prior to selecting a method for handling missing data, followed by a discussion of likely missing data scenarios for social scientists. Preliminary steps include identifying relevant study variables, specifying the level of analysis, conducting missing data diagnostics (detailed in Chapters 3 and 5), selecting relevant statistical models and tests, and using the appropriate statistical software. We then discuss how to use the results from the preliminary steps to guide decision making.

PRELIMINARY STEPS

Step 1: Identify the Relevant Variables

It is not unusual for researchers to collect information from study participants that is never analyzed. Many times, these data are collected "just in case" or because at the time of the study, they were deemed important. When the time comes to analyze the data, the researcher may decide to analyze data only for subjects with complete data. In making such a determination, the entire data set is subjected to a search for missing data, and cases with missing values are deleted. In general, this type of deletion is needless and wasteful, particularly with respect to participants' efforts to provide the data and the effort researchers expend to collect it.

Although it might seem to be an obvious first step, we recommend that researchers first identify the specific variables for analysis before considering what might be missing. It makes no difference if some participants have failed to provide information about their income if that variable is not going to be used in the analysis.

We emphasize the identification of relevant variables as the first step only to avoid common problems associated with statistical techniques that rely on complete cases. In such analyses, any *case* (e.g., research participant) with missing data is deleted. This can be a problem if variables that will not be part of the analyses of interest are included in the determination of complete cases. The primary goal of reducing the data set to only theoretically and analytically meaningful variables, therefore, is to simplify both diagnosing and treating missing data.

Step 2: Specify the Level of Analysis at Which Data Are Missing

Data are sometimes characterized as having hierarchical structure, with micro and macro units. Macro units are formed by aggregates or groupings of the micro units. For example, in a multisite study, we might collect data from individuals (micro units) as well as larger organizations like schools or hospitals (macro units). Although we have data from individuals, the analysis might be aimed at comparing the sites. Thus the level of analysis (sometimes referred to as the unit of analysis) in this example would be the site. Conversely, analyses might be aimed at explaining individuals' outcomes, and site characteristics then serve merely as covariates that might account for a portion of the individuals' outcomes.

Similarly, in a factor analytic study, item values versus factor scores could be the level of analysis, while in meta-analyses, data from each study versus aggregates of the data from each study could be the level of analysis. It should be noted that identification of the level of analysis is not necessarily a "this or that" decision. There can be and often are analyses that focus on several levels simultaneously (e.g., multilevel models), such as patients and hospital sites.

Identification of the level of analysis is an important preliminary step in the missing data decision-making process for several reasons. In some cases, when micro level data are aggregated and the aggregate is the focus of analysis (e.g., in which items are aggregated to create factor scores), missing data at the micro level may not be worrisome. In other cases, missing micro level data can create strong biases in macro level analyses, for example, missing data for occasions of measurement (micro level) in longitudinal studies when estimating change parameters (macro level). The reverse is true as well; that is, biased results may occur when the micro level is the unit of analysis and when macro level data are missing. Some determining factors for whether data missing at a particular level of analysis will result in bias are the amount and pattern of the missing data and the variances/covariances of the variables at those levels. Attention to the level of missing data will help inform the data analyst about the nature of the missing data and the potential impact on study outcomes.

Step 3: Conduct Missing Data Diagnostics

Missing data diagnostics refers to a broad range of procedures used to identify the mechanism, level, pattern, and amount of missing data. Because diagnostics are discussed in detail in Chapter 5, we attend to them only briefly here, with a focus on how they might influence the selection of techniques to address missing data.

If the Missing Data Mechanism Is Known

Almost all missing data handling techniques require that missing data be of the ignorable type. Therefore, it is important to carefully assess and diagnose the study data as MCAR (missing completely at random), MAR (missing at random) and/or MNAR (missing not at random) before making the judgment that missing data are indeed ignorable (see Chapter 3 for a detailed discussion of mechanisms). If ignorability is likely, certain methods are preferred, such as imputation and model-based parameterization methods (see Chapters 8–10). Similarly, missing data that are of the nonignorable type present a variety of decision-making difficulties, and those are addressed later in this chapter.

As discussed in Chapters 3 and 5, missing data diagnosed as MCAR or MAR are considered to be ignorable. When the mechanism is known, the mechanism can be modeled statistically and therefore accounted for in the planned analyses of interest for a particular study. However, when missing data are MNAR, the relevant variables needed to model how they are missing are not available (because the data have not been collected). The extent of ignorability of missing data plays a large role in the decision-making process, which we discuss in the second section of this chapter. Therefore, understanding the missing data mechanisms present in one's study data will help inform the researcher and data analyst about the nature of the missing data and the potential impact on study outcomes and interpretation of results.

Amount of Missing Data

The amount of missing data refers to the percentage of cases without complete observations for all variables included in the analysis. The percentage may vary across levels of analysis, variables, and occasions of measurement, and the amount of missing data has an impact on statistical power as well as precision of parameter estimates. Since statistical power is a function of sample size, effect size, and significance levels (alpha, specified a priori), a large percentage of missing data results in a small sample on which analyses can be profitably performed. With a small sample size, statistical power is reduced. The selection of techniques for handling missing data depends, to some extent, on the amount of missing data and the study sample size. For instance, when the sample size is large and the percentage of cases with incomplete data is small (i.e., ≤ 1%), data deletion may be a reasonable solution if the missing data are ignorable. In contrast, studies that are underpowered to begin with cannot afford case deletion. Alternative techniques, that incorporate methods for replacing or imputing values for incomplete cases, are needed to maintain acceptable statistical power.

The amount of missing data can affect statistical power in several ways when cases with missing data are deleted. When sample size decreases due to deletion of incomplete cases, statistical power decreases. Additionally, as the amount of available data decreases, measurement error increases. Larger measurement error leads to smaller effect sizes, and smaller effect sizes are more difficult to detect and thus require more statistical power. Furthermore, as sample size decreases, standard errors increase and therefore the precision of parameter estimates suffers. That is, there is less information on which to estimate parameters of interest, so estimates are less precise and the expected error about those estimates is increased. In the end, less precision can lead to more tenuous statistical conclusions.

Missing Data versus Missing Information

Dempster, Laird, and Rubin (1977) distinguish between the amount of missing *data* and the amount of missing *information*. The two concepts are related but not equal. Consider an example from the field of paleontology. The data are the remains (e.g., bones, tracks) of extinct dinosaurs, and the information provided by those data might include the stature of the beast, whether it was carnivorous, its communication systems, and so on. Thus, data are collected to provide scientists with information about a phenomenon. Information can include, but is not limited to (1) measurement (are we measuring what we hope to be measuring?), (2) structure (are we capturing the relationships between variables accurately?), and (3) samples, populations, and causal generalization (are we able to generalize beyond the boundaries of our study to other samples and conditions?). Given the distinction between data and information, the relation between missing data and missing information can be varied and perhaps not entirely intuitive. For example, a great deal of data may be missing from the observed data matrix, but if the data are MCAR, little information is lost. That is, the observed data sufficiently capture the information of interest because there are no systematic reasons why data are missing. Conversely, when missing data are MNAR and even small amounts of data are missing, the amount of missing information is likely to be high. For example, in a longitudinal study aimed at understanding delinquency trajectories, if the few youths with criminal records refuse to provide data about delinquent behaviors, only a small amount of data are missing, but vital information about trajectories for that subgroup of juveniles is missing. Therefore the combination of missing data and the missing data mechanism affects the amount of missing information. Most missing data handling techniques will be more sensitive to the amount of missing information than to the amount of missing data. Both data and information are important to account for in the decision-making process.

When a large amount of data are missing, few if any procedures can completely rectify the situation without error. Deletion procedures may render the available, complete case sample size so small that statistical power suffers greatly. Moreover, all imputation procedures require a reasonable pool of available information from which to draw imputed values. When the proportion of missing data is large relative to the observed information, the pool may be insufficient to provide reasonable draws. Even in circumstances where missing data are MCAR and only a few missing data patterns exist, the pool of available information may have so many "holes" that draws from the pool are biased. In such a case, multiple imputation (MI) is the only reasonable solution, since MI allows the estimation of the error attributable to imputation.

Facets of Missing Data

One should also identify the facets and level at which data are missing, as discussed in Chapter 3. The facets include the person, variable, and occasion dimensions of Cattell's data cube, and the various possible combinations of the three. As noted previously here and in Chapter 3, hierarchies within those facets are important as well for the selection of the most appropriate missing data procedure(s). In general, data missing at the micro level may not need to be replaced or imputed if the data are to be aggregated and the analysis is to be done at a macro level. Simple techniques have been suggested to replace data missing at the micro level. For example, with missing item values, the item mean score, the case mean score (based on the average across all items making up a scale for a given individual), and the midpoint on the scale are commonly used to replace the missing item value. These techniques can also be used when data are missing for persons and for occasions. Each technique has advantages and disadvantages that should be taken into consideration before making a final decision. For example, data missing at the item level likely should be treated differently from data missing at an endpoint in a longitudinal study due to dropout.

Pattern of Missing Data

Diagnostics indicating the pattern of missing data are also important when deciding on the appropriate missing data procedures. The pattern of missing data dictates whether missing data are "messy" versus systematic (also referred to as *unstructured* vs. *structured*). Missing data are unstructured when there are multiple patterns of missing values across all participants in a study. The most extreme case occurs when there is a different pattern of missing data for each participant. Referring back to Table 5.2 in Chapter 5, one participant might be missing data for *IV*1 and *IV*2, while another might be missing data for *Age* and another might be missing data for *DV*1. In such cases, data appear to be missing randomly. At the other extreme, a consistent, *structured* pattern of being missing emerges, reflecting some systematic and possibly nonignorable mechanism (as discussed in Chapters 3 and 5). For example, numerous individuals could be missing data at 6-month follow-up due to attrition or the fact that data for the last few items on a speeded test are absent because time ran out. Both examples show a *monotonic* pattern in how the data are missing, detailed in Chapter 5. Figure 6.1 illustrates a structured missing data pattern graphically. In this missing data matrix, there are five patterns (represented by the five white boxes), each made up of missing data for a single variable. As the matrix illustrates, the patterns appear to be structured, as opposed to in the matrix illustrated in Fig-

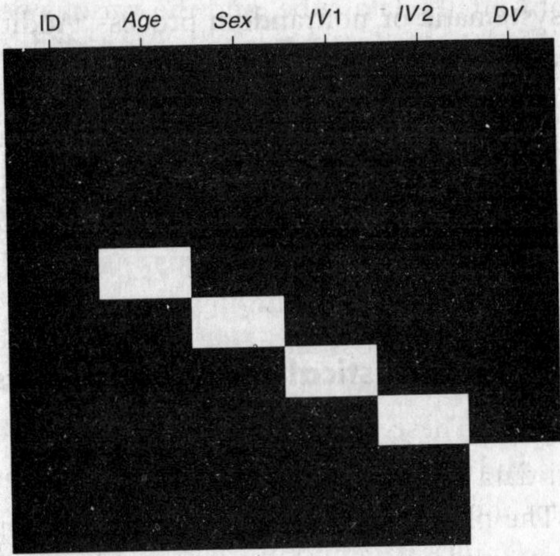

FIGURE 6.1. "Clean," or "structured," missing data.

ure 6.2. The numerous missing data patterns reflect missing data for a variety of variables and for numerous cases.

Missing data patterns are important for several reasons. They help in the detection of the mechanisms of missing data. Messy missing data is an indicator that the mechanism might be random, while patterns that are concentrated or limited in certain ways or in which patterns are con-

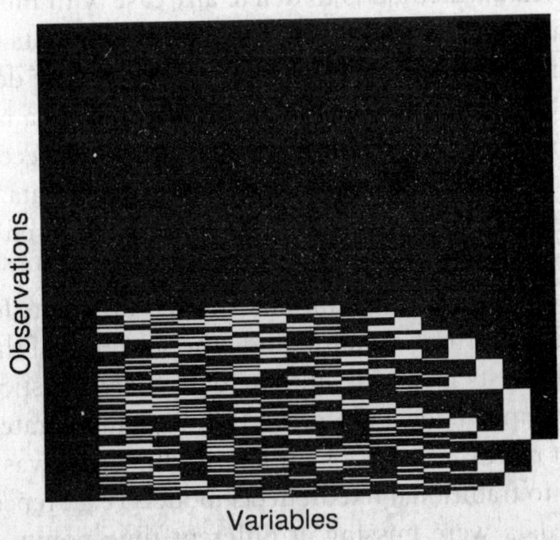

FIGURE 6.2. "Messy," or "unstructured," missing data.

sistent suggest a systematic or nonrandom process. Additionally, patterns govern what is feasible with respect to missing data solutions. For example, regression imputation is more feasible when data are missing for only a few variables (i.e., a structured missing data pattern) versus many variables (i.e., an unstructured missing data pattern) due to the difficulties associated with regression models involving a large number of predictors.

Step 4: Identify the Statistical Model and Tests to Be Used

Prior to the actual data analysis, researchers should have a plan for data analysis in mind. The plan involves identifying the appropriate statistical models and tests to employ given the questions the study is seeking to answer. Some familiarity with the requirements and assumptions of the available statistical procedures is important in order to guide decision-making with respect to missing data, because some of those requirements and assumptions are directly related to missing data characteristics. For example, procedures that rely on covariance matrices as the basis for parameter estimation generally require complete cases to estimate the matrix (although methods have been developed to bypass this problem, e.g., Tomarken & Waller, 2005).[1] Examples of these analytic methods include structural equation modeling (SEM) and factor analysis. Traditionally, in these procedures, when the covariance matrix is estimated, the most common default method is to delete any case with missing data (i.e., listwise deletion). This is problematic if the missing data characteristics (e.g., pattern, amount, mechanism) are such that listwise deletion is inappropriate. On the other hand, methods that use raw data as the basis for estimating parameters, such as linear models, may not necessarily require complete cases. Thus at the technical level, all present data (e.g., pairwise deletion) can be used in these less finicky procedures, even if cell sizes or group levels are unequal.

Awareness of the basic assumptions and requirements for a particular statistical model and/or test can also guide the selection of the most appropriate models and tests given the missing data characteristics of a particular study. For example, Nich and Carroll (1997) demonstrated how the use of random-effect regression models for longitudinal data was advantageous when compared to traditional fixed-effects models (e.g., repeated measures ANOVA) when data were missing at different time points. The random-effects models could handle "unbalanced" data as well as "time unstructured" data, both of which occur frequently in longitudinal studies.[2] These types of missing data violate the assumptions of traditional fixed-effects models in which data analysts typically must delete cases for which observations are missing. These deletion methods are known to be problematic under certain conditions of missing data (i.e., MAR and MNAR—the very conditions that are common in longitudinal studies in which data are frequently missing due to attrition).

Another advantage of familiarity with statistical models and tests is knowledge about the manner in which missing data are traditionally handled in those models and tests. For example, those who employ SEM models should be aware that the default procedure for missing data is listwise deletion. For linear regression models, either pairwise or listwise deletion is traditionally used. This is also the case for calculating Pearson's Product–Moment correlation coefficients (Pearson's *r*). Knowledge of the traditional methods for handling missing data is useful because the researcher can determine if these methods are appropriate and if the data set, given the missing data characteristics, is appropriate for a particular analytic procedure.

Parameter Estimation

Statistical models are generally associated with parameter estimation procedures. For example, ANOVA models (e.g., ANOVA, repeated measures ANOVA, MANOVA) are associated with least squares estimation procedures, while structural equation models and multilevel models (e.g., hierarchical linear models [HLM]) are generally associated with maximum likelihood procedures. The type of parameter estimation procedure chosen has implications for missing data. Least squares, maximum likelihood (ML), EM (a variant of ML), and Bayesian procedures (e.g., Markov chain Monte Carlo [MCMC]) each handle missing data in different ways and may handle data differently depending on how they are implemented in statistical software programs. Briefly, least squares procedures require complete cases (i.e., no missing data). Therefore, most statistical programs use listwise deletion as the default method for least squares analyses. ML and EM are data augmentation procedures (see Chapter 8) whereby parameters are adjusted using the observed data to counter missing observations. The adjustment procedure is limited by the assumption of an underlying distribution (e.g., Gaussian normal). Bayesian procedures, likewise, are data augmentation procedures, but unlike the ML and EM procedures, they are *not* bound by the same assumptions of distribution.[3] Careful attention to these details facilitates reasonable decision making with respect to techniques for handling missing data.

Regarding planned statistical tests, there are three general divisions that are useful to consider that have implications for missing data handling techniques: between-group comparisons, within-group comparisons, and measures of association. For between-group comparisons (e.g., *t*-tests, ANOVA), the goal is to detect significant differences between groups of subjects. Differences are detected when between-group variance is greater than within-group variance and statistical power is sufficient to detect the difference. When data are missing, deletion of cases is dangerous with respect to statistical power due to decreased sample size and increased error (see the earlier discussion in this chapter and Chapter 2 for more detail). Therefore substituting group means for missing values could be useful, as it decreases within-group variance and increases power in order to detect significant between-group differences. However, mean substitution can also introduce bias (see Chapter 9) in many missing data situations.

For within-group comparisons (e.g., longitudinal or repeated measures studies), the focus is usually on detecting patterns of change in variables of interest. In these types of tests, individual (rather than group) values should be used to replace missing data. This can be done in a number of ways, such as regression imputation procedures (see Chapter 9).

When assessing associations between variables, the interest is in detecting significant relationships (i.e., covariances or correlations) between sets of variables. Therefore in such cases, individual rather than group values should replace missing values since group mean imputation decreases variances/covariances and the ability to detect significant relationships. Chapter 9 addresses strengths and weaknesses of methods for replacing missing values.

Step 5: Identify Statistical Software Default Procedures

Related to step 4, we recommend that researchers and/or data analysts be familiar with the default procedures for handling missing data in light of the statistical software to be employed for analyses. Awareness of default methods is important for the evaluation of appropriateness in particular missing data conditions. For example, listwise deletion is known to be problematic when data are not MCAR and for large amounts of missing data. Yet at the time of this writing, listwise deletion is the default method for handling missing data for many statistical procedures within most statistical software packages. (Because statistical software is updated frequently, we do not provide examples.) Other missing data methods are available within statistical software packages, but the data analyst must specify them.

Some statistical software packages make explicit the default procedures they use for missing data while others do not. Software manuals, printed or online, are generally the best place to find out about the default procedures. These manuals usually specify the available missing data options as well. It is important to be aware of the available default and optional procedures so that the optimal procedures can be used.

DECISION MAKING

After these five preliminary steps have been undertaken, their results can be used for decision making with regard to missing data alternatives. Because a wide variety of missing data conditions are possible when we consider mechanism, amount, level, pattern, and statistical assumptions (and their possible combinations), it is nearly impossible to provide a comprehensive review of all possible missing data problems, their solutions, and alternatives. Therefore, we present examples of missing data conditions that commonly occur within a variety of study designs that are associated with a general set of objectives common to social science research. Those objectives include the following: (1) to describe a sample or phenomenon, (2) to assess relations between variables or items, (3) to assess change over time in the same variable or variables, (4) to compare groups, and (5) to assess change over time *and* compare groups. Within each type of study objective, we discuss missing data conditions that commonly occur and potential solutions for handling the missing data given those conditions. Statistical solutions are described in Chapters 7–10.

Objective 1: Describing a Phenomenon or a Sample

When the study objective is to describe a phenomenon or sample, the design is often correlational and cross-sectional (i.e., one occasion of measurement). Often survey research designs are used for this objective. For these types of studies, missing data occur at the person and/or variable facet (but not the occasion since there is only one) and can occur at the micro or macro level—for example, items versus scales—depending on the purpose and design of the study. Statistics are usually descriptive; however, inferential statistics (e.g., bivariate correlations) might be used as well. In these types of studies, there are a variety of possible missing data scenarios. The amount and pattern of missing data can vary widely, and the mechanism can be ignorable (MCAR or MAR) or nonignorable (MNAR).

There are many possible reasons why data are missing in these designs. Data can be missing for *reactive* reasons; in other words, studies that place a high burden on respondents may cause them to drop out, miss stages of data collection, leave questionnaires incomplete, and so on. Therefore, an investigator's first step should be to assess the missing data mechanism and the ignorability of the missing data. If the amount of missing data is not large and the mechanism is MCAR, the simplest and most available method, listwise deletion (see Chapter 7), is appropriate. If the amount of missing data is worthy of attention and the missing data mechanism is ignorable (MCAR or MAR), several alternatives exist. Maximum likelihood (Chapter 8) and multiple imputation procedures (Chapter 10) are just two of many options that might be suitable for these conditions. When the mechanism is nonignorable (MNAR) and other observations in the data set do not provide insight into why data are missing (i.e., the mechanism is not MAR), fewer options exist. If the amount of missing data is minimal (e.g., less than 5% of cases), listwise deletion can be a suitable method in some cases. When the mechanism is nonignorable and the amount of missing data is not trivial, any alternative is questionable that fails to include the variables or the mechanism that account for the missing data.

Objective 2: Assessing Relations between Variables

Another common objective of social science studies is to assess the relations between variables. The study design is usually observational or correlational, and for the purposes of this discussion, we assume a cross-sectional design (longitudinal designs are discussed later). Missing data occur on the person or variable facet, depending on study design. These types of studies might also include psychometric studies that assess relationships between measures, items, or indicators as well as most observational studies that are not longitudinal. These studies differ from the studies discussed in the previous section because they focus on the interrelations between variables or factors rather than on the description of a sample or phenomenon. Statistics are generally inferential and usually include some sort of correlational analysis (e.g., linear regression) or covariance modeling (e.g., path analysis, factor analysis). Because the focus is on relationships between variables, interest should focus on preserving the variability of the factors of interest. Therefore, some missing data options are preferable to others. That is, those that reduce variance, such as mean substitution or listwise deletion, are rarely if ever appropriate.

The amount of variability in the variables of interest is a relevant factor to consider with respect to missing data in any study. If there is little variance in the variable of interest, the amount of missing data is likely to be less problematic than when variance is higher. For example, if many participants fail to report their age but they are all high school sophomores and juniors, there will not be much variability in age, perhaps 2 to 3 years at most. In such cases, it is likely that the missing data are not of much consequence and that the average age for the group can replace the missing values (also known as *mean substitution*).[4] However, if participants ranged in age from 18 to 60, age values would vary widely, and missing data (unless trivial in amount) would likely be of consequence if age was a variable of interest in the study.

Reasons for missing data in correlational studies are often similar to those for descriptive studies. Respondent burden and reactive measures are common problems. Lack of interest in and understanding of the importance of providing complete information can also result in missing data. Depending on the purpose of the study, these reasons may be problematic. The key, as in any type of study, is to ascertain how likely the reasons for missing data are to produce biased study results.

Also common to observational studies that are carried out within an organization (e.g., a classroom, hospital, workplace), are missing data due to absences that have nothing to do with the study. If the absences are unrelated to the study, the mechanism is likely ignorable. If absences are related to the study (e.g., due to illness when the focus of the study is on health-related behaviors), the missing data is likely to be problematic.

Similar to descriptive studies, the first step is to determine the mechanism of the missing data, which can be judged if the reasons for the missing data are known. The same considerations mentioned regarding descriptive studies are relevant with correlational studies. Amount and pattern of missing data should also be determined. These facets are relevant alone, in conjunction with mechanisms, and in light of the magnitude of the expected effects. The type of mechanism is less problematic with trivial amounts of missing data (e.g., a few cases), particularly when moderate to large effects are expected. With correlational studies, effects are measured as covariances or correlations. When small effects (i.e., a weak relationship between variables) are expected, missing data for as little as 10% of the sample can be problematic. Similarly, if a strong relation between variables exists, a larger amount of missing data might not be problematic if the mechanism is ignorable. A large amount of missing data with a nonignorable mechanism is problematic for any study design, and a useful missing data solution might not exist.

Finally, the type of statistical analysis should be considered. As detailed in Chapter 7, analyses involving covariance matrices can be problematic if missing data procedures involve an *available case analysis* (i.e., all available data are used, resulting in unequal sample or cell sizes per variable). To avoid the problems associated with unequal cell sizes, replacement of missing values can be a good option to ensure that all variables have the same number of observations. However, replacement can be problematic if it cannot be done without producing biased estimates. If the mechanism is not MCAR, and if there are nontrivial amounts of missing data and several patterns can be seen in the way data are missing, it is difficult to arrive at suitable values with which to replace missing ones.

Objective 3: Measuring Change over Time

Measuring change has been and continues to be a major concern for social scientists (Gottman, 1995). Change can be associated with an intervention or as a naturally occurring developmental trajectory. The former is discussed in subsequent sections as a mixed design, and thus we focus on naturally occurring change within persons over time. These types of studies often are referred to as within-subjects designs, and the focus is on measuring variability (including stability) in the outcome of interest. Developmental researchers frequently carry out studies in which change or growth in a particular outcome such as development of language, moral reasoning, or self-esteem is measured. Time-to-event studies also fall within this type of objective, where individuals are observed over a specified period of time to determine how long it takes for a particular event (e.g., death, school dropout) to occur. Epidemiologists often use time-to-event designs.

With these types of studies, a new facet—that of occasion—is added. Thus, data can be missing at the person, variable, and/or occasion level. Furthermore, data are structured hierarchically: observations are nested within individuals. Therefore data can be missing at the micro (occasion) level and at the macro (person) level. When individuals are grouped (e.g., males versus females), there is yet another grouping variable, which we address in our discussion of mixed models.

In addition to the reasons for missing data previously discussed, one of the most common reasons for missing data in longitudinal studies is dropout or attrition. When participants drop out of a study, they fail to provide data for subsequent occasions of measurement, producing a pattern of missing data that is monotonic. It is most common that data missing due to dropout are not missing randomly (MNAR), and likely the mechanism is nonignorable.

Special considerations ought to be made for missing data in longitudinal studies. With repeated observations, data can be missing at the ends of the change trajectory (i.e., the start and/or the finish), or in the middle. Special problems occur in any case. When data are missing at the beginning of the study, researchers must estimate initial status from the remaining data points. The same is true if the final observation is missing. When data are missing from the middle of the trajectory, researchers often try to estimate the missing values from the previous values in a process called *last observation carried forward* (see Chapter 9). It is thus important to determine the pattern of missing data prior to selection of the solution.

The amount of missing data is also very important. If a study involves only three repeated measures of an outcome and an individual is missing one observation, a lot of information is missing about the change trajectory for that person, regardless of whether the missing data point is at the first, second, or third observation. Conversely, in a study involving 10 repeated measures, 1 missing observation is less likely to be problematic. In the first scenario, it would be difficult to obtain a reliable estimate of the missing value from the two available observations. It could be higher, lower, or the same as either value. From a series of nine observations, it is likely that a more reliable estimate of the missing tenth observation, whether at the start, middle, or end of the study, could be obtained. And thus, the amount of missing data is an important concern.

The amount of missing data is also of concern for estimating the shape of the change trajectory, depending on the type of statistical analysis to be used. Individual growth modeling approaches, such as mixed model regressions (e.g., hierarchical linear models [HLMs]), random coefficient models, latent growth modeling (an SEM procedure), and slopes as outcomes (or individual regressions) involve estimation of change parameters for each individual from his or her data. These change parameters include initial status (intercept), rate of change (slope), and sometimes curvature and asymptote, depending on the hypothesized shape of the change trajectory. The shape is estimated as a mathematical function, sometimes referred to as a change function. Depending on the type, there are a minimum number of observations required to solve the function. For example, to estimate an intercept and a slope for each individual, there is a minimal requirement of three observations. For a third-order polynomial in which an intercept, a linear slope, and quadratic, cubic, and error terms are estimated, there is a minimal requirement of five observations. If an individual is missing too many observations to meet the minimal requirement, change parameters cannot be estimated for that individual. For statistical methods that "borrow" information from other individuals who have data (e.g., HLM), these missing data might not pose much of a problem, depending on the missing data mechanism at work. However, for the slopes-as-outcomes approach in which a regression model is estimated for each individual based on his or her own data only, the amount of missing data is critical. Unless some sort of replacement of missing values is used, those with too few observations are deleted from all subsequent analyses, because individual change parameters cannot be estimated. Since these regression models are estimated for each individual, data of others is generally not used to estimate replacement values unless the data analyst makes an explicit attempt to do so.

This discussion highlights the importance of considering the statistical analyses to be employed when measuring change. Traditional fixed-effects methods such as repeated measures ANOVA have different assumptions and requirements than do individual growth models. In the traditional models, all observations must be at the same intervals (i.e., time-structured data) for all individuals. Furthermore, cases with missing data are deleted (unless replacement values are substituted). For individual growth models, all available cases can be used (given the aforementioned exceptions) and data are not required to be time-structured. Additionally, because the focus in the traditional fixed-effects models is on average growth, missing data at the individual level might not be as problematic as it is for methods that focus on calculating individual change parameters or trajectories. This depends on the mechanism, amount, and pattern of missing data in both cases. Because some of the individual growth modeling procedures use sample level as well as individual level data to estimate individual change parameters, data missing at the individual level might not be problematic (again, taking into consideration the amount, pattern, and mechanism).

Preserving the variability in outcomes over time is of prime concern with these types of within-subjects studies. Therefore, as is the case with correlational and descriptive studies, it is critical to consider whether missing data solutions artificially alter variability. Methods such as replacing missing values with sample means or previous observations tend to decrease variability within the sample and within individuals. The extent of the decrease depends on the amount of missing data, the true variance in the outcome, the pattern of missing data, and the mechanism. All of these facets should be considered when selecting missing data solutions within these types of studies.

Objective 4: Comparing Groups on Outcomes

Social scientists are often interested in differences in outcomes between groups or between subjects. The groups can be naturally occurring, such as males versus females, or generated for the study, such as experimental versus control groups. Both involve between-subjects designs that are cross-sectional. (Longitudinal between-subjects designs involve within- and between-subjects comparisons, which are discussed next.) Between-subjects studies are either experimental or correlational, depending on how the groups are created. When the grouping variable is a naturally occurring characteristic (often referred to as a *subject variable*), such as gender, race, age group, or socioeconomic status, the interest is in comparing the groups to determine if subject variables produce different outcomes. When groups are created according to the experimental design, such as the treatment versus comparison groups, interest is in comparing the groups to determine if the intervention produces different outcomes. Between-group studies can involve hierarchically nested data, with individuals nested within groups (e.g., patients within different hospitals or students within different classrooms or schools) as long as the group is the unit of analysis.

When group comparisons are of interest, researchers generally want to reduce the variability within groups in order to maximize differences. If there is great variability within each group on the variable of interest, group differences are minimized. That is, when there is more "noise" than "signal," the signal gets lost. Missing data solutions that maintain homogeneity of groups, such as replacing missing values with group means, increase the signal and decrease the noise, thus meeting the goals of these types of studies. However, using these methods to artificially decrease noise would be misleading and produce questionable results.

For between-group comparisons of this type, statistical analyses generally involve hypothesis testing in which group means are compared in order to assess whether they are significantly different from each other. Individual level data are aggregated to create group level data (i.e., group means) for these analyses. With aggregation, it may be the case that data missing at the individual level might not have as significant (i.e., biasing) an impact on study results as would be the case when within-subject analyses are of interest. The impact depends on the amount, pattern, and mechanism of missing data. Group means can be estimated without bias if missing data at the individual level are few, and importantly, if the mechanism is ignorable, preferably MCAR. If the sample size is somewhat small due to missing data, but variability is preserved within groups (i.e., data are MCAR), means can be estimated without bias.

Traditional between-group analyses assume equal sample (cell) sizes for each group. The assumption stems from the fact that cell size relates to variance estimation and cell variances must be equivalent. However, with observed subject variables, participants are not assigned to groups, and therefore equal cell sizes are not guaranteed. For example, when comparing males and females on school outcomes, the number of students in each group is not likely to be equal.

Analytically, linear models are employed in which categorical variables indicating group membership are specified as predictors. The default missing data solution in most statistical software packages is usually *listwise deletion*, in which all cases with missing data are deleted. Listwise deletion is known to be problematic under most conditions of missing data, except when the mechanism is MCAR and the amount of missing data is small.[5] Therefore, other methods should be considered, and their effects on the homogeneity of the groups of interest is of key importance. If the missing data handling procedure increases homogeneity artificially, estimates of group differences can be inflated—that is, group differences look larger than they would have if all the data had been observed.

Objective 5: Monitoring Change, Comparing Conditions, and Comparing Groups

In these types of studies, the interest is in comparing individuals over time (as they undergo varying conditions or naturally occurring change), as well as comparing groups of individuals. These types of studies involve a number of designs broadly referred to as *mixed* designs (due to the focus on both within- and between-subjects comparisons). Repeated measures designs, in which the same participants are monitored on a particular outcome as they are exposed to a variety of conditions, are not uncommon. Cognitive psychologists, for example, often expose individuals to a variety of conditions that interfere with memory formation and measure memory after each stimulus. They might randomly assign one group of participants to receive the conditions in one particular order and another group to receive a different order or a different set of conditions. The repeated observations within individuals are the within-subjects component, while the random assignment to groups is the between-subjects component. Similarly, measuring differences between naturally occurring groups (e.g., males vs. females) on change over time in a particular outcome (e.g., substance use) also employs a mixed design. Intervention studies in which at least two groups (intervention plus a comparison group) are monitored over time also fall within this category of studies. Interventions can be medical treatments, educational programs, or social programs, and can involve large-scale program evaluations.

Because these designs are a combination of between- and within-groups designs, the aforementioned missing data concerns are relevant to mixed designs as well. Mechanism, amount, and pattern of missing data are all study conditions that should be considered as part of the decision-making process. With mixed designs, the most likely missing data conditions are missing occasions (due to dropout) and differential attrition or differential dropout between the groups. The problems with missing data associated with dropout have been addressed in the within-subjects discussion. Differential attrition is a new problem, in which one group experiences a higher rate of dropout than another. Differential attrition violates the assumption of equivalent groups at baseline, a critical component of the logic of experimental designs. To increase the ability to infer a causal link between an intervention and an outcome, it is essential to show that except for the intervention itself, the groups were the same. Differential attrition violates this assumption. In general, differential attrition is not assumed to be the result of random processes, and therefore MCAR is not a likely mechanism. Choosing complete case options for handling missing data will therefore result in biased estimates of the parameters of interest. It is likely that those who remained in the study and provided complete data are not like those who dropped out, and therefore the final sample is not representative of the original sample or of the population.

Some investigators replace missing data with values representing the worst-case outcome. For example, if the outcome were binary, where 0 equals failure to improve and 1 equals improvement, those with missing data would be assigned a value of 0 as a conservative estimate of the intervention's effect. This option is a subset of intent-to-treat analyses in which the subjects (or assigned units) are assumed to be in the treatment group regardless of their successful completion. Subjects failing to even enter into the treatment stage are treated "as if" they actually received the treatment, thus decreasing the expected effect of the treatment.

As with the other study designs, researchers must consider the type of statistical analysis that will be used. Often with these types of designs, mixed models are employed. Mixed models involve estimation of both fixed and random effects, and they have their own default procedures for handling missing data.[6] Mixed models employ a procedure that essentially uses the data that were observed and ignores those values that were not observed. The procedure works in a manner consistent with pairwise deletion, but it invokes the method by requiring that the data are organized in what many statisticians refer to as the *long* (or multiple-record) format. Each subject's data for each measurement occasion is listed on its own separate line. When data are missing on any occasion, the mixed model estimation procedure merely assumes that the parameters ought to be based on the occasions that were available. Mixed models, such as hierarchical linear models (HLMs) or random coefficients models, are known to be flexible with respect to missing data in that they allow for time-unstructured data (i.e., varying intervals between occasions of measurement across individuals and within groups). They allow for this due to the nature of the data format. Furthermore, many of the mixed model procedures involve maximum likelihood (ML) for parameter estimation, and the missing data handling procedures within these mixed model procedures are sufficient for treating data that are MAR. These procedures are considered to be more flexible and robust for handling missing data problems when compared to traditional fixed-effects models for handling mixed designs (e.g., repeated measures ANOVA; Nich & Carroll, 1997) simply because they do not require additional procedures beyond what they employ by default. Of course, data that are not MAR and are not well-behaved according to the ML constraints are not treated kindly by these default methods. Other less constrained methods, such as multiple imputation, might produce more robust estimates either if data are non-normal or if there is any uncertainty about the ignorability of the missing data mechanism (see Chapter 10).

Theory Testing versus Generating Hypotheses

Another important distinction to make between types of studies in the social and behavioral sciences is the difference between those that are focused on testing theory (i.e., confirmatory) and those that are focused on generating hypotheses (i.e., exploratory). Karl Popper (1959) referred to these two situations as the *context of justification* and the *context of discovery*, respectively, and we adopt his terminology. Consider two scenarios that distinguish these aims. A local arthritis center collects data for every patient on as many variables as possible, adding new variables as deemed appropriate. The data are made available for exploration to find out if relationships exist between variables or, more specifically, for generating hypotheses about relationships between variables (e.g., variables related to disease severity). Due to the exploratory nature of the data collection and analyses, the researchers emphasize that the data are not appropriate for theory testing. In the second scenario, the same arthritis center has a research grant to collect data to test competing theories regarding variables related to the onset of symptoms and disease severity. In this case, the design of the study and data analyses would be different, because the theory to be tested would dictate the variables for data collection and the types of relationships to test. Therefore the impact of missing data would be different. When data are used to generate hypotheses, data missing at any level and for almost any reason are likely to be less problematic than when the goal is theory testing. Naturally, if the data are badly tainted by missing observations, hypotheses generated from the source will be adversely affected, but the consequences are not dire. In the context of discovery, exploratory hypotheses are generated and will ideally be put to the test in a subsequent confirmatory study. Although it is not ideal, mistakes can be made in hypothesis generation.

In contrast, studies designed to test theory (Popper's *context of justification*) are more conservative, and therefore missing data are more likely to be problematic. Statisticians are trained to be cautious of making errors on the side of accepting a theory; that is, they prefer to make a Type II error (reject a true theory) over a Type I error (accept a false theory). Both types of errors can have negative consequences, depending on the purpose of the study. If missing data result in reduced statistical power, for example, the statistician is more likely to make a Type II error. If the rejection of a true theory leads to negative consequences, and that error is due to the missing data, those missing data had a strong impact on study results. Conversely, missing data could lead to biased parameter estimates, causing researchers to believe that a relationship exists between variables when in fact it does not (a Type I error). If acceptance of this false theory leads to negative consequences and the Type I error is due to the missing data, then the missing data had a strong impact on study results. It is important to note that missing data do not favor one error over another, and therefore researchers engaged in either conservative (avoiding Type I errors) or more liberal (avoiding Type II errors) theory testing ought to be concerned about missing data. A researcher's confidence in the data will necessarily affect confidence in the theory.

SUMMARY

Decision making regarding the selection of solutions for handling missing data is a complex process. According to the decision-making literature, there are several steps involved in any decision-making endeavor: (1) having a reasonable idea of the problem at hand, (2) clear specification of objectives, (3) maximizing the number of alternatives, (4) awareness of the consequences of each alternative, (5) compromising between tradeoffs to meet objectives, and (6) avoiding common traps that can lead to poor decisions. This chapter accomplishes step 1 by specifying a set of preliminary steps each investigator should undertake to have a better understanding of the missing data problem at hand. These steps involve the identification of relevant study variables, specifying the level of analysis, performing missing data diagnostics, identifying relevant statistical models and tests, and selecting statistical software. Step 2, in which the importance of handling missing data in a manner that decreases the negative consequences of missing data (e.g., biased parameter estimates, faulty study conclusions), has been repeatedly discussed in this text. Steps 3 through 6 are addressed within this chapter with regard to solutions for handling missing data at the analysis stage of the study when prevention efforts have failed. A discussion was presented of the types of missing data conditions likely to be encountered within five broad categories of objectives for social science studies. Common missing data concerns associated with these broad categories of studies were presented to illustrate tradeoffs and common traps with respect to missing data solutions. Alternative solutions were briefly presented, with their strengths and weaknesses discussed in light of the missing data conditions and objectives of the study.

The next four chapters introduce the types of statistical solutions for missing data that are available to the social scientist. Consistent with the current chapter, those solutions are appropriate when efforts to prevent missing data fail. The best overall solution to the problem of missing data is still to plan for it and prevent it in the first place. When prevention efforts fail, as they most invariably do, then analytic methods for handling missing data must be employed. However, as noted throughout this book, there is no panacea for handling missing data, and therefore each procedure must be considered in light of its strengths and weaknesses in terms of the objectives and design of a particular study.

NOTES

1. Complete cases are usually required for estimating covariance matrices due to the mathematical properties of matrices and how they behave when they are manipulated, the technical details of which are not necessary to discuss for the purposes of this chapter.

2. Unbalanced data are those for which some subjects have fewer repeated observations than others due to missing data. When data are time structured, all subjects are measured at the same intervals over time, such as every 6 months. When data are unstructured, subjects are measured at varying intervals.

3. For a more complete description of the handling of missing data in these parameter estimation procedures, see Schafer (1997) and Allison (2002).

4. This solution would work best if age is being used as a grouping variable. With such little variance in age in this example, it would be difficult and likely fruitless to assess the extent to which age covaries with other variables. The example offers a rare situation in which mean substitution might be advisable. Years of Monte Carlo simulations (for an early reference, see Haitovsky, 1968) indicate that mean substitution is rarely, if ever, appropriate. Additionally, Little and Rubin (1987) provide a formula (p. 44) for calculating the extent to which the variance is underestimated with mean substitution. The formula shows that underestimating variance is a critical problem with using mean substitution for handling missing data.

5. What dictates whether the amount of missing data is trivial cannot be determined merely by the proportion of missing cases. For example, the size of the expected effect dictates whether a particular amount of missing data is trivial: if a small effect is expected, even a few missing cases can be detrimental. The variances of the variables of interest, the covariances among them, and other study conditions determine the impact of the quantity of missing data.

6. Fixed effects are parameter estimates associated with levels of a classification factor (e.g., males and females), and we wish to make inferences about only those particular levels of the classification factor that were used in the experiment. Random effects are parameters associated with individual experimental units drawn *at random* from the population. These are *effects* because they represent deviation from an overall mean. Random effects models are used when we wish to make inferences about the population from which the levels of the classification factor were drawn.

7

Data Deletion Methods for Handling Missing Data

The simplest and most commonly used method for handling missing data is some type of data deletion procedure. The five deletion methods we address in this chapter are (1) listwise deletion, (2) pairwise deletion, (3) available item analysis, (4) individual growth curve analysis (the longitudinal counterpart to available item analysis), and (5) multisample analysis. Although these methods might appear to have little in common, they all use procedures that do not replace missing values and do not make other adjustments to account for missing values, unlike the model-based procedures discussed in Chapter 8. Deletion methods, although often criticized, are easily implemented; when they are used appropriately they provide suitable parameter estimates. The primary advantage of deletion procedures is ease of use. We discuss each deletion method, explaining its use and its strengths and weaknesses.

DATA SETS

Prior to our discussion of each of the deletion methods, we briefly review the data sets used to illustrate the statistical methods for handling missing data in this and the following chapters. We use the same three data sets across Chapters 7–10 to illustrate each of the statistical methods, facilitate comparison of the methods, and simplify presentation. These three data sets involve content that is easy to understand. The three content areas are (1) blood screening for carriers of a rare disease (the Biomed data set), (2) juvenile delinquency (the Delinquency data set), and (3) body composition (the Body Comp data set). Each data set represents different types of studies and different types of missing data. Blood screening data are from a repeated measures study, delinquency data are from a longitudinal study, and body composition data are from a cross-sectional design. All three studies are nonexperimental, although the blood screening study is quasi-experimental, because although participants are not randomly assigned to groups, a naturally occurring grouping or subject variable (i.e., "normal" vs. "carrier") is used as the grouping factor.

Prior to reporting results for these and the methods discussed in Chapters 8–10, we see it as *critical* to remind the reader that although we include the full data set as a comparison for our results, techniques for handling missing data are not aimed at reproducing the parameter estimates from the complete data set. Rather, they are aimed at reproducing parameter estimates that accurately reflect the true *population* values. Missing data techniques try to produce, for example, the true correlation between abdominal circumference and percent body fat in the population rather than the correlation between these two variables as calculated in the fully observed Body Comp data set. Therefore, the demonstrations in this chapter as well as those in Chapters 8–10 are aimed merely at showing the differences between estimates provided by the fully observed data and those provided by data that were modified to take account of missing values. The reader is cautioned against regarding the results from the fully observed data as the "right" answer. Although fully observed, these data might not be an accurate representation of the population to which the researcher plans to generalize findings.

COMPLETE CASE METHOD

As the name implies, the complete case method, referred to as *listwise deletion*, drops all cases with any missing data. Specifically, any "case" (e.g., participant) with at least one missing value is dropped from the analysis.[1]

As a default routine for most statistical software packages, this procedure requires very little effort on the part of the data analyst. That is, analysts need not bother with procedures for replacing missing values prior to carrying out the analyses of interest. However, when used without regard for the mechanism or the amount of missing data, listwise deletion will often lead to biased parameter estimates and decreased statistical power, respectively. Both can have a deleterious effect on the validity of statistical conclusions.

Listwise deletion is appropriate when data are MCAR (Little & Rubin, 1987; Schafer & Graham, 2002). In fact, when data are MCAR, the reduced sample size due to listwise deletion is a random subset of the original sample, and therefore if parameter estimates would be unbiased for the full data set, they will remain so for the listwise deleted data set. However, as noted in Chapter 3, the likelihood that data are MCAR is small, and the effect of deletion on statistical power is still relevant, regardless of the missing data mechanism. Thus, careful consideration is necessary before selecting this procedure, regardless of the ease of implementation.

We demonstrate the process and results of listwise deletion with a data example, using the aforementioned Biomed data set. The data were collected in a study aimed at developing screening methods to identify carriers of a rare genetic disorder (Cox, Johnson, & Kafadar, 1982). Four repeated measures (*m*1, *m*2, *m*3, *m*4) were made on blood samples, and one of these measures, *m*1, has been used before. The original data set contains 209 observations (75 for "carriers" and 134 for "normals"). Because the disease is rare, there are only a few carriers of the disease from whom data are available. The purpose for collecting the data was to develop a screening procedure to detect carriers and to assess its effectiveness as a screening tool.[2] The data set includes age and disease classification ("carrier" vs. "normal") as well as the repeated blood sample measures (*m*1–*m*4).

We analyzed these data with a General Linear Model (GLM), where the grouping factor has two levels—normal versus carrier—and age is treated as a covariate due to its known effect on *m*1–*m*4 levels. The dependent variable is a unit-weighted factor created by converting *m*1, *m*2, *m*3, and *m*4 into *z*-scores, summing them and taking the mean *z*-score. The goal was to see if group (normal vs. carrier) predicted scores on the blood sample measures, taking into account the individual's age.

Initially, we conducted the GLM for the Biomed data set on a fully observed data set with 50 participants (25 normals and 25 carriers).[3] This data set is presented in Table 7.1.

Next, we created missing data to reflect an MAR mechanism, the most common missing data mechanism in the social sciences. To do this, we

TABLE 7.1. Biomed Data Set with Fully Observed Data

Row ID	*Age*	*m1*	*m2*	*m3*	*m4*	*Normal*
52	36	30	66.7	15.3	124	1
95	32	56	72	9.9	227	1
125	25	34	92	12.1	217	1
99	33	28.8	104	6.9	169	1
88	38	26	109	8.9	163	1
17	31	34	92.7	7.9	140	1
31	34	73	57.4	7.4	107	1
33	25	35	71	8.8	186	1
91	39	23	111.5	10	133	1
45	26	34	78	8	140	1
74	27	24	89.5	16.1	176	1
90	39	21	92.4	10.3	197	1
30	25	37	73.3	13	254	1
65	22	35	59.4	11.3	130	1
49	25	72	80.5	12	225	1
119	32	35	97	14.5	137	1
35	20	62	81	10.2	181	1
54	33	67	98	9.3	225	1
102	22	21	74.5	12.2	163	1
29	27	34	86.3	11.8	120	1
53	36	23	66.3	4.4	142	1
131	32	43	87.5	6	136	1
24	27	30	80.2	8.1	100	1
126	20	30	80	12.9	129	1
79	25	30	77	16.2	124	1
10	35	122	88.5	21.6	263	0
47	35	1288	82	51.6	368	0
62	52	242	85.5	16.6	168	0
34	58	34	98.5	19.9	299	0
51	30	363	91.3	36	325	0
20	30	41	90	9.7	342	0
22	31	657	104	110	358	0
7	59	58	88.2	11	259	0
72	26	700	90	49.1	343	0
61	52	197	91.5	25.2	236	0
8	35	129	93.1	18.3	188	0
69	45	35	86.3	14.4	184	0
58	31	85	94	20.1	198	0
12	29	265	83.5	16.1	136	0
301	34	73	105.5	17	285	0
56	42	52	93.3	11.2	272	0
60	32	72	88	8.3	166	0
15	27	25	91	49.1	209	0

(cont.)

TABLE 7.1. *(cont.)*

Row ID	*Age*	*m*1	*m*2	*m*3	*m*4	*Normal*
651	39	228	104	10.2	236	0
491	53	59	93	22.2	240	0
43	35	34	96.5	10.4	122	0
291	39	148	105.2	18.8	221	0
1	30	167	89	25.6	364	0
331	58	19	100.5	10.9	196	0
541	41	99	93.2	18.6	156	0

Note. Row ID refers to the row number for each participant in the original data set. *Normal* refers to the grouping variable where 1 is "normal" and 0 is "carrier."

conditioned missing data for the *m*1–*m*4 measures on the *Age* variable. Specifically, if participants were 29 years old or older, there is a 70% chance that they would have missing data for *m*1, *m*2, *m*3, or *m*4. This MAR data set is presented in Table 7.2. The missing data matrix for this data set is presented in Figure 7.1. The white cells indicate missing data. The top 30% of the matrix (the solid black area at the top) represents those who are under 29 years of age and therefore have no missing data for this demonstration.

It is useful to compare the GLM results without the missing data to those with the listwise deleted data. The results are presented in Table 7.3. Recall that with listwise deletion *all* cases with missing data, even if for a single variable, are deleted. Therefore, 70% (35 from 50) of the cases in the missing-data version of the Biomed data set were deleted! A comparison of the results in Table 7.3 shows the effects of listwise deletion on parameter estimation (by examining the "Estimate" column) as well as hypothesis testing (by examining the *p*-values). Parameter estimates are different for the two data sets, and, as expected due to the smaller sample size, standard errors are much larger for the listwise deleted data set. Therefore, results for hypothesis tests are different (e.g., see the results for Intercept). Finally, the amount of explained variance indicated by Adjusted R^2 is different between the two models, with the listwise value almost twice that of the fully observed data set.

In short, although listwise deletion is simple to understand and implement, it often leads to a substantial reduction in sample size (in this case, 70%) and thus in statistical power. Furthermore, unless it is used under MCAR conditions, it produces biased parameter estimates.

TABLE 7.2. Biomed Data Set with Data MAR

Row ID	*Age*	*m1*	*m2*	*m3*	*m4*	*Normal*
52	36	30		15.3		1
95	32	56		9.9	227	1
125	25	34	92	12.1	217	1
99	33	28.8			169	1
88	38	26	109			1
17	31	92.7	7.9			1
31	34	73			107	1
33	25	35	71	8.8	186	1
91	39	23	111.5	10		1
45	26	34	78	8	140	1
74	27	24	89.5	16.1	176	1
90	39		92.4	10.3		1
30	25	37	73.3	13	254	1
65	22	35	59.4	11.3	130	1
49	25	72	80.5	12	225	1
119	32	35		14.5		1
35	20	62	81	10.2	181	1
54	33			9.3	225	1
102	22	21	74.5	12.2	163	1
29	27	34	86.3	11.8	120	1
53	36	23	66.3			1
131	32			6	136	1
24	27	30	80.2	8.1	100	1
126	20	30	80	12.9	129	1
79	25	30	77	16.2	124	1
10	35		88.5		263	0
47	35	1288			368	0
62	52	242	85.5			0
34	58	34	98.5			0
51	30		91.3		325	0
20	30	41	90			0
22	31			110	358	0
7	59	58			259	0
72	26	700	90	49.1	343	0
61	52		91.5		236	0
8	35			18.3	188	0
69	45	35	86.3		184	0
58	31	85	94			0
12	29	265	83.5			0
301	34			17	285	0
56	42	52	93.3	11.2		0
60	32		88		166	0
15	27	25	91	49.1	209	0

(cont.)

TABLE 7.2. *(cont.)*

Row ID	*Age*	*m*1	*m*2	*m*3	*m*4	*Normal*
651	39			10.2	236	0
491	53			22.2	240	0
43	35		96.5	10.4		0
291	39	148			221	0
1	30		89	25.6		0
331	58		100.5	10.9	196	0
541	41	99	93.2			0

Note. Row ID refers to the row number for each participant in the original data set. *Normal* refers to the grouping variable where 1 is "normal" and 0 is "carrier."

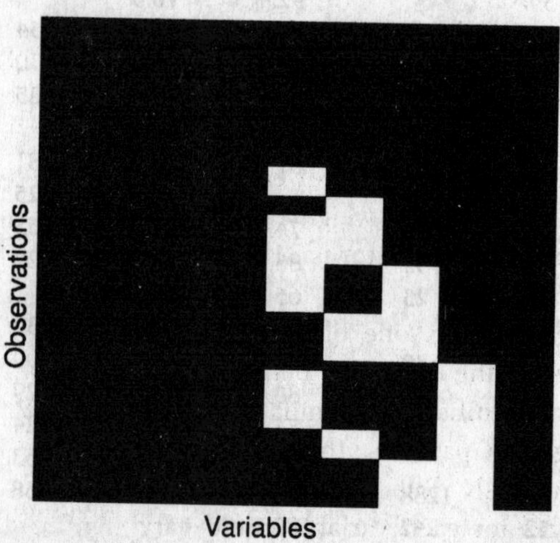

FIGURE 7.1. Missing data matrix for MAR, Biomed data set.

TABLE 7.3. GLM Results for Biomed Data Set

	Estimate		Standard Error		Model Adjusted R^2	
Coefficients	Full	Listwise	Full	Listwise	Full	Listwise
Intercept	1.01*	1.10	.41	1.42	.37	.68
Age	–0.01	0.02	.01	.05		
Group (normal vs. carrier)	–1.04**	–1.90**	.19	.36		

Note. "Full," data set with fully observed data (i.e., no missing values) (*N* = 50); "Listwise," data set with listwise deleted data (*N* = 15).
$^*p < .01$; $^{**}p < .001$.

AVAILABLE CASE METHOD

In contrast to the complete case method, the *available case* method, referred to as pairwise deletion, uses data when they are available and discards data only at the level of the variable, not the observation. To demonstrate this method, we again use our Biomed data set. The same fully observed (Table 7.1) and MAR data sets (Table 7.2) were used to compare results for a simple psychometric analysis in which two indices were the focus: item-total correlations and Cronbach's alpha (an index of internal consistency). Item-total correlations were calculated by correlating *m*1, *m*2, *m*3, and *m*4 with the unit-weighted factor score or average *z*-score previously described. Cronbach's alpha was computed for a scale made up of *m*1–*m*4.

In the pairwise analysis, all observed data are used. Therefore, to calculate item-total correlations, for example, there might be a different number of observations for *m*1 than for *m*2. In essence, two somewhat different samples would provide the data for each variable (*m*1 and *m*2) to estimate its correlation with the unit-weighted factor. The sample size for correlations between *m*1 and the factor is 31, and for *m*2 and the factor it is 35, as presented in Table 7.4.

Table 7.4 illustrates one of the problems associated with pairwise deletion. Although the difference between sample sizes of 31 and 35 does not appear to be significant, when data sets are large and there are a number of missing data patterns, the cases providing data for one variable could be dramatically different from those providing data for the other. The sample sizes for each variable could vary significantly as well. The imbalance in sample size for each parameter leads to many problems when

TABLE 7.4. Results of Correlational Analyses Using Pairwise Deletion for Biomed Data

	Item-total correlations (*N*)		Cronbach's alpha	
Variables	Full	Pairwise	Full	Pairwise
*m*1	.75 (*N* = 50)	.83 (*N* = 31)	.44	.52
*m*2	.53 (*N* = 50)	.67 (*N* = 35)		
*m*3	.84 (*N* = 50)	.86 (*N* = 35)		
*m*4	.82 (*N* = 50)	.84 (*N* = 35)		

Note. Item-total correlations represent the bivariate correlation between the variable (*m*1, *m*2, *m*3, or *m*4) and the unit-weighted factor. Cronbach's alpha was calculated with all four of these variables.

analyzing a covariance or correlation matrix. Frequently, pairwise deletion leads to singular or indeterminate matrices—a problem that plagues many who attempt complex analyses using covariance matrices.

Results from the psychometric analyses are presented in Table 7.4. Item-total correlations for $m1$ and $m2$ are substantially different for the fully observed versus pairwise deleted data. Due to the MAR procedure for creating missing data, carriers (who tend to be older) were disproportionately deleted compared to normals—a scenario that is not uncommon with social science data. Thus the sample composition changed, resulting in different parameter estimates from those for the fully observed data set. Moreover, the index of reliability for these analyses (Cronbach's alpha) was substantially different as well, reflecting different covariances between items for the fully observed versus pairwise deleted data.

These results illustrate some of the problems with pairwise deletion. The method is often used when computing simple bivariate relationships (e.g., correlations). In contrast to complete case methods, available case methods preserve a larger proportion of the sample. However, pairwise deletion can result in problems due to differences in the number of observations used in the analysis. If a correlation matrix is computed using the available case method, each correlation may be based on different observations and a different sample size for each variable. The differing number of observations affects the stability of the estimate while also affecting the characteristics of the matrix. Therefore, available case methods can interfere with statistical procedures, such as SEM, that require well-behaved correlation matrices. As with complete case methods, great care ought to be used when implementing available case methods.

AVAILABLE ITEM METHOD

Another method that uses available information is the *available item* method. This is a specialized type of data deletion method that is used when missing data occur at the item or indicator level—from here on referred to simply as "items"—and those items are used to create a composite variable similar to that used in factor analysis, where the items are expected to be correlated. Researchers often combine multiple items to measure an underlying, unobservable latent construct (as described in Chapter 3). Measures of self-esteem, depression, and intelligence, for example, employ multiple items to measure these latent constructs. One or more items within these measures are often missing data. With item-level missing data, researchers often employ methods that use the observed values of other correlated items to estimate the latent variable score (see Schafer & Graham, 2002). Because the items are correlated, their missing values are expected to be consistent with those observed.

The available item method involves sensible aggregation across correlated items for calculating latent variable scores that involve missing data. One such method requires taking the mean *z*-score of correlated items. Standardizing item values (transforming items to have a mean of 0 and a standard deviation of 1) creates a common metric known as a *z*-score. (*z*-score transformation is often recommended even when items have a common metric in order to adjust for different item variances.) Once differences in scaling are eliminated, the transformed values can be combined to form a composite variable score for each person. Rather than the composite score being a sum of all the items, the composite score is the mean item *z*-score. Because this method makes no explicit attempt to replace missing values, it is known as a deletion method. The mean *z*-score can be computed "as if" the missing item or indicator had been observed. This "as if observed" notion is the underlying principle of deletion techniques.

Caution must be taken when using the available item method for calculating composite scores when item-level data are missing. This method is appropriate only when items are intersubstitutable or correlated with each other, as in the case of a common factor. For composite variables made up of uncorrelated items, it is not tenable to assume that missing values for a particular item would be consistent with the observed values for other, unrelated items. For example, a composite index measuring quality of places to live might be composed of indicators such as climate, population, quality of local schools, employment opportunities, and cost of living. These indicators are not interchangeable—they measure different and often unrelated dimensions of the quality of places to live. The indicators themselves may be of many different types, such as a sliding scale between three choices (mild, moderate, extreme, for climate) versus a rate (e.g., the jobless rate). An indicator like the jobless rate may have a great deal of variance among cities; whereas the values for another indicator may be fairly close together, given the range of possible values (e.g., the climate of cities tends to be mild or moderate when possible). Therefore, taking the average *z*-score of each indicator makes little sense with these types of measures. Classical test theory (CTT) holds that items are a random subset from a universe of "like" items. If items are randomly selected from this theoretical universe, the omission of any one item ought to be suitably treated by inferring its missing value based on available items. However, composite variables that are not composed of like items (i.e., they are multidimensional), such as the quality of places to live index, do not meet the assumption of intersubstitutability of items or indicators.

To demonstrate the available item method, the following simple analysis was used. A unit-weighted factor score (i.e., the mean *z*-score for *m*1–*m*4) was already created for the previous pairwise deletion demonstration. If an individual was missing data for any one of the four items, *m*1–*m*4, the mean *z*-score was computed based on only those items with observed data. This is the available item method. To assess the utility of this method, we correlated the factor scores from the fully observed data with those from the available item analysis. Results show a high level of agreement between the two factor scores ($r = .94$). A plot of the fully observed factor scores versus those produced with the available items is presented in Figure 7.2. As illustrated, the available item analysis is capturing the variability in the factor, although not all of the indicators are available for each case. These results demonstrate that when items are intercorrelated and measure a single common factor, the available item method can be a viable option that does not produce biased estimates (assuming that the full data set produced unbiased estimates).

As a missing data handling technique, Schafer and Graham (2002) note that the available item method violates the principle that an esti-

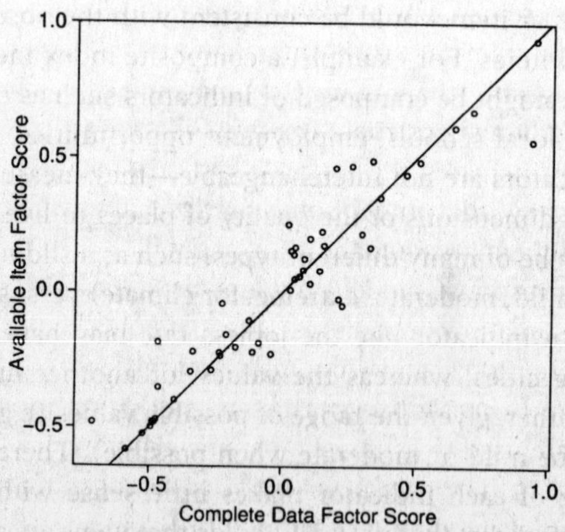

FIGURE 7.2. Bivariate correlation between unit-weighted factor scores for fully observed and available item analysis methods.

mand be a well-defined aspect of a population rather than an artifact of a specific data set. The skepticism these authors apply to this procedure is appropriate, because the imputed values come directly from the observed data, and this may produce biased estimates of population values. In other words, estimates are sample-specific. Another disadvantage of this procedure is that the available item method may decrease the variance between items.

Additionally, the argument against using the available item method makes sense in situations where items or indicators are not intersubstitutable, as noted previously. Specifically, for composite variables in which each indicator is measuring the same underlying unidimensional construct, items are intercorrelated and are thus intersubstitutable. This explains the high correlation between the factor scores produced by the fully observed versus the available item methods in our demonstration in Figure 7.2. In the case of an underlying multidimensional construct, however, items measuring different dimensions should not be used interchangeably. For example, in a "Quality of Life" scale, an item measuring quality of education ought not to be replaced by an item measuring climate desirability.

Schafer and Graham (2002) note that the available item method also reduces a measure's reliability. This is because reliability is directly related to the number of items in a measure, according to the Spearman-Brown prediction formula, which states that as the number of items increases, scale reliability increases. The available item method may reduce estimates of reliability if the items are truly interchangeable. However, when items are not interchangeable, the missing item may in fact be an unreliable indicator of the underlying construct. The missing item then, distorts the data less and actually increases the estimate of scale reliability. We offer this clarification to show that under some limited circumstances, this procedure may actually enhance reliability.

Many latent response model programs make use of the available data for parameter estimation procedures. These include Rasch software (e.g., Winsteps; Linacre, 2002, and ConQuest; Wu, Adams, & Wilson, 1997), and IRT software (e.g., Multilog; Thissen, 1991). Within these analyses, available items are used to estimate a parameter known as "ability" (theta) for each respondent. The parameter estimation procedures usually involve either some form of maximum likelihood or Bayesian algorithms (see the discussion in Chapter 8) that are well suited for treating missing data at the item level.

INDIVIDUAL GROWTH CURVE ANALYSIS

A different procedure that is conceptually similar to the available item method is the use of available repeated measures (analogous to items) to estimate growth curve, or change, parameters. This approach specifically addresses a method of individual growth curve analysis using individual linear regressions to estimate growth parameters such as intercepts and slopes separately for each individual (e.g., Rogosa, 1995). Although individual growth curve analysis is not technically a missing data handling method, it makes use of available data in much the same ways that available item analyses do. Because social scientists make use of repeated measures data frequently, it is important to address this technique.

When repeated measures are collected on a single variable or a set of variables to measure change over time in those variables, and missing values at some time points are evident, available data from other time points are often used to estimate the overall change trajectory. For example, if participants are measured at five different occasions and some are missing values from some of those occasions, their individual change trajectories can still be computed. These change trajectories are characterized by an intercept and a slope, referred to as growth curve parameters.[4] The process of estimating growth curve parameters separately for each individual, and then combining those estimates in a single model as outcomes to be predicted, is known as slopes-as-outcomes analysis, meta-analytic growth curve analysis (Figueredo, Sales, Russell, Becker, & Kaplan, 2000), and individual growth curves (Rogosa, 1995).

Similar to available item analysis, growth curve parameters are estimated for each individual based on available observations, provided that there are sufficient observations to yield the hypothesized change function.[5] If not, the entire case is deleted (i.e., no growth parameters are estimated for that individual). The procedure, therefore, does not replace missing values but uses observed values to estimate individual growth parameters instead.

The individual growth curve procedure is likely to produce biased results if missing values alter the overall trajectory. That is, if an individual's trajectory appears to be a steadily increasing linear slope, but the missing value would have shown a dramatic drop (as would happen, e.g., in a drug treatment failure), using the existing values would lead to the incorrect estimation of a positive linear slope.

The point along the change trajectory where values are missing can have a differential impact using this missing data handling procedure.

Values that are missing at the end of a longitudinal study (often associated with dropout) can lead to large errors of estimation. Conversely, values missing between the baseline and last observations might be less prone to catastrophic error or influence, particularly if the "true" trajectory is a straight line. Again, the impact of the missing data on biases in parameter estimation will be related to the underlying change trajectory.

When using this method for handling missing data for estimating change parameters, it is critical to remember that the method assumes that the missing data are correlated with the observed data. If this assumption is not true, the method will most likely produce biased growth parameter estimates and therefore a misunderstanding of change trajectories.

Results from our demonstration using the available item approach to estimating change should help illustrate the method and its strengths and weaknesses. We use the Delinquency data set. It includes a subset of data that were collected as part of the National Youth Survey (NYS), a longitudinal study involving a national sample of American youth selected by area probability sampling (Elliott, 1976). The data were collected at the beginning of each year from 1977 through 1981, and then in 1984 and in 1987 (for a total of seven data collection periods). The data covered events and behavior that occurred during the previous year. For the purpose of this demonstration, only data from the youngest age cohort (11 years old at baseline) were included. The sample size for the fully observed data for this demonstration was 158.

For the current example, the focus was on characterizing and predicting youths' perceptions of how their parents viewed them over the 10-year period, measured at seven time points. Responses to only the negative labels (e.g., "messed up," "needs help") were summed to create the dependent variable, *BDKID*. *BDKID* was transformed into a *z*-score for each time point. Gender, family income, and parental education were tested as predictors of change in the dependent variable over time.

To create the missing data, we deleted values for the *BDKID* variable at any one of the seven time points to mimic the MAR mechanism, again, because MAR is the most likely missing data mechanism in social science research. Missing data for any one of these values was conditioned on parental education: those reporting a low education level had a 60% probability of missing data on any one of the seven observations for the variable *BDKID*.

Individual growth curve analyses require two steps: modeling change trajectories to obtain individual growth parameters (previously discussed) and using the growth parameters as dependent variables to be predicted in a subsequent model. Step 1 models the shape of change (also known as the

Level 1 model) and step 2 predicts the change trajectory (also known as the Level 2 model).

Figure 7.3 illustrates the shape of the change function for the average trajectory for the 158 fully observed cases, specified as a second-order polynomial. As Figure 7.3 illustrates, a second-order polynomial function allows for a shift in the direction of the trajectory (illustrated by the solid line), rather than a monotonic (i.e., single direction, increasing or decreasing) path, illustrated by the dashed line.

With a second-order polynomial growth function, three growth parameters are estimated: the intercept, which estimates the baseline; the linear component, which represents the early trend of the direction (in the *BDKID* example, a decrease); and the quadratic component, which represents the curvature, or change, in the direction (the plateau in the *BDKID* example). The three growth parameters are estimated based on the present or available observations for the repeated measures of *BDKID*, analogous to the available item method. Thus for one individual, these parameters might be estimated on only four of the seven observations, while for another, they might be estimated on six of the seven observations. As discussed earlier, if an individual does not have the minimal number of obser-

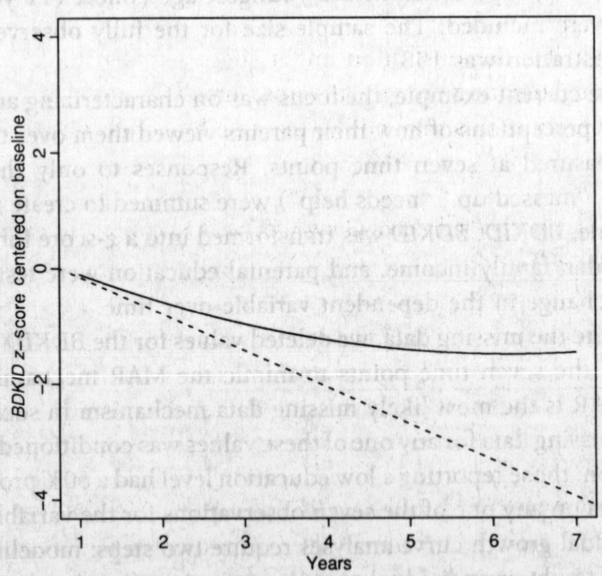

FIGURE 7.3. Average growth trajectory (for *BDKID* variable) versus monotonic linear function.

vations required for estimating the parameters, that case is dropped from the analyses or listwise deleted. With missing data, growth parameters are estimated using varying numbers of observations per individual.

The growth parameters serve as dependent variables to be predicted by relevant covariates in the Level 2 models described previously. For our example, we focus on the Level 2 models in which we predict the quadratic growth parameter, an index of curvature or plateau, with linear change (measured by the linear growth parameter), baseline status (measured by the intercept growth parameter), sex, and family income. We analyzed the data using Ordinary Least Squares (OLS) multiple regression. We conducted these analyses on the two data sets: the fully observed (N = 158) and the MAR data set (N = 157; one individual did not have the minimal requirement of four observations for estimating the change parameters).

Table 7.5 compares the results of these Level 2 analyses for the two data sets. The most notable aspect of this comparison is that the results differ trivially in that the *p*-values for the parameter estimate for the variable *Sex* differ, although both are statistically significant. This is reflected in the slightly larger standard errors for the MAR data set, due to the missing observations. These minor differences would not likely yield any change in the information we glean from the analyses or in the interpretation of results.

Although this demonstration might suggest that using available observations for estimating growth curve parameters is a useful missing data handling technique, this may not be the case for other longitudinal stud-

TABLE 7.5. Results from Individual Growth Curve Analyses of Fully Observed and MAR Data Sets

	Estimate		Standard error		Adjusted R^2 for the model	
Coefficient	Full	MAR	Full	MAR	Full	MAR
Model intercept	–.005	–.009	.006	.007	.96	.96
Linear growth parameter	–.14**	–.14**	.003	.004		
Intercept growth parameter	–.01**	–.02**	.002	.002		
Sex	–.01**	–.01*	.003	.004		
Family income	–.001*	–.002*	.001	.001		

*$p < .01$; **$p < .001$.

ies. In particular, this study has seven repeated observations, exceeding that for most longitudinal studies in the social sciences, which most often make use of only two observations, pre and post (see Rogosa, 1995, for an excellent discussion on measuring change). Missing several observations of seven likely does not have the same impact as missing several of only four observations, for example. As noted previously, data deletion methods are known to be problematic in many missing data situations and therefore must be used with caution.[6]

MULTISAMPLE ANALYSES

A final deletion method that shares a great deal in common with both available case and available item methods is *multisample* analysis (MSA). MSA is a procedure that can be used in SEM to handle missing data. In MSA, missing data patterns can be used to form groups of respondents. These groups can then be analyzed according to the available data. For example, consider a simple two-factor model in which Factor *A* (e.g., poor physical health) leads to Factor *B* (e.g., depression). These are latent factors, meaning they are not directly observed, represented by the circles in Figure 7.4. Each latent factor has three indicators—physical symptoms for Factor *A* and symptoms of depression for Factor *B*—represented in Figure 7.4 as boxes. One group of respondents fails to respond to the indicators for Factor *B*. In MSA, the measurement model for Factor *A* would be estimated using all cases in the data set (because they have fully observed data for Factor *A*), identified as Subsample 2, Figure 7.5. The structural model—that is, the relationship between Factors *A* and *B* depicted by the arrow from *A* to *B* in Figure 7.4—and the measurement model for Factor *B* would be estimated with the data for only those subjects who provided data for both Factors *A* and *B*. This is Subsample 1, Figure 7.4.

Thus, MSA is similar to available case methods. The common parameters—that is, those that can be estimated for both subsamples—are the path coefficients a, b, and c, portrayed in Figures 7.4 and 7.5. In MSA, these coefficients are constrained to be equal. These equality constraints are then assessed to see whether the parameters from each group differ significantly. If the equality constraints are rejected (i.e., the parameters differ significantly across groups), the missing data are likely responsible for the parameter differences and the mechanism is likely nonignorable.

The advantage of multisample analyses is that missing data do not threaten parameter estimation for those variables that are fully observed.

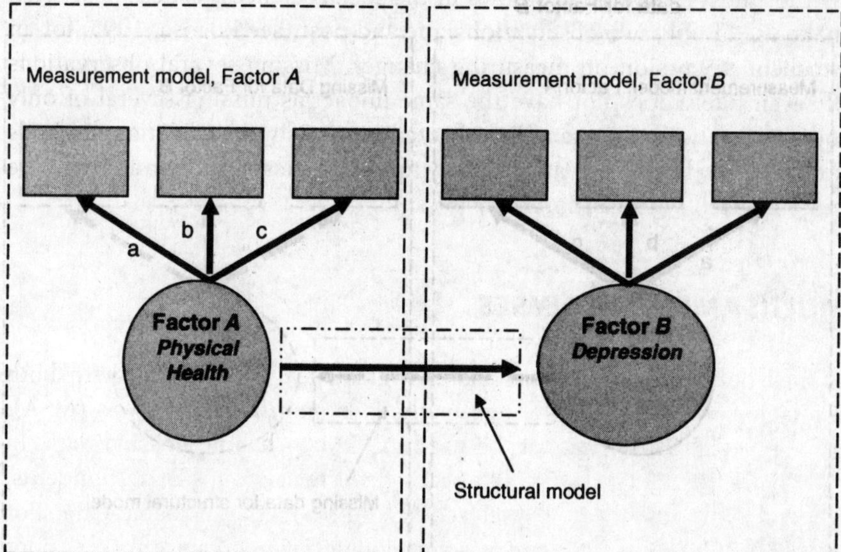

FIGURE 7.4. Multisample analysis, Subsample 1.

Furthermore, parameters that involve variables with missing data can be estimated. In a sense, this procedure is somewhat akin to a multivariate pairwise deletion. MSA is preferable to pairwise deletion due to the aforementioned problems inherent in covariance matrices when variables are pairwise deleted (i.e., differing numbers of observations for each variable being correlated). Additionally, MSA does not require assumptions about the missing data mechanism. Therefore, MSA can be a useful method for handling missing data in structural equation models. MSA can also provide insight into missing data mechanisms, as previously noted.

Two serious limitations exist with MSA. First, the number of patterns of missing data is often limited to the number of multisamples the software can handle. For example, at the writing of this book, the maximum number of samples EQS (Bentler, 1995) will handle is nine. In an MSA of missing data, the number of samples is determined by the number of missing data patterns. It is unlikely that a small number of missing data patterns exist in complicated or even routine social science studies; therefore, nine groups in an MSA is limiting. Second, parameter estimates for small group samples can be suspect and can lead to erroneous rejection of equality constraints. When missing data patterns contain only a small number of

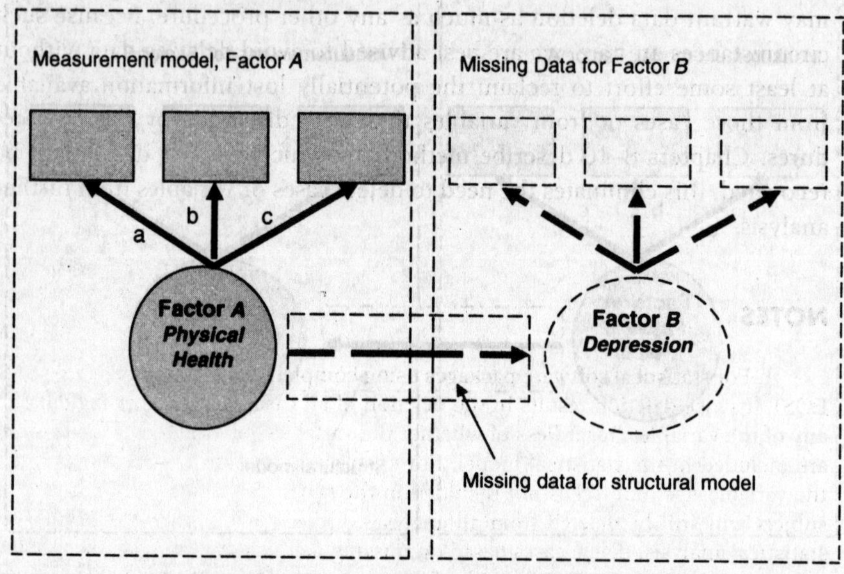

FIGURE 7.5. Multisample analysis, Subsample 2.

observations, the parameters associated with that sample may be skewed in relation to the other samples. MSA requires a large overall sample size to have pattern samples large enough to provide reasonable estimates. Therefore, for many missing data patterns or a small overall sample size, MSA is most likely ill suited for treating missing data in structural equation models.

SUMMARY

Deletion procedures, while commonly used and easily implemented, rarely can be justified. Some missing data experts (e.g., Brown, 1983; Allison, 2002) regard procedures such as listwise and even pairwise deletion as viable options, but under very limited circumstances (e.g., small amounts of missing data and when data are MCAR). Yet due to the sensitivity that all deletion procedures share, with respect to missing data mechanisms and the inefficiencies inherent in losing data for statistical power, these procedures ought to be avoided whenever possible. Circumstances exist, although rare, when few data are missing and their loss is not likely to have an impact on the validity of study conclusions. These circumstances may warrant data deletion as much as any other procedure. Because such circumstances are rare, we are best advised to avoid deleting data without at least some effort to reclaim the potentially lost information available from those cases or from variables that were discarded by these procedures. Chapters 8–10 describe methods by which missing data might be recovered; this eliminates the need to delete cases or variables from further analysis.

NOTES

1. For statistical software packages using complete matrix methods (e.g., SAS, EQS), listwise deletion results in the deletion of all cases that are missing data for any of the variables, regardless of whether the variables for which data are missing are included in the statistical model. For example, if a subject is missing data for the variable *Age*, but *Age* is not included in the statistical model to be tested, that subject will still be deleted from all analyses. Other packages, depending on the statistical analysis, delete cases based on missing data for the variables included in the statistical model.

2. These data and their description were obtained from *http://lib.stat.cmu.edu/datasets/biomed.desc*. The data set was distributed as part of the proceedings of the American Statistical Association (ASA) annual meeting, 1982.

3. Although the original data set included 209 observations, for ease of presentation we randomly selected 25 "normals" and 25 "carriers" for a total of 50 cases.

4. Depending on the hypothesized change function or shape of the growth trajectory, other growth parameters can also be assessed, such as curvature (as in the case of a quadratic change function) or asymptote (as in the case of a logarithmic function). Most often, change is characterized as a monotonic linear function (i.e., a straight line), and therefore intercept and slope are the most commonly estimated growth parameters.

5. A minimal number of observations is required to estimate slopes as well as other growth parameters (e.g., curvature), depending on the change function. For example, to estimate the slope for a linear function, at least two observations are required, or three if one desires an estimate of error. To estimate the slope and curvature for a second-order polynomial function, at least three observations are required (or four, if one wishes to estimate error).

6. In the present example, we estimate change over time using OLS regression for each individual. Other methods used to analyze individual growth curves include hierarchical linear models (HLMs) that generally make use of augmentation methods (see Chapter 8) for handling missing data.

8

Data Augmentation Procedures

Several loosely related missing data procedures fall under the general heading of data augmentation. These methods avoid many of the inherent problems of deletion procedures described in Chapter 7 because they derive parameter estimates (e.g., means, variances, covariances) from the available data and from an underlying distribution or probability model. It is critical to note that data augmentation does not explicitly replace missing values. Instead, an algorithm is invoked that takes into account the observed data, the missing data, the relationships among the observed data, and some underlying statistical assumptions when estimating parameters. In other words, parameter estimates based on observed data are augmented by the extra information provided by an assumed underlying distribution or probability model.

Procedures such as maximum likelihood (ML), expectation maximization (EM), Markov chain Monte Carlo (MCMC), weighting, and dummy code adjustment are considered to be augmentation procedures in the context of missing data. Little and Rubin (1987) describe the ML and EM procedures as model-based procedures, and we conform to their classification, to maintain consistency with the missing data literature. Schafer (1997) refers to these procedures under the more general heading of data augmentation. In this chapter, we discuss the following as augmentation methods: two model-based procedures, maximum likelihood (ML) and expectation-maximization (EM); Markov chain Monte Carlo (MCMC); weighting; and dummy variable adjustment. It is important to note that classification of some of these procedures as augmentation methods is not clear-cut. Specifically, MCMC is referred to as a data augmentation procedure within the process of multiple imputation (e.g., Allison, 2002).

We discuss each method and either provide a specific example (as in Chapter 7) to demonstrate outcomes or refer readers to the extant literature for a more thorough illustration. Because a wide range of procedures fall under this broad category of missing data handling techniques, we limit our focus to some of the methods more commonly used by social scientists.

MODEL-BASED PROCEDURES

Model-based procedures are used to generate parameter estimates given the observed data, the relationships among observed variables, and constraints imposed by underlying distribution.[1] It is this underlying distributional model that gives these procedures the name "model-based." For the procedures on which we focus in this section, the assumed underlying distribution is normal. There are many alternatives to the normal distribution, including but not limited to (1) the Bernoulli or binomial distribution (for dichotomous outcomes), (2) the Poisson distribution for counted variables (e.g., rare outcomes such as juvenile criminality), (3) the multinomial distribution for unordered categorical values, and (4) the Dirichlet model for Bayesian categorical estimation. These distributions are beyond the scope of our discussion, but interested readers can refer to Schafer (1997) for a more detailed explanation of their use and relevance to missing data.

Unlike the empirical methods discussed in Chapters 9 and 10, model-based procedures do not actually impute any values the user can see. Rather, these methods treat the data "as if" all values were observed, and parameters or statistics are estimated in that manner. The allure of model-based procedures is their ability to produce *robust* parameter estimates under conditions of missing data. That is, the methods reliably estimate expected values.

Whereas imputation procedures (see Chapters 9 and 10) rely solely on observed data to impute values to replace missing observations prior to further analysis, model-based procedures combine those data with a theoretical model (e.g., multivariate normal), and they base resulting parameter estimates, *without* replacing missing values, on that combination of information. One concern regarding imputation methods, as we discuss in Chapters 9 and 10, is that when imputed values do not correspond well with what would have been observed had the data not been missing, the results will depart from those that would have occurred with complete data, and more important, they will produce biased parameter estimates.

At this point, we step aside and clarify what is meant by "expected" or "expectation," a term we use repeatedly in this chapter. *Expectation*, when used in the statistical sense, refers to the predictions one would make given the theoretical model with which we are working. For example, in the model-based procedures of focus in this section, normal distribution theory provides an expectation (or prediction) of what statistics (e.g., variance) would most likely occur in a set of observations. In simplified terms, because normal distribution theory specifies that the most likely observation is the mean, one would predict or expect that when randomly sampling values from a population, the most likely value to be observed is the mean. With respect to missing data and parameter estimation, model-based procedures provide an expectation for a statistic rather than for the raw data. Thus, unlike the imputation methods discussed in the following chapters, the model-based procedures base parameter estimation not only on what is observed, but also on what is expected (determined by the assumed underlying distribution or *likelihood* function).

Model-based procedures determine what constitutes "suitable" statistics from which parameter estimates are derived, based on whether they fall in the range of likely (i.e., expected) values, given a particular distribution. Establishing the likelihood of suitable statistics is often carried out by first assuming an underlying distribution (e.g., Gaussian normal) and then selecting values that are most likely representative of the missing values, but without replacing missing data. Parameter estimates are chosen by considering the observed values in the data as well as the theoretical distribution assumed to be underlying the observed data. Although technically this theoretical distribution applies to the more abstract concept of the "population" rather than the actual observed data from the study sample, it is assumed that the observed data come from a sample that was selected randomly from the population of interest. Thus, the theoretical distribution can be applied to the observed data.

Maximum Likelihood

The most popular model-based procedure for handling missing data is *maximum likelihood* (ML). We want to emphasize that ML is not a method that was designed specifically to handle missing data in the way that single or multiple imputation are, for example. ML is a method for estimating parameters in a variety of models such as hierarchical linear models (HLM) and structural equation models (SEM). In fact, the most frequently used estimation method—least squares—is an ML procedure that assumes errors to be normally distributed, and parameter estimates are derived that conform to that constraint. When this assumption is met, least squares and ML parameter estimates are identical. When this assumption is not met, as is often the case with social science data, ML procedures are regarded as more robust estimators. In fact, ML estimators, as they are called, are advantageous in that they produce unbiased estimates in large samples, they are efficient (small standard errors), and in repeated samplings the estimates approximate a normal distribution (which we can use for calculating confidence intervals and *p*-values).

ML is a general estimation procedure found in common statistical software packages including SPSS, SAS, S-Plus, R, LISREL, EQS, AMOS, Mx, and others. Different ML algorithms can be used, such as restricted ML or REML, and full information ML or FIML (frequently referred to as raw ML). Data simulations suggest that some algorithms are more efficient than others under certain data conditions (Kreft & de Leeuw, 1998). For purposes of our discussion, we discuss ML as a general procedure.

In the past, ML estimation procedures could be quite cumbersome for complex analyses where multiple iterations (i.e., repeated attempts) are necessary to obtain stable parameter estimates. Yet with the vast improvement in computers, these methods are not nearly as prohibitive as they used to be. As noted in Chapter 6, ML estimation procedures are associated with a number of statistical models, including SEM, HLM, and other mixed models as well as item-response theory (IRT). One advantage of using ML for parameter estimation is that it handles missing data quite well. Specifically, when missing data are ignorable (i.e., MAR), ML produces unbiased estimates (Allison, 2002; Arbuckle, 1996).

The basic principle of ML is to choose estimates with values that maximize the probability of obtaining the observed data. This is accomplished by the use of a formula (the likelihood function) that estimates the probability or likelihood of the data as a function of both the data and the unknown parameters. When data are missing and the mechanism is ignorable, the likelihood can be obtained by estimating probabilities over all possible values of the missing data and summing them (Allison, 2002; Schafer & Graham, 2002).[2]

It is often the case that ML is best understood through a specific example, so we present a simple example based on the Biomed data set described in Chapter 7. We compare the ML estimates for the population means (μ) and variances (σ^2) for the variables *Age* and *m*1–*m*4. Table 8.1 illustrates these results. Although the estimates of μ from the full data set (Full in Table 8.1) are somewhat different, especially for *m*1 and *m*4, the differences between the estimates of σ^2 are noticeably different for *m*1–*m*4. It is important to note that ML is not trying to recapture the complete data matrix obtained from the sample but rather the population values, which should be estimable from this sample data. Thus, the differences between the estimates of μ and σ^2 in our example may be due not to problems inherent in the ML procedure for handling missing data but to problems in the sample from which the data were derived. In other words, these sample data might not be representative of the population values, and the ML estimates for the MAR data set might actually be better.

Expectation Maximization Method

The EM algorithm is a general method for obtaining ML estimates when data are missing (Dempster, Laird, & Rubin, 1977). Because ML estimates can be difficult to obtain for complex or "real world" data, a procedure is

TABLE 8.1. Comparison of ML Estimates with and without Missing Data

	Mean (μ)		Variance (σ^2)	
Variable	Full	MAR	Full	MAR
Age	34.18	34.01	95.37	93.35
*m*1	122.60	113.12	47881.27	71362.63
*m*2	88.06	86.92	148.33	107.65
*m*3	17.71	17.51	287.12	454.56
*m*4	203.58	208.36	5398.26	4018.92

Note. These data are from the Biomed data set introduced in Chapter 7. Full, the fully observed data set; MAR, the same data set with the missing values that were deleted to mimic the MAR mechanism (see Chapter 7 for details).

necessary to reduce the difficulty of obtaining those estimates. EM handles the problem of missing data and the complications of parameter estimation associated with ML alone by attempting to solve smaller, complete data problems. These complete data problems lead to estimates for the entire data set, including both observed and unobserved values. It is called EM because it consists of two steps: expectation and maximization. These steps repeat multiple times in an iterative process that eventually converges on ML estimates.

The basic steps are (1) to impute values for missing data using ML (by sampling a model-based set of expected values, in combination with the observed data), (2) to generate parameter estimates (means, variances, and covariances) based on step 1, (3) to reimpute values based on the parameter estimates obtained in step 2, and (4) to reestimate parameters based on the reimputed data from step 3. The loop continues until the final step converges on a solution that differs very little from the previous solution. EM treats missing data by making model-based guesses about the data (i.e., expectations, as described previously) and relationships between variables. For data that are assumed to be multivariate normal, imputation in the expectations step is essentially the same as performing regression on the missing values (Allison, 2002). Our description of EM is an oversimplification, but it serves the purpose of introducing and providing a brief overview of the method.

Software specifically designed to implement EM estimation with missing data is available in both commercial and freely distributed statistical software packages. Some of the most popular social science statistical software packages—for example, SPSS, SAS (Yuan, 2000), and S-Plus (Schimert, Schafer, Hesterberg, Fraley, & Clarkson, 2001)—use the EM algorithm in their respective missing data packages. Stand-alone software packages including EMCOV (Graham & Hofer, 1991) and Amelia (King, Honaker, Joseph, & Scheve, 2001) implement the EM algorithm. SEM software packages like AMOS, EQS, LISREL, and Mplus offer ML estimation with missing data using the EM algorithm as well. The software automates the EM steps and produces the ML parameter estimates for the statistical models of interest.

What is advantageous about ML and the EM algorithm for handling missing data are their desirable estimation properties for when missing data are ignorable. In this situation, ML estimates are known to be optimal (i.e., consistent and efficient, as previously noted) for large samples. Where model-based procedures offer little help is in the area of statistical hypothesis testing. Specifically, the EM procedure tends to underestimate standard errors, which are critical to hypothesis testing (Allison, 2002). These underestimates lead to a greater likelihood of Type I errors. Partly to blame for the underestimation of standard errors is the fact that the influence of the missing data is not estimated and therefore cannot be used to correct the standard error estimates. Incorrect standard errors, therefore, adversely affect hypothesis testing, which leads to a greater likelihood of inferential errors. Missing data experts such as Allison (e.g., Allison, 2002) recommend using a different ML method to obtain correct standard errors (the *direct ML* method). Software for analyzing SEM with latent variables is available for this purpose. For details, see Allison (2002).

MARKOV CHAIN MONTE CARLO

One limitation of the ML model-based methods is that they are constrained by distributional assumptions (e.g., multivariate normality). The increasingly popular Markov chain Monte Carlo (MCMC) procedure promises greater flexibility when underlying distributions are unknown. MCMC covers a diffuse set of procedures. *Gibbs sampling* is the most commonly used method for applying MCMC (and the most available in terms of statistical software), although it is often cited without reference to the fact that it is an MCMC procedure. MCMC procedures are loosely allied with Bayesian estimation procedures, but Schafer (1997) argues that MCMC might be somewhat mislabeled as Bayesian. Most readers are likely to see MCMC described as inherently Bayesian. For more detailed information regarding MCMC, we refer the reader to Gelfand and Smith (1990) and Gilks, Richardson, and Spiegelhalter (1996).

MCMC was developed in physics to investigate equilibrium distributions of interacting molecules. For statisticians, the MCMC process has the desirable quality of enabling parameter estimates under difficult data conditions, including when data are missing and when underlying distributions do not fit the assumptions of ML procedures. The process is characterized as Bayesian in that the ultimate goal is to obtain a desired probability distribution known as a *posterior* distribution that can be used for parameter estimation. A posterior distribution is the distribution of unknown parameters after observing data and using the information gained from the data to update the statistical model (Gill, 2002).

Standard Monte Carlo methods are used to generate simulated values *independently* according to some desired probability distribution. MCMC methods generate simulated values in a Markov chain, which is a sequence of random values whose probabilities depend only on the values at the previous step. Therefore, MCMC simulated values are not completely independent. A Markov chain is characterized as a stochastic process that "wanders" around, moving from value to value until it "finds its way" to the desired posterior distribution (Gill, 2002). A simple example is the nonreturning random walk, where the only restriction is to not go back to the location just visited. Markov chains are stochastic (probabilistic) processes that are conditional only on the previous value, a property that is enormously useful for generating the posterior distribution for parameter estimation.

In statistical situations with missing data, the goal is to generate unbiased parameter estimates. This can be difficult when using only the observed data. Thus, much like the EM algorithm, with MCMC the observed data (Y_{obs}) are augmented with simulated values of the missing data (Y_{mis}) to handle this parameter estimation problem. Repeating two steps augments the data: the imputing, or I-step, and the posterior, or P-step. The I-step starts with an estimated mean vector and covariance matrix and simulates missing values for each observation independently given the observed data. The P-step takes this now-complete data set (the observed plus the estimated missing values) and generates new estimates for the mean vector and covariance matrix (which are to be used as the starting point in the next I-step). The repetition or iteration of I-steps followed by P-steps creates the Markov chain, the goal of which is to generate a distribution of values from which to randomly draw the simulated missing values. These values are used in multiple imputation procedures (Chapter 10) when estimating parameters in the presence of missing data. Experts emphasize that the MCMC process ought to be repeated with different random number generators and starting values (based on different initial parameter estimates) in order to validate the multiple imputation results (e.g., see *http://support.sas.com/rnd/app/da/new/802ce/stat/chap9/sect20.htm* for SAS online help suggestions).

While MCMC procedures are pervasive in the statistical literature, they are relatively unused by social scientists compared to the ML-based procedures. However, MCMC procedures are gaining in popularity as software developers include Bayesian methods in standard software packages. Evidence of the growing popularity can be seen in the inclusion of MCMC in the SAS PROC MI (multiple imputation procedure), new R/S-Plus functions, and stand-alone programs such as WinBugs (Gilks, Thomas, & Spiegelhalter, 1994) and MLWin (Multilevel Models Project, 1996).

A thorough description of MCMC procedures falls outside the scope of this book. Even the most useful tutorials (e.g., Gill, 2002) require a more statistically sophisticated knowledge base. Understanding of stochastic processes, posterior distributions, and prior probabilities (concepts from the Bayesian literature) as well as abstract concepts such as "state space" are essential for making sense of these tutorials; therefore, our discussion is limited.

The advantages of the general MCMC procedure over the ML model-based procedures are efficiency and flexibility. MCMC procedures are efficient in the sense that they allow data analysts to estimate parameters when underlying distributions are either unknown or clearly non-normal. Computationally, these procedures tend to offer solutions to even the most complicated missing data problems, particularly when distributions are not well understood or when they deviate from the traditional multivariate normal distribution. Procedurally, these methods work similarly to the model-based procedures, but they are not limited to the expectations (in the statistical sense) of a specific distribution (e.g., Gaussian normal). Like EM estimation, these are iterative processes. Yet the iterative process is different in that EM is limited by the expectation derived from a specific distribution underlying the parameter estimates (the E-step) while the MCMC procedures are not. In fact, Gill (2002) describes the Markov chain process of MCMC as wandering around, "remembering only where it has been in the last period." This process is characterized as a "random walk" and, as noted previously, has the overarching rule that one cannot go back to where one has already been.

Besides their advantage in efficiency and flexibility, MCMC methods are more available to data analysts. Software implementations are now almost universal throughout the mainstream statistical packages and computing platforms, making these methods even more attractive. Despite these advantages, however, the methods are difficult to implement in most cases and continue to remain somewhat elusive for the novice data analyst. As Gill (2002) notes, these methods have been around for a long time (citing a 1953 essay by Metropolis, Rosenbluth, Rosenbluth, Teller, and Teller), and their lack of recognition and use in the past is likely due, at least in part, to the barriers between statistical physics where the earlier work on MCMC originated, and other fields.

ADJUSTMENT METHODS

In contrast to model-based and MCMC procedures, adjustment methods are empirical ways of augmenting parameter estimation. The methods correct parameter estimates so as to prevent or decrease expected biases. For example, if the proportion of males in a sample is greater than what would occur in the population, parameter estimates based on this sample can be corrected for the unintended oversampling of males. These adjustment methods are used primarily in survey research, and there are many of them. Therefore, we provide only a brief discussion.

Dummy Variable Adjustment

Dummy variable adjustment (Cohen & Cohen, 1985) is a method by which to adjust parameters to account for missing data. Generally used in regression analyses when a single predictor is missing, the procedure can be applied to more complex situations as well. The method involves creating two variables that correspond with the variable that is missing data: a binary dummy variable and a variable that replicates the observed values and replaces the missing values with a constant. Suppose we have a simple regression model in which Y is regressed on independent variables X and Z, and X is missing data. Using our previously described notation, we create the dummy variable D, coding the missing data for X as 1s and the observed data as 0s. We also create X^*, in which the observed values of X are replicated and missing values of X are replaced with a constant, such as the mean of those with complete data. We then regress Y on D, X^*, and any other predictors in the intended model (in this example, the other predictor is Z). The logic behind this method is that the dummy variable "partials out" or eliminates the variance in the dependent variable that is attributable to missing data. The regression coefficients for the predictors of interest (X and Z in the example) are estimated with D in the model and therefore these parameters are adjusted for the missing data.

To illustrate the procedure, consider the data in Table 8.2 (using data from Table 5.2). The model is a multiple regression model in which we wish to assess whether *DV* is predicted by *IV*1, *IV*2, *Age*, and *Sex*. There are missing data for the predictors and the *DV* (indicated by the empty cells in Table 8.2), so we create dummy codes for each of these variables (the columns on the right side of the table). Next, we replace the missing data with a constant, the mean of the observed scores for each variable.

Each dummy variable corresponding to a variable with missing data is entered into the regression model prior to entering the predictors of interest. Where the adjustment enters the analysis is through the hierarchical partitioning of variance. In hierarchically partitioned models, the variables entered first into the model are given priority over subsequent variables, to

TABLE 8.2. Illustrative Data Set with Dummy Codes Added (from Table 5.2, Chapter 5)

						Dummy Codes				
Subject	*Age*	*Sex*	*IV*1	*IV*2	*DV*	*DAge*	*DSex*	*DIV*1	*DIV*2	*DDV*
01	25	M	3		25	0	0	0	1	0
02	29	F	2	3	22	0	0	0	0	0
03	20	M	4	8	23	0	0	0	0	0
04	21	M	5	9		0	0	0	0	1
05	20	F	1	1	15	0	0	0	0	0
06	24		3	2	16	0	1	0	0	0
07	26	F	7	3	22	0	0	0	0	0
08	29	F	8	5		0	0	0	0	1
09		M	9	7	30	1	0	0	0	0
10	30	M		9	26	0	0	1	0	0

Note. DAge, dummy code for missing data for the *Age* variable; *DSex*, dummy code for missing data for the *Sex* variable; *DIV*1, dummy code for missing data for the first independent variable; *DIV*2, dummy code for missing data for the second independent variable; *DDV*, dummy code for missing data for the dependent variable.

account for variance in the dependent variable. The explained variance is partialed out, and regression coefficients are adjusted accordingly for the remaining predictors. The dummy variables therefore adjust the parameters for the theoretically relevant predictors (e.g., *Age*, *Sex*, *IV*1, and *IV*2) by removing variance attributable to missing data that is lurking in the dependent variable. This leaves the remaining variability in the *DV* to be explained by the predictors of interest, which is the focus of the study in the first place.

Although it appears to be a reasonable method for handling missing data, Jones (1996) and Allison (2002) showed that this procedure generally produces biased parameter estimates regardless of the mechanism of missing data (MCAR, MAR, or MNAR). For example, Allison (2002) conducted simulations with MCAR data for 10,000 cases and found the regression coefficients to be both underestimated and overestimated. Readers interested in the details are referred to the original source (Cohen & Cohen, 1985) and critiques (e.g., Allison, 2002; Jones, 1996).

Weighting Procedures

One method for addressing the problems associated with deletion procedures (e.g., smaller sample size and decreased statistical power) is weighting cases or parameters based on the observed data. After deleting all incomplete cases, the remaining complete cases are weighted so that their distribution approximates that of the full sample or population. The weights are employed to correct for either the population variability or standard errors associated with the parameters. To derive suitable weights, the probability of each potential response for the variable with missing data is estimated from the data. For example, if a variable is measured on a 5-point Likert scale ranging from *strongly disagree* to *strongly agree*, the researcher must estimate the response probability of each of the five options. As Schafer and Graham (2002) note, weighting can eliminate bias associated with differential response rates for the variables used to estimate the response probabilities, but it cannot correct for biases related to unused or unmeasured variables.

Little and Rubin (1987) discuss several methods for estimating and applying weights for survey data. In general, these methods are fairly easy to apply for a limited number of situations. Specifically, in situations with monotonic missing data patterns or in univariate analyses, weighting procedures are a viable option. As described in Chapters 3 and 5, monotonic patterns are those in which data that are missing for one variable (e.g., an item or repeated measure) are missing for all subsequent variables. A monotonic pattern is reflected in attrition, when respondents drop out and do not return for subsequent observations. Univariate analyses are those in which statistics are computed or estimated for single variables, as is often the case in survey research, where interest lies in describing responses to single items (e.g., percentage of people who smoke cigarettes).

While these methods do not require a model for the underlying distribution like the model-based procedures, applying the response probability can become quite cumbersome when multiple variables have different response probabilities and/or when many missing data patterns exist (e.g., *arbitrary* missing data). Therefore, weighting is rarely a suitable option for most social scientists unless under fairly constrained conditions, that is, when missing data patterns are few and when response probabilities are known and are relatively uniform across variables. Schafer and Graham (2002) note a renewed interest in weighting procedures, particularly in the field of biostatistics, with new methods appearing for parametric and semiparametric regression that extend generalized estimating equations (or GEE). For a review of these methods, see Meng (1999) and Schafer and Graham (2002). In general, these reviewers conclude that under rare circumstances these models outperform Bayesian multiple imputation (MI) methods (discussed in Chapter 10).

SUMMARY

This has hardly been an exhaustive account of data augmentation, but we have taken a brief look at the available tools for handling missing data. The general approach of maximum likelihood and the Bayesian-like approaches of MCMC offer the greatest promise, but, like all missing data handling procedures, they are not without their flaws. Unsuspecting users have to contend with the fact that assumptions they make about distribution may be wrong, these methods entail computational complexity, and statistical software is not universally available for the better of these methods, though there is software for the weaker ones (e.g., dummy code adjustment).

NOTES

1. Not all of the model-based procedures make use of the same set of observed data. For example, full information maximum likelihood (FIML, also known as raw ML) uses the *entire* data matrix (hence, "full information"), even when some of the variables in the matrix are not included in the statistical analyses of interest.

2. For a more complete treatment of the advantages and disadvantages of ML procedures, we refer the reader to Enders (2001), who offers a useful primer on ML procedures with missing data.

9

Single Imputation Procedures

In our discussion of statistical methods for handling missing data thus far, we have addressed procedures that, in principle, do *not* replace missing data with actual values prior to further analyses and interpretation. In contrast, the methods in this and the following chapter *do* provide actual values for those that are missing. The basic principle for imputation methods is to substitute a value for each missing one and carry out the analysis as if there were no missing data. In contrast to the multiple imputation procedures discussed in Chapter 10, single imputation methods replace a missing value with a single value rather than with multiple values. In this chapter, we focus on procedures that replace the missing value with either (1) a constant, (2) a randomly selected value, or (3) a nonrandomly derived value. Table 9.1 outlines the single imputation procedures we address in this chapter.

To briefly summarize these methods, the general method of *constant replacement* involves imputing a constant to replace the missing value. These methods frequently call for substituting the missing value with the mean—either the arithmetic mean (known as *mean substitution*) or the estimated population mean (known as *ML mean* or μ)—but may also

TABLE 9.1. Single Imputation Procedures

General procedures	Specific procedure	Type of data
Constant	Mean substitution	Continuous normal
	ML mean substitution	Continuous normal
	Median substitution	Continuous
	Zero imputation	Categorical or continuous
Random		
Data-based	Hot deck	Any
	Cold deck	Any
Model-based	Bayesian (MCMC)	Any
	ML	Continuous normal
Nonrandom		
One condition	Group mean	Continuous with groups
	Group median	Continuous with groups
	Last observation carried forward (LOCF)	Longitudinal
	Next observation carried backward (NOCB)	Longitudinal
Multiple conditions	Mean previous observations	Longitudinal
	Mean subsequent observations	Longitudinal
	Last and next average	Longitudinal
	Regression	Multivariate continuous
	Regression with error	Multivariate continuous

include *median substitution* and *zero imputation*. The two major random selection procedures are called *hot deck* and *cold deck* imputation, for reasons detailed later. Finally, nonrandomly derived values can come from regression, conditional imputation, or previously recorded values for the subject. We discuss each of these procedures, provide a discussion of their strengths and weaknesses, and, in some cases, illustrate the method using data sets introduced in Chapter 7. As with all data demonstrations throughout this book, our intention is to illustrate the procedure and its outcomes, not to justify or criticize its use. That is better accomplished by rigorous data simulation studies (e.g., Monte Carlo simulations) that go beyond the scope of this book.

CONSTANT REPLACEMENT METHODS

The most common method of single imputation is constant replacement. This procedure requires a single value to be computed and then subsequently imputed for (i.e., to replace) a missing value. The best thing about imputing constants is that it is easy; however, there are numerous disadvantages to constant replacement. Constant replacement methods tend to be most widely used in social and behavioral sciences, and they require close scrutiny. We demonstrate mean substitution, ML mean imputation, median substitution, and zero imputation by presenting the means, the standard deviations, and the parameter estimates that were obtained using these methods for a regression model that predicts body fat percentage, so that the reader can note the effects of each procedure on these parameters.

The Demonstration Data Set

The data set (entitled "Body Comp") from which we carry out our demonstration includes measures of percentage of body fat (measured through the underwater weighing technique), age, weight, height, and 10 body circumference measurements (e.g., abdomen, chest, wrist) obtained with a tape measure. These data were recorded for 252 men and as part of an earlier study (Penrose, Nelson, & Fisher, 1985).[1] Body fat was calculated from underwater weighing using two different formulas, the Siri and the Brozec algorithms. Both values were available for each subject in the data set. The purpose for collecting the 10 body circumference measures is to estimate body fat for men using only a scale and a measuring tape (vs. underwater weighing). The data set was used by Johnson (1996) to demonstrate to students the utility of multiple regression.

To generate the missing data for this example, we maintained consistency with missing data demonstrations in Chapters 7 and 8 by taking the fully observed "Body Comp" data set and deleting values to mimic an MAR mechanism. This was accomplished by conditioning the missing data on higher values of the Brozec measure of body fat (i.e., ≥21% body fat). Specifically, those with values ≥21% had a 60% probability of missing data on at least 1 of the body circumference measures, but on no more than 6 of the 10. The Brozec measure is almost perfectly correlated with the Siri measure of body fat ($r = .99$). The Siri measure was used as the dependent variable to be predicted by the 10 measures of body circumference. Therefore, missing data in this example are related to body fat content, the dependent variable of interest.

To demonstrate the constant replacement methods, we conducted a multiple regression analysis in which we predicted body fat (the Siri value) with the 10 body circumference measures. Parameters of interest in this analysis are the regression coefficients for each of the 10 predictors, their standard errors (which influence tests of statistical significance), and the amount of explained variance in the dependent variable, or adjusted R^2. Table 9.2 presents these parameters (in the interest of space, only 3 of the 10 predictor variables are included), for the fully observed and the MAR data sets using the different constant replacement methods. The mean, ML mean, and median calculated for each of these 3 predictor variables (abdominal, bicep, and wrist circumferences), as well as the standard devi-

TABLE 9.2. Results for Constant Replacement Methods

		Constant replacement method		
	Full	MAR data set		
Statistic	data	Mean	ML mean (μ)	Median
Means				
Abdomen	92.56	91.34	91.36	91.19
Bicep	32.27	31.94	31.94	31.90
Wrist	18.23	18.22	18.21	18.23
Standard deviations (*sd*)				
Abdomen	10.78	9.79	9.79	9.80
Bicep	3.02	2.72	2.72	2.72
Wrist	.93	.87	.87	.87
Unstandardized regression coefficients (*B*)				
B_0—Model intercept	6.64	–19.11	–17.71	–22.02
B_1—Abdomen	1.04	.65	.66	.60
B_2—Bicep	.14	.07	.09	.05
B_3—Wrist	–1.49	–1.69	–1.69	–1.52
Standard error for β				
se_0—Model intercept	6.71	8.51	8.44	8.65
se_1—Abdomen	.08	.07	.07	.07
se_2—Bicep	.17	.20	.20	.20
se_3—Wrist	.51	.62	.61	.64

Note. MAR, missing at random; the MAR data set was created by deleting missing values to mimic a MAR mechanism. Full, values produced via the fully observed data; Mean, values produced via the mean substitution method; ML mean, values produced via the ML mean substitution method; and Median, values produced via the median substitution method.

ation for these variables, are also reported so that the reader can see the actual values that were substituted for the missing data.

The following describes the missing data procedures and presents the results from these analyses. As noted in Chapters 7 and 8, it is *critical* to remind the reader that results from the full data set are included merely to show the differences between estimates provided by the fully observed data and those provided by data adjusted for missing values. Again, the reader should not regard the results from the fully observed data as the "right" answer, because they might not be an accurate representation of the population to which the researcher plans to generalize findings.

Mean Substitution (Between-Subjects Imputation, Fill In with Means, and Imputing Unconditional Means)

Mean substitution is the procedure whereby missing values for a variable are replaced by the observed mean for that particular variable. Although popular in social sciences (see Roth, 1994) and easy to implement in most statistical software packages, mean substitution is a poor choice for handling missing data under most circumstances. If mean values are imputed, extreme values are underrepresented and therefore the variable with missing values will decrease in variance (Little & Rubin, 1987). The method is known to generate biased estimates of variances and covariances and generally should be avoided. However, if there are few missing values that are replaced by the mean, the deleterious effect of mean substitution is reduced.

Table 9.2 contains the results of the aforementioned regression analyses for complete and single imputation methods. The means, standard deviations, and regression parameters with their associated standard errors for 3 of the 10 predictor variables (abdomen, bicep, and wrist circumference) were computed for the fully observed data set with no missing data, and for the MAR data set after the missing data was replaced using a particular method (i.e., mean, ML mean, or median). We focus on these parameters to illustrate the differences a researcher might expect when comparing these methods.

As Table 9.2 demonstrates, mean substitution has little effect on calculating the means for each of the predictors in this example (which are the values we used to replace missing data for each of the predictor variables). It can have substantial effect if the mean were computed on a non-normally distributed variable, where the mean is not the best measure of central tendency for that set of data. Otherwise, the expectation ought to be that means remain fairly constant with mean imputation.

The real difference between the results for the fully observed data versus the data with mean substitution is reflected in the other parameters. First, as expected, standard deviations for the "Mean" substitution data are smaller: smaller standard deviations reflect less variability, and when all missing values for a variable are replaced with a constant—for example, the mean—there is less variability in scores.

Next, we turn our attention to the unstandardized regression coefficients (B_0, B_1, B_2, and B_3). These are the parameters of focus for the regression model, and therefore it is important that they be good estimates of the population parameters. It is noteworthy how they differ from the coefficients derived from the complete data, particularly B_0, the regression coefficient for the model intercept. The magnitude and the sign of this parameter do not resemble the value for the full data set, in part due to the mechanism of missing data. The MAR data were conditioned on the outcome variable and hence restricted the range of values for the sample. The model intercept is based on the grand mean of the dependent variable. Conditioning missing data on the higher values of the dependent variable disproportionately deleted values from the predictors for the sample with higher body fat, resulting in a corresponding shift in the intercept. Note also the differences in standard errors (se_0–se_3). Smaller standard errors mean more precision of the estimate (although this does not necessarily translate to more accuracy), and smaller standard errors increase the likelihood of obtaining statistical significance. Except for the model intercept (i.e., se_0), the standard errors for the mean substitution method are larger than those for the full data set.

Our example suggests that mean substitution produces somewhat mixed results but that the results are fairly predictable. As expected, variability in the three predictors of interest decreases with this method, and regression coefficients change in odd ways. Furthermore, certain standard errors are generally larger, which becomes a problem for tests of statistical significance.

ML Estimated Mean Substitution

In contrast to the traditional method of computing arithmetic means for a variable with missing data, the relatively newer method of computing expected means (or μ) is based on the maximum likelihood (ML) algorithm. Arithmetic means tend to be sample-dependent and sensitive to outlier values. All parameters from the ML algorithm are estimates from the available data but rely on the underlying assumption that the data come from a normally distributed population distribution (see our discussion in Chapter 8). Thus ML provides an estimate of the population mean (μ) rather than calculating the sample mean. For ML estimates, substantial deviations from the assumed distribution tend to render poor estimates of the mean and offer few or no advantages over the arithmetic mean.

For our demonstration, we calculated the ML means for the three predictors as depicted in Table 9.2. This estimate of the mean is virtually the same as the arithmetic mean for both the MAR data set (see the "Mean" column) and the full data set. Similar to the mean substitution method, variance is decreased when compared to the full data set (as indicated by the smaller standard deviations).

For the regression coefficients and their standard errors, the ML mean method produced estimates similar to those of the mean substitution method. Standard errors were larger, except for the abdomen measure, and the regression coefficients were different, particularly for the model intercept (B_0).

Median Substitution

The two previous methods impute a single value that is assumed to best represent the underlying distribution of values for the variable of interest. As noted in Chapter 8, when data are normally distributed, the mean is the most likely value to be observed and therefore serves as the best estimate when values are missing. However, the mean may be an inappropriate characterization of data that are not normally distributed, especially when the distribution deviates strongly from Gaussian normal. Underlying distributions that are skewed (either positively or negatively) as well as those that are flat or peaked (platykurtic and leptokurtic, respectively) are at risk for being poorly represented by a mean. Therefore, an alternative measure of central tendency provides a better summary of the underlying distribution and thus a better estimate for missing values. The median, in particular, frequently performs well as a measure of central tendency when distributions deviate greatly from the standard normal distribution. The procedure for substituting the median for missing values for a particular variable follows the same logic and protocol for the two substitution methods previously presented.

Results of our demonstration of this method are included in Table 9.2 in the "Median" column. Because these data for the three circumference measures were normally distributed, the median is virtually the same as the mean. Similarly, the standard deviations for each of the three predictors are the same as those for the mean and ML mean substitution methods for the same reason. As with the other two methods, they show less variability than the full data set, except for the abdomen measure.

In comparison to the mean and ML mean methods, the regression coefficients and their standard errors for median substitution are different, and standard errors for the model intercept and wrist measure are the largest of all the constant replacement methods. Again, these larger standard errors are less optimal for rejecting the null hypothesis in significance tests but may be seen by some as an improvement over previous methods for protecting against Type II errors.

Zero Imputation

A common practice in the social sciences and in psychometric work is to replace missing data with a value of 0, where 0 might indicate failure on the measure of interest. Of course, this method is only appropriate in cases where 0 is a plausible value. For example, 0s are assigned for treatment dropouts when measuring positive outcomes, for skipped items on achievement tests, for experimental protocol compliance data, and for binary outcomes in which the value 0 indicates the most conservative outcome. In each case, a 0 means that the individual did poorly on the measure or construct. Many researchers justify this imputation by stating that the missing data were handled in the most conservative manner.

If missing data were always indicative of poor outcomes, zero imputation would have no bearing on the results of the analysis. However, missing data are missing for a variety of reasons, as discussed previously, and not all of these reasons justify assuming the worst or most conservative outcome. Moreover, differential dropout between treatment and control groups may be a situation in which zero imputation creates an artifact that says little about substantive interests and reflects merely the imputation procedure. Specifically, if a larger proportion of individuals in the control versus treatment group drop out from a study, then the mean of the outcome measures for the control group will be influenced by the greater number of 0s. Hence the treatment effect may appear greater due solely to the imputation procedure.

Zero imputation is the most common procedure in achievement testing or binary response measures. In speeded tests, respondents who fail to complete items or omit responses to an item are almost always assigned a

0, indicating item failure. The items that were not completed are by definition considered to be incorrect or failed, and in these circumstances, zero imputation appears justifiable. In contrast, when used to indicate failure in intervention studies simply because individuals have dropped out, zero imputation might not be an appropriate method. This sort of method is often used for intent-to-treat analyses, in which individuals assigned to the treatment condition have dropped out of the study and are considered to be treatment failures. They are assigned 0s for all missing outcome measures. However, as noted in Chapter 4, individuals drop out of intervention studies for a variety of reasons, some of which may not be related to treatment failure. In fact, some might drop out due to treatment success!

Likert scale or polytomous data in which responses are not binary rarely warrant this method since there is no obvious reason why a missing value should be assumed to be the extreme response that corresponds with a value of 0. Consider a set of questions that are mixed with respect to positive and negative wording (e.g., "I consider myself a happy person" vs. "I am often dissatisfied"). If zero imputation were used for all missing data, the net effect rests solely on the proportion of positively worded versus negatively worded questions. Therefore zero imputation should never be used without careful thought given to what a value of 0 means for the given data. Because zero replacement would not be suitable for the Body Comp data set (i.e., 0 is not a valid value for any of the measures of circumference), we do not demonstrate this method with this data. Had we been uncritical in our use of this missing data method with the Body Comp data, the means for all three of the predictor variables would be much lower (reflecting a sample of thinner men) than the other methods and the full data set, because the 0s would "pull" the distribution to the left and lower the means. Furthermore, because 0s would extend the distribution beyond what would normally be a minimal value for each of the circumference measures, the variability in scores would *increase* (approximately three to four times that of the other methods and the full data set). In a data set where 0 is a valid value, this would not necessarily be the case.

RANDOM VALUE IMPUTATION

Another set of single imputation methods involves replacing missing data with randomly generated values. These come from either selecting a random value from those observed in the current data, a method known as *hot deck* imputation, or from a separate but similar data set with matching variables, a method known as *cold deck* imputation. For some of these methods, the process is not entirely random. For example, a random value may be selected after conditioning on another variable (e.g., treatment group, age). The important feature of these procedures is that the exact value imputed cannot be traced to anything but a random selection process.

There are two general approaches for imputing values for missing data within these random imputation methods. The first approach uses available data to estimate suitable replacements for the missing values. We refer to these methods as *empirical* procedures. The second approach makes use of a theoretical distribution (e.g., Gaussian normal) to arrive at imputed values. That is, missing values are imputed based on an expectation that is consistent with the assumptions of a particular type of distribution (e.g., standard normal). The procedures we discuss here are empirical procedures. Chapters 8 and 10 address model-based procedures that may be suitable for random imputation.

Hot Deck Imputation

Little and Rubin (1987) used the term "hot deck" to refer to several single imputation procedures. The term comes from the bygone practice of using computer punch cards to store data. With respect to missing data, selecting replacement values from the stack of cards that are currently in use (i.e., "hot") for the analysis gives us "hot deck" procedures. In contrast, the qualifier "cold" refers to a stack of computer punch cards that contains data from another sample or study.

With hot deck procedures there are several methods to impute values. One involves randomly selecting a value from the observed data to replace a missing value. For example, if an individual failed to provide his age, we could randomly select a value for that individual from all of the reported ages. The probability of selecting one observed value over another will be based on the rate at which the different values occur. If only 3 individuals in the sample of 100 are 15 years old and 30 of them are 35 years old, it is 10 times as likely that the value of 35 will be selected to replace the missing value. A related method, *hot deck within adjustment cells*, involves doing the same but only after blocking on relevant covariates. For example, if we believe the sex (gender) of respondents is relevant to why data are missing and we are mostly missing age data from females, we would randomly select only from the observed ages of the females, thus blocking on the sex variable. A third hot deck method is to use the nearest neighbor's value to replace the missing data. For example, if Subject 11's age is missing, we use either Subject 10's or Subject 12's age as a replacement.

Hot deck procedures were originally intended for survey research; hence, these terms or procedures are rarely referenced outside the survey research field. One known problem with these procedures is the underestimation of standard errors. This is due to decreased variability in scores on variables with missing data because the missing values are replaced with values that already exist in the distribution of scores. As noted previously, smaller standard errors lead to a greater likelihood of Type I errors (i.e., the missing data manipulation is likely to increase the likelihood of detecting a difference when no difference exists). Moreover, unless the missing data are MCAR (which, as noted in Chapter 3, is not common for social science data), these procedures may introduce biases that are unpredictable. A brief demonstration illustrates both the hot and cold deck procedures.

The data set we use to demonstrate this procedure is the Biomed data set discussed in detail in Chapter 7. Briefly, four repeated measures (*m*1, *m*2, *m*3, *m*4) were made on blood samples of 209 individuals (75 "carriers" and 134 "normals") in order to develop a screening method to identify carriers of a rare genetic disorder. The data set includes age and disease classification ("carrier" vs. "normal") as well as the repeated blood sample measures (*m*1–*m*4).

As in Chapter 7, we analyzed these data with a general linear model (GLM), treating disease classification as the factor ("normal" vs. "carrier") and age as the covariate. The dependent variable is a unit-weighted factor created by converting *m*1, *m*2, *m*3, and *m*4 into *z*-scores, summing them, and taking the mean *z*-score.

As described in Chapter 7, we initially conducted the GLM on a fully observed data set with only 50 participants (25 normals and 25 carriers), that is, the Full data set. We created missing data to reflect an MAR mechanism by conditioning the missing data for the *m*1 through *m*4 measures on age (i.e., participants 29 years or older had a 70% chance of missing data for *m*1, *m*2, *m*3, or *m*4). For the hot deck demonstration, missing values for *m*1–*m*4 were randomly selected from the observed values for each of those variables in the MAR data set. After replacing the missing data, we created the unit-weighted factor score and conducted the GLM.

Table 9.3 shows the results for hot deck and cold deck imputation methods. We focus on the GLM parameter estimates, their standard errors, and the explained variance of the model, when compared to the fully observed data set ("Full" in Table 9.3). The parameter estimates ("Esti-

TABLE 9.3. Hot and Cold Deck Imputation Procedures

	Estimate			Standard Error			Adjusted R^2		
Coefficients	Full	Hot	Cold	Full	Hot	Cold	Full	Hot	Cold
Intercept	1.01*	.46	.29	.41	.39	.38	.37	.24	.26
Age	–0.01	–.003	.001	.01	.01	.01			
Group (normal vs. carrier)	–1.04**	–.692**	–.667**	.19	.18	.18			

Note. Full, full data set; Hot, MAR data set with missing values replaced using hot deck imputation; Cold, MAR data set with missing values replaced using cold deck imputation. The sample size for each data set is 50.
*$p < .01$; **$p < .001$.

mate" in Table 9.3) are smaller for the hot deck procedure when compared to the "Full" data set. Substantively, this means a weaker relationship between the experimental factor (Group) as well as a weaker relationship between the covariate (Age) and the dependent variable. This is because MAR data reduce variability in the outcome variable, and this is compounded by randomly selecting values to replace missing data with observed values, which further reduces variability. The reduced variability is further reflected in the model adjusted R^2, which is substantially smaller for the MAR data set with hot deck imputation. Of the variance in the outcome variable, 37% is explained by the model with fully observed data, while only 24% is explained in the model using the hot deck procedure.

The standard errors are somewhat comparable to those of the full data set, but as noted previously with hot deck procedures the imputation method reduced the observed standard errors. Again, these reduced variability in the hot deck data. The concern with smaller standard errors is that they can lead to an increase in Type I errors. The example, although limited, shows the potential effects of hot deck imputation on a simple model. The next procedure aims at eliminating some of these problems by using data that do not inherently restrict the variance.

Cold Deck Imputation

There are situations where it may be possible to use data sets other than the current one to provide values for the missing data in the current, incomplete data set. Rubin (1987) referred to using values from another data set to replace missing values from the current set as "cold deck" imputation. The most likely situation where cold deck imputation would be possible is survey research. However, there are studies where researchers split data sets to conduct exploratory and confirmatory model tests. Briefly, investigators split the entire data set into two subsets: one on which to conduct exploratory analyses and the other on which to conduct analyses to confirm the results of the exploratory analyses. In these circumstances, the partial data set for the confirmatory analyses may serve as the cold deck for imputation in the hot (i.e., exploratory) deck and vice versa.

Results of the demonstration of the cold deck procedure are also reported in Table 9.3 to facilitate comparison with the hot deck procedure and with the fully observed results. The procedures were the same as those described for the hot deck imputation demonstration. For the cold deck procedure, recall that there is another available data set from which to impute missing values: the remaining 159 cases from the original data set.[2] Values randomly selected for the variables *m*1–*m*4 from that data set were used to replace missing values for those variables in the MAR data set with 50 cases. After replacing the missing data, the GLM was conducted.

Similar to the hot deck procedure, the cold deck approach resulted in smaller parameter estimates, and notably one estimate (for "age") was in the opposite direction when compared to the full data set (i.e., –0.01 vs. 0.001, respectively). A change in magnitude and direction would lead to substantively different conclusions based on these results. As with the hot deck procedure, standard errors are slightly smaller than those for the full data set, and the adjusted R^2 is substantially smaller, again, denoting decreased variability in the data used for these analyses.

NONRANDOM VALUE IMPUTATION: SINGLE CONDITION

Conditional Mean Imputation (Within-Subjects Imputation, Regression Imputation, Buck's Method)

The methods we refer to as *conditional mean* imputation require empirical procedures to estimate missing values from observed data that are not limited to only the data for the missing variable. If values are missing for a theoretically relevant variable, missing values can be imputed from other related variables, including predictors, covariates, and perhaps even non-model-specific variables. Additionally, these conditional procedures can employ single or multiple observed variables. We restrict our current discussion to only the cases where a single value is used to generate the imputed value (the multiple method is covered in Chapter 10).

This approach employs a substitution method whereby means are estimated by using a classification variable in the data set. For example, the mean value for just the males in the Delinquency data set for the outcome variable *BDKID* (described in Chapter 7) could replace missing data for all males who are missing data for *BDKID*. Comparing this method to the earlier discussion of *mean substitution*, the conditional method differs in that the mean to be used for replacing missing values for a particular variable is not calculated using the entire sample. Instead, the means for the different groups within a classification variable (e.g., males vs. females) are used to replace missing data for members of those groups.

With the conditioned means method, a key area of concern is the relationship between the classification variable (e.g., *Sex*) and the variable with missing data (e.g., *Drug abuse*). The weaker the relationship, the more the mean imputation procedure mimics a random process (like hot deck imputation). To use the method effectively, it is important that the classification variable be strongly related to the variable for which the missing data are imputed. However, there can be problems associated with this procedure when strong relationships exist between the variable from which the replacement is derived and the variable with the missing data. If a classification variable is relevant to the analytic model, the data analyst may end up either reifying the model (i.e., confirming a model by replacing missing values with data that are based on that same model) or reducing its chances for success—depending on the nature of the relationship.

For example, consider a situation where missing data are restricted to the dependent variable (e.g., *Drug use*) and we conditionally impute missing data values based on the level of a predictor we think is relevant (e.g., *Age*). Furthermore, we are interested in predicting drug use with a variety of predictors, including age, because, as noted before, we think it is relevant. In such situations, the statistical model would likely be strengthened by imputation. Specifically, if we were to test the relationship between age and drug use but used age to conditionally impute the missing values for drug use, the relationship between drug use and age would be artificially increased due solely to the imputation method. Even if the imputed values were based on another variable (e.g., *Education*) and that variable had a strong relationship with the model predictor (i.e., *Age*), the overall model strength would be increased.

The alternative would be to condition on a variable that has little to no relationship with the predictors but is conditionally important for the outcome. In our example, if biological sex was not theoretically important in the model, that variable might be a good conditioning variable to impute missing values of drug use. There is no reason to suspect that sex and age would necessarily correlate in the population, and therefore the conditional imputation would have little to no effect on the model test.[3]

Asymptotic Imputation: Last Value Carried Forward

For longitudinal data analyses, attrition is the primary reason for missing data. One method for replacing missing values in longitudinal data is to use previous observations to replace later missing values. The previous observations are almost always limited to the participant's last or most recent observation; hence these methods are usually referred to as "last value carried forward" (LVCF), sometimes referred to as "last observation carried forward." For example, if we measured adolescent drug use every year for 5 years and some individuals were missing data for the fifth year, LVCF would dictate replacing that missing data with observations from the fourth year (if available). The underlying assumption is that the most recent observation is the best guess for subsequent missing values.

With LVCF, there are choices to be made by the data analyst regarding how recent an observation must be in order to be carried forward to replace missing data. Using the same example, assume that some of the adolescents are missing data for the fourth and fifth measurement occasions (or "waves"). The analyst could choose to carry the observation from the third wave forward to the fourth and fifth waves, but if the waves were judged to be too far apart, the data analyst might opt for a different method for handling the missing data. Thus, it must be determined how much time between observed and missing measurement occasions is allowed for the last observations to be carried forward. The most extreme example is for an individual to provide baseline data and have missing data for all subsequent waves. The researcher must consider whether it is tenable to replace those missing values with the baseline data. In many cases, it is not.

Lavori (1992) provides an excellent description of the problems associated with this LVCF. To summarize, LVCF tends to bias parameter estimates and increase Type I errors. Additionally, logic dictates that LVCF may introduce biases that interfere with inference. Consider a situation where data were MCAR and missing only on the last of three observations. Three general situations are possible for each individual with missing data: the person would have had a higher, lower, or same standing (or score) for that variable had the data been observed. The proportion of the sample that is at each of these three levels dictates the direction of bias in the results. If the majority of those with missing data actually had a lower standing on the outcome variable, LVCF would result in biased higher values. For longitudinal analyses where the relationship between the repeated observations is the focus (e.g., individual growth curve analyses) and the majority of missing data is from the final measurement occasion, these imputation biases add error to the end of the trajectories, where the influence is greatest.

Regarding significance testing, LVCF results in unpredictable changes. For example, if individuals tend to drop out of a treatment protocol, it may well be that those individuals voluntarily left the study due to adverse effects from the treatment, symptom improvement, or no change. The extent to which they drop out for those reasons dictates the appropriateness of LVCF with respect to significance testing. Significance testing is based on standard errors and variance. When variance is underestimated, correlations suffer and significance testing tends to result in more Type II errors. Conversely, when standard errors are underestimated, significance testing tends to result in Type I errors. Since the effects of LVCF are not predictable, it is difficult to forecast the direction of the bias or error. However, this method is likely to lead to errors in significance testing, regardless of the direction.

We illustrate the probable effects of LVCF on a simple longitudinal data set where we have six repeated measures for a hypothetical outcome variable (see Figure 9.1). The observed points are indicated by the empty circles, and the linear regression line (i.e., the line that best fits or summarizes the six data points) for the trajectory is indicated by the solid line. If only the last two observations are missing, the fourth observation carries forward and the new points are indicated by the letter *F.* The linear slope for the LVCF (shown as the dotted line) illustrates the potential effect of seriously altering both the slope and intercept parameters. In this example, the slope moves in the opposite direction to the original regression line (the solid black line), suggesting an increase rather than a decrease over time in the outcome being measured. Furthermore, the intercept for this model (where the dotted line crosses the *Y*-axis) is about 4, which is lower than for the original model. Lavori (1992) discusses these effects in detail.

Next Value Carried Backward

Similar to LVCF, the method of carrying subsequent values backward aids in the imputation of longitudinal data where early observations are miss-

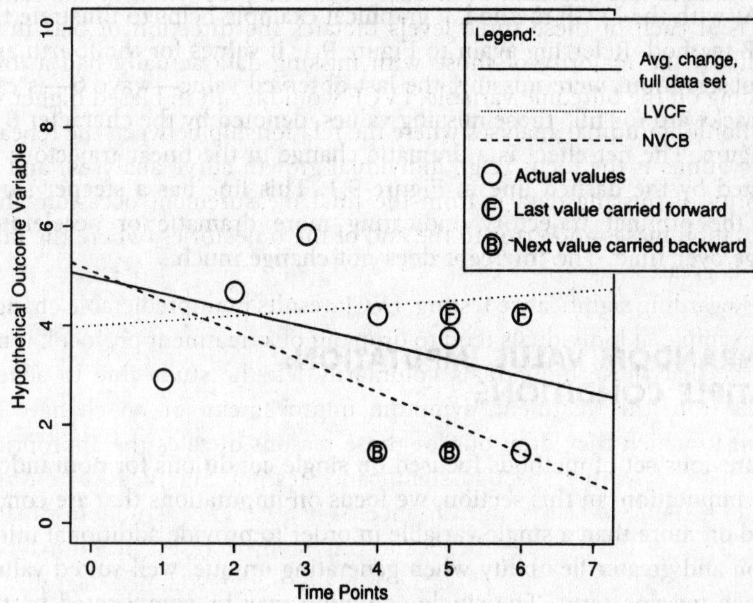

FIGURE 9.1. Illustration of LVCF and NVCB.

ing. The process of "back filling" is frequently referred to as next value carried backward (NVCB). Situations where subjects fail to complete baseline information or where a long buildup to the study leads to incomplete data might benefit from this procedure. Simulation results tend to support the use of NVCB, whereas LVCF is more problematic, as implied in our discussion of it (see Engels & Diehr, 2003).

LVCF and NVCB both rely on within-subject imputation (i.e., using a subject's own data for imputing missing data) and make use of only observed values (i.e., they are not model-based procedures, see Chapter 8). Thus, when subjects are missing data for the first of five waves of data collection (i.e. baseline data are missing), those values can be imputed from their own observed data at the second wave. The two methods are also similar in that they both require the data analyst to make decisions about the distance between missing observations and how recently an observation must be made in order to serve as a suitable estimate for the missing data. Other methods, such as data augmentation (see Chapter 8) and multiple imputation (see Chapter 10), tend to be easier to implement and provide more robust parameter estimates for a wider range of models. Lavori (1992) and Engels and Diehr (2003) offer more complete coverage of these methods.

As with the LVCF method, a graphical example helps to illustrate the NVCB method. Referring again to Figure 9.1, if values for the fourth and fifth observations were missing, the last observed value—wave 6—is carried backward to "fill" those missing values, denoted by the character *B* in the figure. The net effect is a dramatic change in the linear trajectory, as depicted by the dashed line in Figure 9.1. This line has a steeper slope than the original trajectory, indicating more dramatic or accelerated change over time. The intercept does not change much.

NONRANDOM VALUE IMPUTATION: MULTIPLE CONDITIONS

The previous set of methods focused on single conditions for nonrandom value imputation. In this section, we focus on imputations that are conditioned on more than a single variable in order to provide additional information and greater flexibility when generating unique, well-suited values for each missing term. The single condition may be complicated by the fact that some participants may be missing data for the conditioning variable as well. For those cases, there is not enough information by which to impute missing values. Therefore, acquiring information from multiple sources can be useful. There are several methods that make use of multiple variables to conditionally derive values for each missing value, and we briefly address them in this section. The advantage of these methods over the single-condition values is just that more is better than less, particularly with respect to information for imputing values. That said, the following procedures perform only marginally better than the single-condition values. An excellent review of these procedures and the associated biases from each can be found in Engels and Diehr (2003).

Mean Previous Observations

In longitudinal data analyses, an individual's data can be aggregated to form an estimate for subsequent missing values. One method for aggregation is the mean of all previously observed values. For example, if an individual is missing data for the last of five waves of data collection, the missing value could be imputed by taking the mean of the observations at the first through fourth waves. Engels and Diehr (2003) demonstrate that this imputation method performs poorly across a range of missing data conditions and produces biases similar in magnitude to mean substitution.

Therefore, not only does this procedure require somewhat laborious programming, but it also provides almost no benefit over even the most rudimentary single-condition imputation methods.

Last and Next Average

A logical method for dealing with the vagaries of longitudinal missing data is to average values around those that are missing. By averaging the last observed value and the next value observed after the missing value, the data analyst can take advantage of the fact that individual change may be described best by multiple indicators that share common time-related variance. For example, for an individual missing data for the fourth of five waves of data collection, the missing value can be imputed by taking the mean of the values observed at the third and fifth waves.

Engels and Diehr (2003) show that averaging these two values tends to produce the least amount of error or bias while retaining the expected variance in both the model and the variable for which data are missing. The *last and next average* appears to be one of few methods in which the benefit of improved parameter estimation is worth the investment in statistical programming required to conduct the missing data analysis. As with the previous method, this type of missing data handling procedure is not a stand-alone program that merely requires plugging in numbers. This is because decisions must be made when there are a variety of patterns of missing data.

Regression and Regression with Error

Regression methods share similar characteristics with the single-condition, mean imputation method. However, in contrast to conditioning on a single value, individual values for replacing missing data are imputed based on multiple variables. The prediction equation comes from a least squares procedure of a complete-case regression whereby parameters (regression coefficients) are used to weight each of the variables. For every missing value, a regression equation is used to provide a predicted value. The predicted value may be based on all available variables in the data set, only those variables specified in the model, or only those variables not specified in the theoretical model. For example, if an adolescent's age and parents' education are used as predictors of his or her drug use, missing values for drug use at any time point can be imputed from the unstandardized regression parameters associated with those two variables. Note that these regression parameters are computed with listwise deletion procedures (i.e., the imputation parameters are based on complete case methods). Likewise, the regression imputation may be used with or without adding random error to the model. The error term allows for a greater range in the stochastic element of imputation, thereby eliminating some threat that the model will be reified (as discussed previously regarding single-conditioned approaches).

While the general multivariate or multiple-conditioned imputation regression method appears to be easy enough, there are several important details about conditional imputation methods that need to be considered prior to implementation. First, the method of deriving the parameters (e.g., the unstandardized regression coefficients) can be either theoretically or empirically driven. That is, we justify the variables we use to predict missing values theoretically, or we let the data specify the variables we choose. If we believe that age and parental education should be related to adolescent drug use at the onset of a study, our theory guides us to select those two variables to predict missing values for drug use at the first measurement occasion (baseline). Conversely, if we have little idea regarding which variables in our data set should be related to baseline drug use, we can select the variables based on an empirical analysis of the covariance matrix for all of the variables, which would include baseline drug use. We would select those that are highly correlated with baseline drug use as predictors of missing data for that variable.

One problem associated with the empirical selection of variables for imputing missing data is the increased likelihood of imputing meaningless and even invalid values because the resultant regression model for predicting those values is not likely to be related to the "true" underlying model of why values are missing. These "illegal" values in turn cause problems with further statistical analyses (e.g., unstable covariance matrices and their attendant problems). For example, a model using age and parents' education to predict a value for baseline drug use might not model accurately why data are missing; it might therefore predict values that fall outside the valid range given the scale in which drug use is measured. If drug use were measured in days out of the past 30 in which the respondent used drugs, a faulty prediction model might predict a value of –10—a value that makes no sense in terms of number of days. Likewise, values greater than 31 would make no sense for this scale.

A second consideration involves understanding the potential for bias if conditional imputation is misused. The variables used to estimate the missing values should not come from the pool of variables that are part of the statistical model being tested for a given study. We addressed this previously for single-conditioned means, but the issue is even more important when multiple variables are used to predict missing values. Specifically, if a dependent variable were missing and the only available variables to condition the imputed values were the independent variables in the statistical model, the method would inflate the relationship between the independent and dependent variables.[4] We mention this limitation to highlight the fact that when few variables are available, the opportunity to use variables that are related to but not part of the model being tested diminishes.

A third consideration relates to the number of variables with missing data. Conditional imputation requires a separate procedure for each variable with missing data. Although this may seem trivial, in large studies with hundreds of measured variables, the number of regression procedures required may become unwieldy (see Schafer, 1997). In an age of high-speed computers and sophisticated statistical scripting languages, coping with this limitation may be more manageable than it once was, but it still might be impractical for many researchers. Consider the case where only a few variables exist to condition missing values, as we see in the Biomed data set. This data set involves few variables: age, disease category, and the four blood samples, *m*1–*m*4. If data were missing for *m*1, for example, we could possibly use *m*2, *m*3, and *m*4 to predict the missing value, but not age or disease category, because they are the predictors in the statistical model of interest. The same can be done for missing values for *m*2, *m*3, and *m*4. Social science data sets are generally much larger than the Biomed data set, and therefore the number of missing data equations increases substantially. Under these circumstances, with many relevant variables or too few irrelevant variables, conditional imputation may be an inefficient and perhaps inappropriate method for handling missing data.

Finally, conditional imputation assumes an ignorable missing data mechanism—MAR or MCAR. Regression imputation, however, has been shown to be problematic even under MCAR conditions (see Allison, 2002, for a discussion). If these procedures are likely to be difficult to implement, potentially biased, and limited to only a few circumstances, we find no compelling reason to recommend these procedures alone. There are situations where these procedures can be used effectively along with others, and therefore they should not be overlooked. For example, when only a small proportion of the data is missing in a longitudinal study and yet every individual has at least one missing value, a single, conditional imputed value based on the within-subject data (i.e., other wave data) may be the most efficient and most readily explainable method to choose.

SUMMARY

The single imputation procedures discussed in this chapter are known to lead to several problems. First, each procedure tends to underestimate standard errors, resulting in a greater likelihood of rejecting the null hypothesis when it is true (i.e., Type I errors). Second, the single imputation procedures introduce biases that may or may not be predictable and are not treatable by conventional methods. Finally, these procedures tend to perform poorly even when the missing data mechanism is ignorable (MCAR or MAR), a situation that makes their suitability limited to quite a restricted set of assumptions. As Allison (2002) notes,

> All the common methods for salvaging information from cases with missing data typically make things worse: They introduce substantial bias, make the analysis more sensitive to departures from MCAR, or yield standard error estimates that are incorrect (usually too low). (p. 12)

In short, although with some exceptions they are generally simple to implement, single imputation procedures are often likely to lead to more problems than they solve. In very limited missing data conditions (e.g., MCAR with a small portion of missing data), these methods can be useful, and, in general, they are relatively easy to implement. However, listwise deletion is the easiest method to implement, and in light of the shortcomings associated with the single imputation methods, listwise deletion "does not look so bad" (Allison, 2002). Model-based (Chapter 8) and multiple imputation procedures (Chapter 10) are considered to be superior alternatives for handling missing data, particularly when the missing data are MAR. The following chapter addresses multiple imputation, a method that tends to perform better across a wide array of data situations and provides greater insight into the potential effects of missing data on parameter estimation and hypothesis testing.

NOTES

1. These data and their description were obtained from *http://www.amstat.org/publications/jse/v4n1/datasets.johnson.html*. The data come from a previous study (Penrose, Nelson, & Fisher, 1985), and are used at this website for demonstration purposes.

2. Recall that the fully observed data set Full in Table 9.3 was created by selecting 25 normals and 25 carriers from the original data set of 209. Because cold

deck imputation procedures require data from a different sample than the one being used for the analysis, the 159 remaining cases with observations for the variables in the model (*Age*, group, and the unit-weighted factor combining *m*1–*m*4) serve as the cold deck from which missing data values can be obtained.

3. Economists use "instrumental variables" for the same purpose we use conditional imputation here. The instrumental variable is one that bears a relationship to the predictors (*IVs*) but no relationship with the outcome variable, or dependent variable (*DV*). Instrumental variables adjust for bias in nonrandom assignment. Since that same bias may be present in the data that are missing, it might be best to conduct conditional imputation adhering to the same guidelines economists insist on for instrumental variables; however, those guidelines are stringent, to the point of perhaps rendering conditional imputation impractical.

4. When values are missing for the dependent variable (*DV*), imputation from other related variables that are not being used as predictors in the statistical model of interest can be useful. In studies involving multiple *DVs* that are correlated, for example, missing data on one *DV* can be imputed from the others.

10

Multiple Imputation

Multiple imputation (MI) has become the most highly praised method for statistically handling missing data (Allison, 2002; Rubin, 1996; Schafer & Graham, 2002). According to Rubin (1996), the method provides generalizable estimates and recovers population variance critical to statistical inference. With the proliferation of software to perform MI, it is fast becoming the standard method for handling missing data. In fact, Rubin (1996) stated that the results likely to be obtained from other procedures, or even combinations of other procedures, barely made them worth considering, compared to MI. MI is easily implemented, provides sound parameter estimates (including standard errors), allows for the estimation of missing information and its impact on parameter estimation, and can be applied to many different missing data situations.

In contrast to the single imputation methods (Chapter 9), in which only a single value is imputed for each missing datum, MI makes use of several imputed values, usually from 3 to 10. For example, if an individual were missing data for abdominal circumference in a body composition study, an MI procedure would produce 3–10 estimates of that missing value. (The reasons for the 3–10 range we discuss shortly.) Single imputation methods would produce only one value for that missing datum.

The multiply imputed values are derived from an iterative process that uses the observed data (i.e., both the individual and sample values). Each set of imputed values is then used separately to replace the missing values in order to create a complete data set. For each set of imputed values, there is a separate complete data set. Thus, for five MI imputations, there are five sets of values to replace the missing values, resulting in five complete data sets. The multiple data sets are then used in complete case analyses to test the statistical models of interest for the study (e.g., a multiple regression predicting percentage of body fat from body circumference measures). The multiple analyses produce multiple parameter estimates (e.g., regression coefficients estimating the relation between body circumference and percentage of body fat). Those multiple estimates are combined to obtain a single best estimate of the parameter of interest. For example, with five imputations, five multiple regression models would be carried out, one for each of the complete data sets. As a result, there would be five separate parameter estimates for the regression coefficient and standard error for each predictor variable. The mean of the five estimates and the associated standard errors would serve as the single best estimate of each regression coefficient and each standard error. Because MI produces multiple (versus single) estimates for each parameter, the increased variability can be used to adjust standard errors upward (i.e., they are larger), which in turn reduces the likelihood of a Type I error. Conversely, single imputation methods produce a single parameter estimate and are known to underestimate standard errors and inflate test statistics.

A critical feature of MI that is absent from other statistical methods for handling missing data is the ability to estimate the influence of the missing data on parameter estimation. The variability in the parameter estimates across each of the imputed data sets provides clues about how the missing data are affecting the rate of meaningful *information* that is missing. The rate of missing information gives the researcher a sense of the impact the missing data have on parameter estimates and ultimately on statistical conclusions. Higher rates of missing information suggest that the missing data have a larger impact on parameter estimates and that therefore statistical conclusions may be suspect. In essence, the rate of missing information serves as an indicator of statistical uncertainty due to the missing data.

Rubin (1987) provides diagnostic measures for assessing the extent to which the quantity being estimated (e.g., regression coefficients) is influenced by the missing data, known as the estimated *rate of missing information*, or gamma (γ). In our demonstration of MI in the following section, we show how to calculate γ. Using γ, Rubin introduced the following formula to estimate the efficiency of MI for parameter estimation with missing data:

$$\frac{1}{1+\gamma/m} \tag{10.1}$$

where γ equals the rate of missing information for the quantity being estimated and m equals the number of imputations. Values of γ can range from 0 to 1.0, where 1.0 means there is 100% missing information. In a later example, we calculate a maximum value of .04 for γ, or a 4% rate of missing information, which in this example is regarded as trivial.[1]

As formula 10.1 shows, the relative efficiency of the MI inference is related to the rate of missing information (γ) in combination with the number of imputations (m). The rate of missing information is related to the increase in variance due to missing data. Unless there is a tremendous amount of missing information, Rubin's (1987) simulations indicate that the number of imputations can generally be constrained to fewer than 10. Hershberger and Fisher (2003), however, show that these estimates might not necessarily be correct for some models. In general, however, the statistical field tends to support Rubin's heuristic of 3–10 imputations.

Once it has been decided that an MI procedure for handling missing data should be employed, one much choose which MI procedure to use. The researcher must first ascertain the distributional assumptions underlying the data to be analyzed and the type of data (e.g., categorical vs. continuous). In MI procedures, an individual's missing values are replaced by values that are imputed using his or her own observed data for other variables, with error added to ensure conformity with an assumed underlying distribution. Making assumptions about the distribution, therefore, is critical to the success of this procedure. The most commonly assumed underlying distribution is normal. Yet social and behavioral scientists often study phenomena in which the data are not expected to have normal distribution (e.g., study of rare phenomena, frequency count data, or deviant samples). In some circumstances, the observed data can be transformed to appear normal.[2] However, when data are not distributed normally, alternative models must be applied. There are methods, for example, for nonindependently sampled data (e.g., longitudinal and linear models with clustered or nested factors; see Liu, Taylor, & Belin, 2000, and Schafer, 2001).[3] Rubin (1987) and Lavori, Dawson, and Shera (1995) use a method called approximate Bayesian bootstrap, a two-cycle hot deck (see Chapter 9) imputation approach to create multiple imputations without an underlying distributional model.[4] Categorical, mixed categorical, and continuous data also reflect different underlying distributions, and there are methods for handling these types of data as well (Schafer, 1997).

As the variety of approaches for handling distributional assumptions suggests, MI is not just one method but rather a general term for many different approaches. The unifying concept for all MI procedures is the general process of selecting values to impute (to be described shortly), imputing multiple values to replace the missing data, analyzing the focal model with each complete data set, and aggregating the results from the analyses. The selection process for the appropriate MI procedure is guided by distributional assumptions and data types (e.g., continuous vs. categorical).

Regarding distributional assumptions, consider an example involving two different types of distributions—normal and Poisson.[5] For the normal distribution, values in the center of the distribution occur most often, by definition, and therefore have the highest probability of being selected as values to impute. For the Poisson distribution, scores at the low end of the distribution (i.e., low counts) are most frequent, by definition, and therefore have the highest probability of being selected. With respect to data types, MI with continuous data may, in fact, select values that were never directly observed in the data set (e.g., selecting a value of 101 from a distribution of IQ scores in which no individual actually scored 101). MI with categorical data, however, is restricted to those categories that were observed. For example, if data were missing for smoking status where 1 equals "nonsmoker," 2 equals "occasional smoker," and 3 equals "current smoker," imputed values would be 1, 2, or 3 only. Thus with MI procedures, distributional assumptions and data types are key components in determining the proper MI procedure to use for imputing missing values.

To illustrate the steps involved in MI procedures, we provide an example and describe the procedure in greater detail. Multiple imputation involves several steps, each requiring some explanation. The following example is far from a complete illustration of the flexibility of MI, but it serves to introduce the reader to the general process.

THE MI PROCESS

Imputing values, conducting analyses with the complete case data, aggregating the results from each analysis, and analyzing the aggregated results constitute a very general description of the multiple imputation process. We describe the steps involved with an example where the outcome of interest is the percentage of body fat and the predictors are multiple measures of body circumference from different areas of the body (e.g., abdomen, chest, wrist, and so on).

The Body Comp data set used in this example was also used in Chapter 9 to illustrate single imputation procedures. Briefly, the data set (described more fully in Chapters 7 and 9) includes measures of percentage of body fat (obtained with the underwater weighing technique), age, weight, height, and 10 body circumference measurements (e.g., abdomen, chest, wrist) for 252 men. Body fat was calculated using the Siri and the Brozec algorithms, and both results were available for each participant. We took the fully observed data set and deleted values to mimic an MAR mechanism by conditioning the missing data on higher values of the Brozec measure of body fat (i.e., ≥ 21% body fat). That is, those with ≥ 21% body fat had a 60% probability of missing data on at least 1, but no more than 6 of the 10 body circumference measures. The Brozec measure is almost perfectly correlated with the Siri measure of body fat ($r = .99$), which was used as the dependent variable. Therefore, missing data in this example were related to the dependent variable.

As in Chapter 9, we conducted a multiple regression analysis in which we predicted body fat (the Siri value) with the 10 body circumference measures. Parameters of interest in this analysis are the regression coefficients for each of the 10 predictors and their standard errors. Missing values for the MAR data set were imputed using Schafer's NORM procedure (described shortly) in the statistical package R.[6]

Prior to carrying out the MI procedure, it is necessary to choose the variables to use for imputing the missing values. Along with the variables with missing data, variables from the model to be estimated should be included. Allison (2002) also recommends including variables that are not part of the focal model but are highly correlated with the variables that have missing data or are associated with the probability that those variables have missing data. In our example, the 10 body circumference measures and the two different body composition estimates (the two dependent variables) were included in the multiple imputation procedure. We were limited to these variables since they were all that were available from the database.

Step 1: Imputation

The specific process of the first MI step, imputation, is similar to single imputation, detailed in Chapter 9. Where MI differs is that there is no necessary restriction on the procedure selected; that is, values may be imputed using random normal values (e.g., ML estimates), hot deck values, or MCMC-method-derived Bayesian estimated values, described in Chapter 8. Mixing single imputation methods in MI, however, is generally not wise, since the single imputation methods produce somewhat different results (e.g., mean substitution vs. hot deck imputation). Those differences would then be reflected in the estimate of missing information by yielding larger estimates due to the increased variability. Most MI experts recommend an iterative procedure that is not limited to only a specific group of imputed values (e.g., the mean and values found only within the data set). Instead, a more random process is preferable so that values are unique between each imputed set but share a common underlying relationship to the data (e.g., if all of the data were used for one imputation, they should be used for all imputations). Because it is an iterative process, MI can allow for the flexibility of multiple methods, provided they conform to the standards just mentioned. In other words, values may be imputed (1) by conditioning on other variables, (2) unconditionally, (3) theoretically, or (4) purely empirically.

For our example, we use Schafer's (1997) NORM procedure to demonstrate MI. Recall that imputation accounts for both the underlying distribution and the type of data. NORM assumes that data have an underlying normal distribution, which happens to be true for the Body Comp data set. If our data did not meet the normality assumption, procedures that are not bound by that distributional assumption (e.g., multiple imputation with chained equations [MICE], or Markov chain Monte Carlo [MCMC] methods) would be more suitable. Additionally, because the Body Comp data are interval-level measures, we are able to use a more straightforward procedure such as NORM. If the data were mixed, with both continuous and categorical values, those options would be restricted to only the MIX procedure (also part of Schafer's library) for the entire data set, or a combination of imputation procedures, each purposely selected according to the variable.

Using NORM to impute missing values for the 10 body circumference variables, we produced five complete data sets. That is, for each missing value for the body circumference variables, five values were imputed to replace the missing value, and five complete data sets were produced from the five separate replacements. Five imputations was the number chosen, based on Rubin's (1987) recommendation, discussed previously. The five complete data sets provide the basis for step 2.

Step 2: Routine Analysis

The second step in MI simply involves traditional data analyses using the complete data sets provided after imputation. There are no constraints on the types of statistical analyses that can be performed on the MI data sets: univariate and multivariate analyses are equally suitable. For our illustration, we conducted a multiple regression using the 10 body circumference measures (e.g., abdomen, chest, wrist) to predict the percentage of body fat as measured by water tank testing. The parameters resulting from each of the five complete case analyses are listed in Table 10.1.

A scan of the 5 values for each of the 10 regression coefficients and the model intercept indicates some variability in the estimates resulting from the different imputed values. The variability is also reflected in the standard errors associated with each of these regression coefficients. For example, values for the intercept range from .79 to 5.0, and for the slope of the thigh measure range from –.113 to .061. The multiple parameter estimates in Table 10.1 are used for the next step in the MI procedure.

Step 3: Parameter Estimation from Aggregated Results

The third step in the multiple imputation procedure is to analyze the aggregate results (listed in Table 10.1) and compute an overall estimate for each parameter of interest and for the standard errors, respectively. According to Rubin's (1987) original method, to obtain a single estimate for each parameter in the statistical analysis (e.g., each of the 10 regression coefficients in our regression analysis), we simply take the mean of the estimates produced by each of the imputed data sets.

Each parameter estimate is referred to as $\hat{Q}$, and the overall estimate or mean of the $\hat{Q}$s is referred to as $\overline{Q}$. In our example, we add up the five regression coefficient estimates ($\hat{Q}$s) for the abdominal circumference measure and divide by 5 to obtain a mean value ($\overline{Q}$) of 1.051, which then serves as our overall estimate of the regression coefficient for abdominal circumference. In our example, we calculate 11 $\overline{Q}$s, one for each of the 10 predictors and one for the model intercept, taking the mean for each from the five data sets. Table 10.2 shows the overall estimate for the intercept and 10 predictors in the far right column.

To compute the overall standard error, which is necessary for significance tests and confidence intervals, there are several steps. First, we compute the within-imputation variance, which is simply the mean of the standard errors associated with each of the parameters of interest in our

TABLE 10.1. Parameter Estimates (Regression Coefficients and Standard Errors) from Each of the Five MI Data Sets

	Data sets				
Coefficient	1	2	3	4	5
Intercept	0.790 (6.676)	3.954 (6.672)	5.000 (6.495)	2.999 (6.741)	2.858 (6.471)
Abdomen	1.041 (.075)	1.068 (.076)	1.061 (.073)	1.026 (.075)	1.057 (.072)
Chest	–0.160 (.094)	–0.171 (.094)	–0.145 (.090)	–0.154 (.095)	–0.154 (.092)
Hip	–0.310 (.130)	–0.262 (.128)	–0.393 (.128)	–0.338 (.123)	–0.323 (.126)
Thigh	–0.016 (.140)	–0.113 (.136)	–0.001 (.135)	0.061 (.138)	–0.002 (.144)
Bicep	0.269 (.180)	0.263 (.170)	0.328 (.168)	0.161 (.179)	0.218 (.180)
Neck	–0.764 (.234)	–0.806 (.228)	–0.699 (.221)	–0.636 (.220)	–0.605 (.231)
Knee	–0.026 (.224)	0.084 (.228)	0.084 (.231)	0.029 (.233)	–0.068 (.231)
Forearm	0.424 (.193)	0.560 (.186)	0.349 (.191)	0.475 (.192)	0.442 (.194)
Ankle	0.264 (.320)	–0.069 (.284)	0.123 (.275)	–0.277 (.286)	–0.085 (.277)
Wrist	–1.173 (.541)	–1.598 (.529)	–1.650 (.526)	–1.230 (.527)	–1.410 (.542)

Note. Values in parentheses are standard errors.

TABLE 10.2. Overall Estimates for 10 Predictors and the Model Intercept

Coefficient	Data sets 1	2	3	4	5	Overall estimate or $\overline{Q}$
Intercept	0.790	3.954	5.000	2.999	2.858	3.120
Abdomen	1.041	1.068	1.061	1.026	1.057	1.051
Chest	–0.160	–0.171	–0.145	–0.154	–0.154	–0.157
Hip	–0.310	–0.262	–0.393	–0.338	–0.323	–0.325
Thigh	–0.016	–0.113	–0.001	0.061	–0.002	–0.014
Bicep	0.269	0.263	0.328	0.161	0.218	0.248
Neck	–0.764	–0.806	–0.699	–0.636	–0.605	–0.702
Knee	–0.026	0.084	0.084	0.029	–0.068	0.021
Forearm	0.424	0.560	0.349	0.475	0.442	0.450
Ankle	0.264	–0.069	0.123	–0.277	–0.085	–0.001
Wrist	–1.173	–1.598	–1.650	–1.230	–1.410	–1.412

statistical model. In our example, we have five estimates each of 11 standard errors (10 predictors and 1 intercept; see Table 10.1). We calculate the mean of the five standard errors for each parameter and obtain the *within-imputation variance*, referred to as $\overline{U}$. That is, $\overline{U}$ represents the variability of the standard errors that are calculated within each of the imputations.

At this point in the process, we have a mean parameter estimate and a mean standard error estimate for each predictor and the intercept in our regression model, a total of 22 values—11 $\overline{Q}$s and 11 $\overline{U}$s. The $\overline{U}$s are presented in Table 10.3 for the intercept and the 10 predictors in the regression model.

After calculating the within-imputation variance (or $\overline{U}$s), the between-imputation variance (or B in Rubin's, 1987, nomenclature) must be estimated. The formula for calculating B is

$$B = \frac{1}{m-1}\sum_{j=1}^{m}(\hat{Q}_j - \overline{Q})^2 \qquad (10.2)$$

Between-imputation variance is calculated by computing the variance for each parameter estimate (all the $\hat{Q}$s). As Equation 10.2 illustrates, variance is nothing more than the sum of the squared deviations (the $\hat{Q}$s minus the $\overline{Q}$s) divided by the number of imputed data sets ($m = 5$ in our example) minus 1. There are five squared deviations to sum for each variable in our example. We obtain a B value for each parameter, as shown in Table 10.4.

Next, we compute the *total variance* for each parameter estimate. Typically, total variance equals *within-variance* ($\overline{U}$) plus *between-variance* (B). However, Rubin's approach is to weight the between-imputation variance according to the number of imputations performed. Thus, the total variance (T) is computed by the following formula:

TABLE 10.3. Within-Imputations Variance for 10 Predictors and the Model Intercept

	Data sets					Within-imputations
Coefficient	1	2	3	4	5	variance or $\overline{U}$
Intercept	6.676	6.672	6.495	6.741	6.471	6.611
Abdomen	0.075	0.076	0.073	0.075	0.072	0.074
Chest	0.094	0.094	0.090	0.095	0.092	0.093
Hip	0.130	0.128	0.128	0.123	0.126	0.127
Thigh	0.140	0.136	0.135	0.138	0.144	0.138
Bicep	0.180	0.170	0.168	0.179	0.180	0.175
Neck	0.234	0.228	0.221	0.220	0.231	0.227
Knee	0.224	0.228	0.231	0.233	0.231	0.229
Forearm	0.193	0.186	0.191	0.192	0.194	0.191
Ankle	0.320	0.284	0.275	0.286	0.277	0.288
Wrist	0.541	0.529	0.526	0.527	0.542	0.533

TABLE 10.4. Between-Imputation Variance (or B) for 10 Predictors and the Intercept

	Data set						
	1	2	3	4	5		Between-imputation
Coefficient	$\hat{Q}_1$	$\hat{Q}_2$	$\hat{Q}_3$	$\hat{Q}_4$	$\hat{Q}_5$	$\overline{Q}$	variance or B
Intercept	0.790	3.954	5.000	2.999	2.858	3.120	2.4355
Abdomen	1.041	1.068	1.061	1.026	1.057	1.051	0.0003
Chest	−0.160	−0.171	−0.145	−0.154	−0.154	−0.157	0.0001
Hip	−0.310	−0.262	−0.393	−0.338	−0.323	−0.325	0.0022
Thigh	−0.016	−0.113	−0.001	0.061	−0.002	−0.014	0.0039
Bicep	0.269	0.263	0.328	0.161	0.218	0.248	0.0039
Neck	−0.764	−0.806	−0.699	−0.636	−0.605	−0.702	0.0071
Knee	−0.026	0.084	0.084	0.029	−0.068	0.021	0.0045
Forearm	0.424	0.560	0.349	0.475	0.442	0.450	0.0059
Ankle	0.264	−0.069	0.123	−0.277	−0.085	−0.001	0.0434
Wrist	−1.173	−1.598	−1.650	−1.230	−1.410	−1.412	0.0454

$$T = \overline{U} + \left(1 + \frac{1}{m}\right)B \tag{10.3}$$

The overall standard error useful in reporting the final model for significance testing is equal to the square root of the total variance (T). Confidence intervals can be computed by taking the mean parameter estimate ($\overline{Q}$) and adding/subtracting a specific number of standard errors to the mean, for example,

$$\overline{Q} \pm 1.96(\sqrt{T})$$

to calculate 95% confidence intervals.

Finally, a t-value similar to the Student's t-test can be computed by dividing each $\overline{Q}$ by the square root of the total variance, or

$$t(df) = \frac{\overline{Q}}{\sqrt{T}}$$

The computation of the degrees of freedom (*df*) requires information about the number of imputations (*m*), $\overline{U}$, and *B*, and is calculated using the formula:

$$df = (m-1)\left(1+\frac{m\overline{U}}{(m+1)B}\right)^2 \qquad (10.4)$$

It might be tempting to use the degrees of freedom from the "complete" data set in which imputed values replace missing data, but we should not. Nor should we use the degrees of freedom from the complete-case-only data set. Instead, we adjust the degrees of freedom based on the number of imputations and the within- and between-imputation variance to correct for the missing data. Comparing the *t*-value and its degrees of freedom against Student's *t*-distribution will allow us to test the null hypothesis that $Q = 0$, where Q is the parameter of interest (e.g., the regression coefficient for wrist circumference).

We carry out this final step for the intercept and 10 predictors in our regression equation and present the results in Table 10.5. According to our results, only the abdomen and wrist measures are significantly ($p < .05$) related to the percentage of body fat.

Step 4: Compute Missing Information

In Chapter 8, we discussed the distinction between missing data and missing information. One of the advantages of MI is that it allows us to estimate the amount of missing information, or statistical uncertainty, that results from our missing data. All the other missing data handling procedures tell us only the amount of missing data. As mentioned in Chapter 6, there is no necessary relationship between the amount of missing data and the true meaning of impact of missing information.

To estimate missing information in our example, we use Rubin's (1987) rules for MI inference. He states that the rate of missing information can be estimated using the degrees of freedom (*df*) and the relative increase in variance (*r*, defined shortly) due to nonresponse, using the following formula:

$$\gamma = \frac{r + 2/(df+3)}{r+1} \qquad (10.5)$$

TABLE 10.5. Tests for Parameter Estimates Produced Using MI

Coefficient	$\overline{Q}$	$\overline{U}$	B	T	t-value	df	Significance
Intercept	3.120	6.611	2.4355	9.5336	1.01	42.55	0.16
Abdomen	1.051	0.074	0.0003	0.0744	3.85	181279.76	<.0001
Chest	–0.157	0.093	0.0001	0.0931	–0.51	2508921.06	0.31
Hip	–0.325	0.127	0.0022	0.1296	–0.90	9024.99	0.18
Thigh	–0.014	0.138	0.0039	0.1427	–0.04	3736.59	0.48
Bicep	0.248	0.175	0.0039	0.1797	0.58	5947.78	0.28
Neck	–0.702	0.227	0.0071	0.2355	–1.45	3062.42	0.07
Knee	0.021	0.229	0.0045	0.2344	0.04	7562.18	0.48
Forearm	0.450	0.191	0.0059	0.1981	1.01	3145.52	0.16
Ankle	–0.001	0.288	0.0434	0.3401	–0.10	543.65	0.46
Wrist	–1.412	0.533	0.0454	0.5875	–1.84	466.85	0.03

where

$$r = \frac{(1+m^{-1})B}{\overline{U}}$$

In Equation 10.5, m is the number of imputations (5 in our example), and r represents the relative increase in variance due to nonresponse. As the formula reflects, r is essentially a weighted F-ratio in which the numerator is the weighted $(1 + m^{-1})$ between-imputation variance (B) and the denominator is the within-imputation variance ($\overline{U}$). Greater variability in parameter estimates (reflected in the numerator) and increased reliability of each parameter estimate (i.e., smaller standard errors, reflected in the denominator) leads to an increase in r, translated as an increase in the variance of the parameter estimates due to missing data. This relative increase in variability provides a clue to the impact of missing data on parameter estimates: less stability in parameter estimates reflects less statistical certainty.

The rate of missing information for the 10 predictors in our regression model is calculated and presented in Table 10.6. As the results suggest, the rate of missing information (γ) is trivial—nearly 0—for all variables. As stated earlier, values of γ can range from 0 to 1.0, where 1.0 means there is 100% missing information. In our example, the maximum value for γ is 0.04, or a 4% rate of missing information. The rate of missing information in this example is trivial, because missing data were generated to mimic an MAR mechanism across all variables with missing data. Recall the discussion in Chapter 3 of *ignorable* missing data, in which it is noted that the MAR data are ignorable because they derive from observed data (Y_{obs}) and can therefore be reproduced. When missing data are ignorable (in the technical sense), the rate of missing information can be negligible and the data replaceable. When missing data are nonignorable, the rate of missing information is likely to be nontrivial. It is important for the reader to note that there is no need to compute missing rate of information values for all parameters—only those that are focal to the analysis. Often researchers are

TABLE 10.6. Rate of Missing Information or γ

Coefficient	*df*	*r*	Rate of missing information or γ
Intercept	42.55	0.4421	0.037178
Abdomen	181279.76	0.0049	0.000011
Chest	2508921.06	0.0013	0.000001
Hip	9024.99	0.0208	0.000219
Thigh	3736.59	0.0339	0.000526
Bicep	5947.78	0.0267	0.000332
Neck	3062.42	0.0375	0.000641
Knee	7562.18	0.0236	0.000261
Forearm	3145.52	0.0371	0.000624
Ankle	543.65	0.1808	0.003379
Wrist	466.85	0.1022	0.004059

interested in only a subset of variables in the study and might exclude covariates and the intercept term, for example, from the secondary analyses in MI described in steps 2 through 4.

SUMMARY

Praise for multiple imputation as a statistical means for handling missing data appears to be well earned. Other statistical procedures for handling missing data tend to be (1) sensitive to the missing data mechanism (i.e., MCAR, MAR, and MNAR) and (2) incapable of providing estimates of missing information. Multiple imputation addresses these two problems and provides a more flexible method for analyzing data. Regarding the missing data mechanism, although MI procedures assume that missing data are MAR, recent results (e.g., Verbeke & Molenberghs, 2000) indicate that MI can be successfully employed in MNAR conditions. Schafer and Graham (2002) note that nothing in the theory of MI requires that missing data are MAR, and they consider MI to be robust enough to compensate for some violations and deviations from MAR into nonrandomness and nonignorable missing data. According to these and other experts (e.g., Rubin, 1996), MI can produce satisfactory results with minor deviations from MAR. The procedures for handling missing data discussed in Chapters 7–9 are not as flexible in this respect.

Regarding the estimation of rate of missing information, Rubin's (1987) formula (Equation 10.5) allows the researcher to assess the influence of missing data on statistical inference using MI procedures—an option as of yet unavailable for other missing data handling procedures. Rate of missing information can provide clues as to the mechanism of missing data as well. When missing data are ignorable, the rate of missing information is likely to be small, whereas nonignorable missing data are associated with higher rates of missing information.

The number of software options leads one to believe that MI not only is regarded as a good option for handling missing data but also is available to most, if not all, researchers. New versions of SAS (PROC MI) and S-Plus include MI routines that automate the procedure. Additionally, more than 15 other stand-alone statistical software packages or routines for the popular statistical packages (SAS and S-Plus, mostly) exist for MI. Stand-alone statistical software packages include MICE (Oudshoorn, van Buuren, & van Rijckevorsel, 1999), Amelia (King, Honaker, Joseph, & Scheve, 2001), SOLAS, and Schafer's (1997) library (NORM, MIX, CAT, and PAN).[7]

Although MI receives high praise from missing data experts, we feel compelled to offer a word of caution. As noted throughout this book, no single method is a panacea for handling missing data. While MI generally offers great advantages over deletion methods, single imputation, and model-based procedures, there are situations where social scientists might find MI to be problematic. MI can provide sound parameter estimates with missing data, but it requires substantial sample sizes that may not always be available in social science research (Schafer & Graham, 2002). At his Multiple Imputation Frequently Asked Questions webpage, *http://www.stat.psu.edu/~jls/mifaq.html#only*, Schafer notes that MI is not the only principled method for handling missing data, nor is it always the best method. Because it is a simulation method, MI can be less efficient under conditions where model-based methods such as EM (see Chapter 8) can calculate parameters directly from incomplete data.

Although MI is becoming more readily available to researchers, there are still nuances to the imputation procedure that tend to confuse less experienced data analysts. The procedures required to carry out MI, though not terribly complicated, are considerably more involved than the standard single-step analysis. The added burden of multiple steps and the potential for computational mistakes may push MI somewhat beyond the reach of novice analysts. MI requires specifying an imputation model (see step 1), such as multivariate normal. Familiarity with the assumptions associated with such models may be difficult for less experienced researchers. The vast improvements in software development for implementing MI have reduced and might someday eliminate the complexities of MI procedures, making MI more accessible to those researchers.

NOTES

1. When presented with an index such as Rubin's *rate of missing information*, we want a heuristic by which to identify values as "large," "medium," or "small," as in the case of Pearson's *r* or Cohen's *d*. Although such a heuristic may exist, we are reluctant to apply it due to the arbitrary nature of delineating these values. To assess the statistical uncertainty due to missing data, researchers should combine Rubin's index with the context and intent of the study. If, for example, a study is exploratory and serves to generate hypotheses for future research, statistical uncertainty is less of a concern than it is for the confirmatory studies that follow.

2. Schafer (1997) illustrates different approaches to these transformations.

3. The assumption of statistical independence basically states that two observations are no more likely to be similar to or different from each other than any other two observations (see Kenny & Judd, 1996; see also David Kenny's Unit of

Analysis website: *http://davidakenny.net/u_o_a.htm*. This assumption is often violated when measures are repeated for the same individual (e.g., in longitudinal studies), or when individuals are grouped into units such as classrooms or health clinics, in which it is assumed that observations from within those units are more likely to be similar to each other than to observations taken from outside the unit. Observations within units are referred to as "nested" data. Thus, students are nested within classrooms, and physicians are nested within clinics, which are nested within hospitals.

4. This procedure is implemented in Rubin's software program SOLAS and referred to as the propensity-score option.

5. The Poisson distribution is most commonly used to model the number of random occurrences of a phenomenon in a specified period of time or unit of space (e.g., number of calls received by an operator in a 2-minute period). Many times, it describes rare occurrences. A typical example of a Poisson distribution is the number of hospital visits individuals make in a year. Most will make 0 visits, and some would make 1 or 2. Only a few individuals will make multiple hospital visits within a year, so the majority of the data are "piled up" at the low end of the scale and only a few observations are at the high end.

6. R is the freeware version of the statistical package S-Plus and is available online at *http://www.r-project.org*. For the demonstration, we used Schafer's (1997) NORM procedure, available in R, and cross-checked the results using MICE (multiple imputation with chained equations), also available in R.

7. At the time of the writing of this book, a current list of statistical software packages for carrying out MI procedures could be found at the website *http://www.multiple-imputation.com*. Also, the Veterans Administration Health Economics Resource Center website lists statistical packages that fully and partially support MI, at *http://www.herc.research.va.gov/resources/faq_i10.asp*. Many of these statistical software packages are reviewed by Horton and Lipsitz (2001).

11

Reporting Missing Data and Results

In this chapter, we present guidelines for reporting study results when missing data are present. We highlight the limitations of current reporting practices and discuss our recommendations, which extend those of the Task Force on Statistical Inference of the American Psychological Association for reporting missing data in empirical studies (Wilkinson & APA Task Force on Statistical Inference, 1999). We discuss the various stages of data collection in a research study, from the recruitment to the analysis phase, and discuss how missing data at these various stages can and often do have a differential impact on study results. We note that reporting missing data at one stage does not necessarily address missing data at another stage. We extend the discussion by addressing and evaluating different types of missing data reporting practices, and conclude the chapter with recommendations for reporting missing data that not only include the appropriate detail but also require little text space, which most book and journal editors should find agreeable.

APA TASK FORCE RECOMMENDATIONS

In 1999, the Task Force on Statistical Inference (TFSI), appointed by the Board of Scientific Affairs of the American Psychological Association, produced a report outlining guidelines for reporting statistical methods and results. This report was published in the *American Psychologist* (Wilkinson & APA Task Force, 1999). Some of these guidelines addressed the reporting of missing data and the impact at various stages of the research process. Although missing data occur at various stages of a study, our preliminary analysis of reporting practices in a top psychology journal suggests that it is common practice to focus on missing data at one or two stages while ignoring it at others. Yet because missing data at different stages likely have different consequences for study results and interpretation (see Chapter 2), we contend that missing data should be attended to at all stages of a study.

While attending to missing data is important at all stages, reporting may be restricted to certain stages, depending on the design and purpose of the study. Study stages that are relevant to the reporting of missing data are the recruitment stage, the stage after recruitment but prior to enrollment in the study, after enrollment during the course of the study, and follow-up. In the following section, we use the format of the TFSI recommendations at each of these stages in turn and expand on them as needed.

MISSING DATA AND STUDY STAGES

Recruitment Stage: Targeted Population and Study Sample

The kinds of missing data problems described in this first section mostly refer to missing data associated with the participant identification and recruitment stage of a study. Missing data at this stage of the investigation are generally at the individuals level of Cattell's data box (Chapter 3). The authors of the TFSI report state that the "interpretation of the results of any study depends on the characteristics of the population *intended* [emphasis added] for analysis. Define the population (participants, stimuli, or studies) clearly" (Wilkinson & APA Task Force, 1999, p. 595). Although here they do not refer to missing data directly, we note that the population "intended" for analysis might not be the same as the actual population that was obtained during the study when data are missing at the recruitment stage. Recruitment methods can unintentionally exclude eligible participants from study enrollment, thus creating missing data. For example, using notices displayed on television monitors in a university hospital to recruit pregnant women for a study excludes pregnant women who have not sought such active prenatal care, thus changing the "intended" population. The TFSI's recommendations should include the need to report that recruitment processes may be responsible for samples not being truly representative—a missing data problem.

Although the TFSI report recommends describing sampling procedures in relation to the representativeness of obtained samples, the report does not frame the issue as one of missing data. Yet we believe it is helpful to think of sampling procedures in the recruitment and pre-enrollment stages of a study as susceptible to missing data, and we recommend reporting it as such. For example, the number of individuals who failed to meet study criteria for inclusion in a study can be a form of missing data and relates to the generalizability of study results beyond the sample obtained. Schwartz and Fox (1995) reported that 1,100 potential subjects with multiple sclerosis were excluded from a trial because they did not meet all study eligibility criteria. This resulted in a sample with a larger proportion of patients with the clearly progressive form of the disease than one would find in the general multiple sclerosis population. Schwartz and Fox concluded that this "over-representation of the more disabled patient population compromised the generalizability of the findings" (p. 367). Providing at least a disclaimer about this important source of missing data allows the consumer to understand the limitations of the study and weigh them in light of study findings. However, it is important to note that in studies where sampling is not likely to or does not affect generalizability (e.g., a census of patients with a rare disease), researchers can safely avoid reporting missing-data risks during the recruitment and pre-enrollment stage of the study.

The Enrollment Stage

Another stage in which researchers rarely report missing data is after recruitment, when participants provide consent to participate.[1] Missing data occur at this stage when individuals who initially showed interest in the study and met criteria for participation decide not to participate after all. These individuals are often referred to as study "refusers." Missing data at this stage may be meaningful, depending on why individuals refuse to participate. If there is a systematic reason for refusal, refusers might represent an important subgroup of the population to which investigators had hoped to generalize. For example, in a study designed to test a new reading curriculum for first graders, parents who refuse to allow their children to participate might be better educated and more involved in their child's education than those who allow participation. As a result, study conclusions might not apply to those children. In such cases, it would be important to know how many refused to participate despite eligibility, and the reasons for refusal. If there appeared to be no systematic reason for refusal, that should be noted. In our aforementioned review of missing data reporting in a prestigious psychology journal, very few investigators reported the number of refusers, much less the reasons for refusal. Therefore, it was difficult to ascertain whether the study participants were a reasonable representation of the population of interest.

Assignment to Study Conditions

In the subsection "Nonrandom assignment" of the TFSI report, Wilkinson and the APA Task Force (1999) recommend describing what "methods [were] used to attenuate sources of bias, including plans for minimizing dropouts, noncompliance, and missing data." We, too, recommend that researchers perform and report procedures to prevent the occurrence of missing data.

One of the major issues with respect to missing data at the assignment stage of the study is differential dropout. When more participants in one group drop out of the study than in another group, it is unclear whether those who remain are representative of the population to which the study is intended to generalize. As discussed at length in Chapter 4, study dropouts are likely to be different from completers on a number of potentially relevant characteristics, such as education, socioeconomic status, gender, and so on. Thus, differential dropout is considered to be a threat to validity, both internal and external. Similarly, in our preliminary analysis of journal articles, the authors found that assignment to treatment condition contributed to dropout in several studies, with a tendency for those assigned to control conditions to have a higher dropout rate compared to those assigned to treatment conditions. The end result is a comparison of groups that might not represent the population to which we hope to generalize and that therefore might not represent the true relationship between the treatment and the observed outcomes. For example, at the conclusion of a recent exercise study with osteoarthritis patients, the retention strategy changed due to the unusually high dropout rate in earlier enrollees. The change in retention strategy likely contaminated the treatment effect for the latter cohorts and confounded the intervention. Reporting not only the rates of retention but also any change in retention strategies can help readers and reviewers fully appreciate the strength of the study's evidence.

Data Collection Stage

The next stage of the research study in which missing data could have important consequences is after participants have enrolled and the study is under way. This is the stage at which missing data are most often reported, and many times this is the only stage at which they are reported. During this stage, missing data can occur at the person, variable, and occasions dimensions of Cattell's data box, as well as at the micro and macro levels of these dimensions (e.g., items vs. factors, individuals vs. groups). For example, during the data collection stage, individuals might skip items on a questionnaire or they might not be present for data collection on particular days, though they have not formally dropped out of the study.

Study Follow-up Stage

A frequently neglected stage of a longitudinal study that is relevant to missing data has to do with study designs that require follow-up data collection. The follow-up phase occurs after the targeted intervention or observation period has been completed. In treatment studies, for example, investigators often follow up with participants after a certain period of time to find out if the treatment effects have been retained. Because it is difficult to locate all participants after a study has long been finished, follow-up data usually have missing observations. We have found that researchers tend to report missing data for the participant and occasion dimensions but are less likely to report data missing at the variable level during this stage (i.e., when participants have been located but have not provided complete data for all follow-up measures). Instead, the reader would have to use the reported degrees of freedom to infer that data were missing at the variable level.

Data Analysis Stage

Wilkinson and the APA Task Force (1999) do not mention the importance of missing data at the data analysis stage of research. Investigators seldom report anything other than the number of participants who were included in the data analyses, if it is fewer than the number who participated, and so on. Thus, the majority of missing data is reported as if it occurred exclusively at the individuals level. It seems that most investigators resort to complete case analyses when data are missing. Missing data at the variable level can thus masquerade as missing data at the person level, because individuals are dropped from the analyses if data are missing for any of the variables.

In our aforementioned analysis of how missing data were reported in a prestigious psychology research journal (see Chapter 1 for a description of our analyis), we found that investigators rarely reported missing data at the variable level unless the focus of the study was on a particular measure or measures. We found that researchers rarely reported how many participants were missing data for a particular variable, especially if that variable was a predictor rather than a dependent variable. Most often, missing data at the variable level had to be inferred based on the reported degrees of freedom for the analyses of focus. Unfortunately, failing to report missing data at any of these levels could be an important oversight on the part of the investigators. Reporting only the number of complete cases for data analyses is often not sufficient information for the reader to evaluate the potential consequences of missing data, particularly with respect to their influence on study conclusions.

TFSI RECOMMENDATIONS AND MISSING DATA

Psychometric Properties and Missing Data

The TFSI report recommends that researchers summarize the psychometric properties of instruments used to collect data, including "measures of validity, reliability, and any other qualities affecting conclusions." Although not mentioned explicitly, missing data is one of the qualities that might affect the psychometric properties of instruments and the conclusions drawn from a study using those instruments. For example, techniques like pairwise deletion may erode the reliability of measures by using incomplete data to estimate the scores of psychometric scales when items are missing. One of us (the authors) observed a study in which a standard measure was used to assess substance use problems by summing available item scores, without missing item level data being taken into account. Thus, some individuals appeared to have improved when in fact their scores were lower due to the missing item-level data. Therefore, we recommend that researchers report the extent to which variable level data are missing and the methods they use for handling missing data (e.g., how skipped items are accounted for in the way a scale is scored).

The Effect of Attrition on Data Analyses

Wilkinson and the APA Task Force (1999) recommend that researchers describe "any anticipated sources of attrition due to noncompliance, dropout, death or other factors" and indicate "how such attrition may affect the generalizability of results" (p. 597). For repeated measures or longitudinal studies, missing data are generally reported at the occasions level, to indicate attrition rates. As with the case of missing items, missing measurement occasions may erode the reliability and validity of individual growth curve parameters, especially if "available data" methods are used (see Chapter 7). Reliability is typically eroded because the individual growth curves are based on fewer observations for some study participants than for others. Validity might be threatened, because in certain cases of attrition it is not logically defensible to extrapolate the missing scores from available scores if a systematic reason for why certain observations were missing, such as a decline in the participant's condition. As with available data methods for psychometric factors, one should report the average number of observations on which the growth curve parameters are based when using available data techniques for longitudinal studies.

Power and Sample Size

Wilkinson and the APA Task Force (1999) recommend that researchers provide "information on sample size and the process that led to sample size decisions" (p. 596). If the loss of subjects due to missing data was not anticipated, any adverse effects of missing data on sample size, and consequently on the desired level of statistical power, should be discussed. For example, assurances should be made, where appropriate, that the sample size actually available for analysis, rather than the one originally intended, is still adequate to test the research hypotheses.

Assessing the Impact of Missing Data

The first paragraph of the section "Complications" of the TFSI report is worth reproducing here in full:

> Before presenting results, report complications, protocol violations, and other unanticipated events in data collection. These include missing data, attrition, and nonresponse. Discuss analytic techniques devised to ameliorate these problems. Describe nonrepresentativeness statistically by reporting patterns and distributions of missing data and contaminations. Document how the

> actual analysis differs from the analysis planned before complications arose. The use of techniques to ensure that the reported results are not produced by anomalies in the data (e.g., outliers, points of high influence, nonrandom missing data, selection bias, attrition problems) should be a standard component of all analyses. (Wilkinson & APA Task Force, 1999, p. 597)

This recommendation clearly goes beyond reporting of the mere *amount* of missing data, as is so often done. What is recommended is that one report the *impact* of the missing data on the interpretation of results. Furthermore, it is recommended that one specify what procedures have been implemented to minimize this impact.

We would add that not only should researchers explicitly identify the techniques they used to handle missing data, but that they should also present satisfactory justifications for using those particular techniques. Chapter 6 on the costs and benefits of different approaches should aid in identifying tradeoffs involved as well as in making decisions and presenting detailed rationales for the choice of missing data handling techniques. The final impact that missing data have on study conclusions is partly contingent on the particular approach that was used to deal with the problem.

Some missing data handling techniques, such as multiple imputation, come with built-in sensitivity analyses that document the impact of making different imputations for the same missing data. Others, such as many single imputation methods and data deletion methods, do not provide this kind of information. Nevertheless, it is usually possible to do some relatively simple analyses that provide useful information regarding the impact of missing data. In Chapter 6, we presented several numerical and graphical procedures for diagnosing missing data and for making inferences from the diagnosis about the impact of the missing data on statistical conclusions and study interpretation. We recommend that researchers not only undertake a diagnosis of missing data but also report the results of the diagnosis to inform the reader of the probable impact of the missing data on statistical results and study conclusions. This information is critical for assessing threats to the internal and external validity of the study conclusions.

Addressing the Impact of Missing Data on Study Conclusions

The "Conclusions" section of the TFSI report does not specifically mention reporting about missing data, but the report does say to researchers, "note the shortcomings of your study" (p. 602). As detailed in this book, missing data may pose a substantial threat to the reliability and validity of the statistical results and thus a threat to the credibility and generalizability of the study conclusions. If researchers follow the recommendations presented in this chapter, which repeat and expand on the recommendations of the TFSI report, it should be easier for the audience of published research to identify the threats posed by missing data problems. Furthermore, in light of what we believe, and what common sense indicates, is the magnitude of the problem (including the amounts and levels of missing data as well as their estimated effect sizes on the major variables of interest), it should be possible for the researcher and the audience to qualify the conclusions with the appropriate level of caution or of confidence, where warranted.

Certainties are rare in science, and it should not be concluded that the presence of missing data invariably disqualifies studies from serious consideration. With the judicious application of appropriate missing data handling methods, empirical support that outweighs missing-data concerns at particular stages of a study should be manageable. There is no reason a study should not be presented in the context of its limitations.

REPORTING FORMAT

In many cases, information about missing data can be reported in the text of the research report. For example, in the Methods section, it is common to discuss how participants were recruited for the study. In that section, it would be important and relevant to note whether there were missing data at recruitment, and why. Again, the need to report missing data for that stage or any stage of the study depends on the purpose of the study. If representativeness of the study sample is an important feature of the study, which is generally the case, missing data should be reported. In the interest of space, it might be useful to report missing data as a footnote or endnote in a written report. If missing data are extensive and/or the researcher believes they have an impact on study results and interpretation, a Missing Data subsection should be included in the Methods section.

Similarly, in the Results section of a report, data missed during the data collection stage of the study should be reported. Investigators should note whether data are missing at the person, variable, and/or occasion level and should report that accordingly. Often, data missing at collection

TABLE 11.1. Example of Several Methods for Reporting Missing Data in a Table Format

	Group A (N = 253)	Group B (N = 153)
Ethnic background (N = 350)[a]		
Caucasian	67%	36%
African American	15%	55%
Other	17%	8%
Marital status (N = 392)[b]		
Never married	17%	17%
Married	66%	67%
Divorced	16%	16%
Military branch service		
Army	52%	78%
Navy	13%	7%
Air Force	24%	8%
Marines	10%	9%
Active duty or reserves		
Active duty	89%	59%
Reserves	11%	41%
Smoking status (N = 371)[c]		
No	66%	75%

[a] Due to missing data for this variable, N = 350.
[b] Due to missing data for this variable, N = 392.
[c] Due to missing data for this variable, N = 371.

would be reported in tables that present study results. For example, some researchers report the sample size for each of the variables of interest, either as a footnote or in the table itself. Table 11.1 illustrates both of these methods. As a table footnote, variables with missing data have a small letter or number (in superscript) next to them, with the explanation presented as a footnote at the base of the table. Table 11.1 illustrates another method where the sample size is presented next to each of the variable names in the table. There are other creative solutions as well, according to the requirements of the publisher.

Not only should the amount of missing data be reported in the Results section, but the actual method for handling missing data should also be reported. The report need not be elaborately detailed. Rather, the results of missing data diagnostics should be presented briefly so as to provide a rationale for the remedy, followed by a brief explanation of the remedy so that it is clear what was done. If sensitivity analyses were performed as part of the missing data remedy, results of those analyses should be noted. These can be presented in table or text format, even as a footnote, endnote, or in an appendix, depending on the extent of the analyses. In table format, the results can be presented with confidence bands based on results from the sensitivity analyses, much in the way 95% confidence intervals about parameter estimates are regularly presented.

In Discussion sections of study reports, missing data reports should probably be included as part of the text, rather than as a footnote, table, or link in a web-based report. In such discussions, the authors should address the nature and extent of the missing data and the assumed impact on study results and conclusions. The assumed impact should be justified. That is, if the investigator claims that missing data are unlikely to have a noticeable impact, he or she should provide evidence to support that judgment. Evidence that patterns in the way data are missing (the mechanism) suggest ignorability (i.e., MCAR or MAR) or that the proportion of missing data is small support of the belief that missing data have a negligible effect on study results.

SUMMARY

In this chapter we have discussed the various stages of studies at which missing data occur and for which it would be appropriate to report the missing data. How important it is to report the missing data depends on the purpose and design of the study, the chosen data analytic method(s), and the potential consequences of the missing data. We contend that reporting missing data at one stage does not necessarily address missing data at other stages. When a researcher reports missing data for the enrollment phase of the study but fails to report missing data from the recruitment stage, for example, the audience cannot know the representativeness of the sample; the missing data picture is incomplete and can lead to misleading inferences and conclusions.

We are not advocating that investigators report every conceivable facet of missing data for every study. Instead, we recommend that researchers carefully consider the consequences of missing data given the results of missing data diagnostics and the stage of the study at which the missing data occur. Wherever possible, any identifiable reasons for the occurrence of missing data should be reported. By attending to missing data and reporting the occurrence as well as the reasons—if understood—scientists provide evidence by which consumers of research can evaluate study results and conclusions. Along with details regarding study methods, instrumentation, and analytic procedures, information about missing data is a critical feature on which to judge the strength of evidence and the plausibility of study conclusions. Without such information, consumers of scientific information cannot be informed sufficiently for making such judgments.

NOTES

1. "Enrollment" refers to the stage when participants formally agree to participate in the study. At a minimum, agreement involves signing a consent form.

12

Epilogue

Readers familiar with the missing data literature will no doubt realize our perspective on missing data differs greatly from other traditional perspectives. Traditional missing data literature focuses primarily on the adverse effects of missing data on statistical power, standard errors, and degrees of freedom. The traditional approach comes from the work of mathematicians and statisticians who proposed various statistical techniques for handling missing data. The techniques are applied after the fact in an attempt to remedy the problem of missing data.

We are methodologists and scientists by training rather than mathematicians or statisticians. Our interests focus on better understanding the phenomena we study, and we aim to enhance the validity of the conclusions we reach in any study. To this end, we have developed and share in this book a methodological perspective on missing data. We consider missing data a threat to validity. Like other threats to validity, the likelihood of its occurrence can be minimized through modifications in study design and methods. Accordingly, we have emphasized prevention rather than treatment of missing data throughout the book. Realizing that missing data may still occur despite the application of appropriate strategies, we have advised the thoughtful use of statistical techniques to address the problem of missing data. We have tried to discuss the available techniques in simple, easy-to-understand terms, to appeal to applied researchers in the biomedical and behavioral sciences.

Our methodological approach to handling missing data is similar to approaches that are designed to address any other threat to validity and that are exemplified in the strategies to minimize selection bias in experimental clinical trials. In such situations, the prevention of missing data as a potential threat involves random assignment of participants to study groups, while its treatment consists of statistical control through the application of proper analytic methods (e.g., controlling for covariates). Our unique contribution to the literature on missing data is to conceptualize missing data as a threat to validity and to emphasize prevention through research methodology and treatment through statistical manipulations, without sacrificing the statistical language. Again, the emphasis is on prevention rather than treatment.

Our methodological perspective was reflected in every chapter of the book. In describing the consequences of missing data, we have focused on the broader scientific implications of this problem. We have classified the effects of missing data in a traditional research methodology that includes internal, construct, and statistical conclusion validity. These aspects might best be defined to fall broadly under the umbrella of causal generalization (Shadish, Cook, & Campbell, 2002)—the extent to which we can generalize our findings beyond the measures, samples, and analyses used in a single study. We have emphasized the effects on causal generalization—though perhaps not by name—throughout the book. For example, by classifying diagnostics into the categories of Cattell's data box, we have showed that when diagnostics go beyond simply identifying the missing data mechanism, they have something to say about causal generalization (Little & Rubin, 1987). Missing data at the levels of observations, constructs, variables, and occasions can have substantially different effects from each other, and the simple language of research methodology makes that point more readily available to a wider audience. The methodology for managing missing data problems, therefore, shows that the ramifications of missing data on scienctific research are broad. Our intent was clear—accounting for missing data is not just a statistical matter but rather is integral to making strong inferences in situations where statistics, per se, may play only a minor role.

We hope that by discussing missing data in the terminology that medical, behavioral, and social scientists understand, those researchers might find the missing data literature more accessible. Greater accessibility might then lead to more attention and greater care regarding missing data in our respective fields. We have little doubt that without adequate attention, missing data will adversely affect the overall scientific utility of many, if not most, studies throughout science. Medical, behavioral, and social sciences tend to bear the brunt of these adverse effects, mostly due to the pitfalls of working with and collecting data from human subjects. Moreover, these scientific disciplines tend to avoid mentioning missing data. Those fields are not only most at risk for missing data but also seem the most avoidant of what the missing data literature implies and cautions against. Our intent was to use methodology—the common language across all scientific disciplines—to form a bridge between the traditional missing data literature and scientists.

We have aimed to reach multiple readers in our discussion of missing data. Those who design and carry out research studies are those who have the greatest opportunity to prevent missing data, so reaching scientists with this information is critical in our eyes. On the other hand, an often neglected but equally important readership is that of research consumers. Consumers may be other scientists who review the work to increase their knowledge about the topic, as peer reviewers for publications, or as reviewers for funding. By understanding the extent of missing data and its potential adverse effects, these consumers can make more informed judgments about the quality of the research and its contribution to their fields. Another set of consumers might be policy makers, whose responsibility is to advocate for or against the application of specific scientific findings. These consumers are less likely to read a book on missing data, but they might find our discussion more accessible than many of the treatments out there, which typically are mathematical.

Where consumers involved in policy making would most likely benefit from the ideas in this book is that they should have more understanding of the need to expect and request clearer communication and reporting by scientists, as advocated in Chapter 11. Only with proper attention can the uninitiated or disinterested consumer appreciate the effects of missing data. That attention must be paid by the original researcher and communicated thoroughly and effectively to the consumer.

Another group of consumers for whom this book may be useful is the public who support research through taxes and contributions. A more informed public may help alleviate some of the strife that exists between the general public and research communities. Attending to missing data by preventing them and reporting them may serve to strengthen findings while also clarifying the limitations imposed by missing data. Inference, therefore, might be stronger from both the researcher's and consumer's point of view if missing data were not simply ignored.

We have presented a methodological perspective and approach to addressing missing data aimed at the broadest possible readership. We did this by reviewing and extending the vast technical literature on missing data in two ways. First, our approach prompts researchers to recognize missing data as a potential threat and to modify research methods in an attempt to reduce it, rather than dealing with missing data after the fact. Researchers have a tendency to ignore missing data, perhaps because they simply do not fully appreciate the potential impact and the steps required to remediate it. We believe that the highly technical ways of handling missing data are not easily accessible to researchers in the behavioral sciences. Second, our approach extends the technical literature by providing a more accessible bridge, where we translate the highly technical material into guidelines that are simple to understand and follow by the less technically inclined researchers. These two extensions to the extant literature serve to make the problem of missing data more available and salient. We hope to have stimulated more interest in the problem of missing data and more care in preventing it.

Our discussion has omitted many technical details. We advise readers interested in the technical treatment of missing data to consult the book's companion website (reachable through *www.guilford.com/pr/mcknight.htm*) for further reading. Yet reading alone might not be as beneficial as simply applying the techniques we document in this book first. In our experience, we have found that the most receptive audience to these missing data ideas were researchers who struggled with missing data in their own work and grew frustrated with the available solutions. They needed something more than just a reading list. The reading list will simply extend the material covered in this text, sometimes providing a more mathematical treatment of the topic. Application of the methods, however, might prove far more valuable, and we strongly recommend that readers apply these tools and provide us with feedback so we can improve our coverage of the topic as well as our delivery.

References

Allison, P. D. (2002). *Missing data*. Thousand Oaks, CA: Sage.

American Psychiatric Association. (2000). *Diagnostic and statistical manual of mental disorders* (4th ed., text rev.). Washington, DC: Author.

Arbuckle, J. L. (1996). Full information estimation in the presence of incomplete data. In G. A. Marcoulides & R. E. Schumacker (Eds.), *Advanced structural equation modeling: Issues and techniques* (pp. 243–277). Mahwah, NJ: Erlbaum.

Aronson, E., & Carlsmith, J. M. (1968). Experimentation in social psychology. In G. Lindzey & E. Aronson (Eds.), *The handbook of social psychology* (2nd ed., Vol. 2, pp. 1–79). Reading, MA: Addison-Wesley.

Awad, M. A., Shapiro, S. H., Lund, J. P., & Feine, J. S. (2000). Determinants of patients' treatment preferences in a clinical trial. *Community Dental and Oral Epidemiology*, 28, 119–125.

Aylward, G. P., Hatcher, R. P., Stripp, B., Gustafson, N. F., & Leavitt, L. A. (1985). Who goes and who stays: Subject loss in a multicenter, longitudinal follow-up study. *Journal of Developmental and Behavioral Pediatrics*, 6, 3–8.

Bacon, F. (1620/2000). *Novum organum (The new organon)* (L. Jardine & M. Silverthorne, Eds.). New York: Cambridge University Press.

Barriball, K. L., & While, A. E. (1999). Exploring variables underlying non-response in a survey of nurses and nurses' aides in practice. *Journal of Advanced Nursing*, 29, 894–904.

Bentler, P. (1995). *EQS program manual*. Encino, CA: Multivariate Software.

Boyd, N. F., Cousins, M., & Kriukov, V. (1992). A randomized controlled trial of dietary fat reduction: The retention of subjects and characteristics of drop outs. *Journal of Clinical Epidemiology*, *45*, 31–38.

Bradburn, N. M. (1992). A response to the nonresponse problem. *Public Opinion Quarterly, 56*, 391–397.

Bradley, C. (1993). Designing medical and educational intervention studies. *Diabetes Care*, *16*, 509–518.

Brewin, C. R., & Bradley, C. (1989). Patient preferences and randomized clinical trials. *British Medical Journal*, *299*, 313–315.

Brown, C. H. (1983). Asymptotic comparison of missing data procedures for estimating factor loadings. *Psychometrika*, *48*, 269–291.

Bryk, A. S., & Raudenbush, S. W. (1992). *Hierarchical linear models*. Thousand Oaks, CA: Sage.

Butcher, J., Dahlstrom, G., Graham, J., Tellegen, A., & Kremmer, B. (1989). *MMPI-2: Manual for administration and scoring*. Minneapolis: University of Minnesota Press.

Byrne, B. M. (1994). *Structural equation modeling with EQS and EQS/Windows: Basic concepts, applications, and programming*. Thousand Oaks, CA: Sage.

Campbell, D. T., & Stanley, J. C. (1966). *Experimental and quasi-experimental designs for research*. Chicago: Rand McNally.

Cattell, R. B. (1966). The data box: Its ordering of total resources in terms of possible relations systems. In R. B. Cattell (Ed.), *Handbook of multivariate experimental psychology* (pp. 67–128). Chicago: Rand McNally.

Cleveland, W. S. (1993). *Visualizing data*. Summit, NJ: Hobart Press

Cochran, W. G. (1977). *Sampling techniques* (3rd ed.). New York: Wiley.

Cohen, J. (1988). *Statistical power analysis for the behavioral sciences* (2nd ed.). London: Erlbaum.

Cohen, J., & Cohen, P. (1985). *Applied multiple regression and correlation analysis for the behavioral sciences* (2nd ed.). Hillsdale, NJ: Erlbaum.

Constantine, W. L., Haynes, C. W., Spiker, D., Kendall-Tackett, K., & Constantine, N. A. (1993). Recruitment and retention in a clinical trial for low-birth-weight, premature infants. *Journal of Developmental and Behavioral Pediatrics*, *14*, 1–7.

Cook, T. D. (1990). The generalization of causal connections: Multiple theories in search of clear practice. In L. Sechrest, J. Bunker, & E. Perrin (Eds.), *Research methodology: Strengthening causal interpretation of non-experimental data* (PHS Pub. No. 90–3454). Rockville, MD: Agency for Health Care Policy and Research.

Cook, T. D. (2004). Causal generalization: How Campbell and Cronbach influenced my theoretical thinking on this topic. In M. C. Alkin (Ed.), *Evaluation roots: Tracing theorists' views and influences*. Thousand Oaks, CA: Sage.

Cook, T. D., & Campbell, D. T. (1979). *Quasi-experimentation: Design and analysis issues for field settings*. Boston: Houghton Mifflin.

Cooper, M. P., & Groves, R. M. (1996). Household-level determinants of survey nonresponse. *New Directions for Evaluation*, *70*, 63–79.

Cox, L. H., Johnson, M. M., & Kafadar, K. (1982). Exposition of statistical graphics technology. In *Proceedings of the annual meeting of the American Statistical Association, Statistical Computation Section* (pp. 55–56), Cincinnati, Ohio.

Crocker, L., & Algina, J. (1986). *Introduction to classical and modern test theory.* Fort Worth, TX: Harcourt.

Cronbach, L. J., & Gleser, G. C. (1957). *Psychological tests and personnel decisions.* Urbana: University of Illinois Press.

Cronbach, L. J., & Meehl, P. (1955). Construct validity in psychological tests. *Psychological Bulletin, 52,* 281–302.

Crowne, D. P., & Marlowe, D. (1960). A new scale of social desirability independent of psychopathology. *Journal of Consulting Psychology*, 24, 349–354.

Dawes, R. (1994). *House of cards: Psychology and psychotherapy built on myth.* New York: Free Press.

Dawkins, R. (1998). *Unweaving the rainbow: Science, delusion and the appetite for wonder.* Boston: Houghton Mifflin.

Dempster, A. P., Laird, N. M., & Rubin, D. B. (1977). Maximum likelihood estimation from incomplete data via the EM algorithm. *Journal of the Royal Statistical Society, Series B*, 39, 1–38.

Dillman, D. A. (1978). *Mail and telephone surveys.* New York: Wiley.

Dillman, D. A. (2000). *Mail and Internet surveys: The tailored design method.* New York:Wiley.

Elliott, D. (1976). *National youth survey (United States): Wave I, 1976 (computer file).* ICPSR version. Boulder, CO: University of Colorado, Behavioral Research Institute (producer), 1977. Ann Arbor, MI: Inter-university Consortium for Political and Social Research (distributor), 1994.

Enders, C. K. (2001). The impact of nonnormality on full information maximum-likelihood estimation for structural equations models with missing data. *Psychological Methods, 6,* 352–370.

Engels, J. M., & Diehr, P. (2003). Imputation of missing longitudinal data: A comparison of methods, *Journal of Clinical Epidemiology, 56*(10), 968–976.

Felson, D. T., & Buckwalter, J. (2002). Debridement and lavage for osteoarthritis of the knee. *New England Journal of Medicine, 347,* 132–133.

Figueredo, A. J., Brooks, A. J., Leff, S., & Sechrest, L. (2000). A meta-analytic approach to growth curve analysis. *Psychological Reports, 87,* 441–465.

Figueredo, A. J., Sales, B. D., Russell, K., Becker, J. V., & Kaplan, M. (2000). A Brunswikian evolutionary-developmental theory of adolescent sex offending. *Behavioral Sciences and the Law, 18,* 309–329.

Gelfand, A. E., & Smith, A. F. M. (1990). Sampling based approaches to calculating marginal densities. *Journal of the American Statistical Association, 85,* 398–409.

Gibbons, R. S., Hedeker, D., Elkin, I., Waternaux, C., Kraemer, H. C., Greenhouse, J. B., Shea, T., Imber, S. D., Stosky, S. M., & Walkings, J. T. (1993). Some conceptual and statistical issues in analysis of longitudinal psychiatric data. *Archives of General Psychiatry*, *50*, 739–750.

Gill, J. (2002). *Bayesian methods: A social and behavioral sciences approach.* New York: Chapman & Hall.

Gilks, W. R., Richardson, S., & Spiegelhalter, D. J. (Eds.). (1996). *Markov chain Monte Carlo in practice.* London: Chapman & Hall.

Gilks, W. R., Thomas, A., & Spiegelhalter, D. J. (1994). A language and program for complex Bayesian modelling. *The Statistician, 43*, 169–178.

Gottman, J. M. (1995). Preface. In J. M. Gottman (Ed.), *The Analysis of Change.* Mahwah, NJ: Erlbaum.

Graham, J. W., & Hofer, S. M. (1991). *EMCOV.EXE User's guide* [Computer software manual]. Unpublished manuscript, University of Southern California, Los Angeles.

Graham, J. W., Hofer, S. M., & Piccinin, A. M. (1994). Analyses with missing data in drug abuse prevention research. In L. M. Collins & L. Seitz (Eds.), *Drug abuse prevention intervention research: Methodological issues* (National Institute on Drug Abuse Research Monograph Series). Washington, DC: National Institute on Drug Abuse.

Haitovsky, Y. (1968). Missing data in regression analysis. *Journal of the Royal Statistical Society, Series B, 30*, 67–82.

Hammond, J. S., Keeney, R. L., & Raiffa, H. (1999). *Smart choices: A practical guide to making better decisions.* Boston: Harvard Business School Press.

Hershberger, S. L., & Fisher, D. G. (2003). A note on determining the number of imputations for missing data. *Structural Equation Modeling, 10*, 648–650.

Horton, N. J., & Lipsitz, S. R. (2001). Multiple imputation in practice: Comparison of software packages for regression models with missing variables. *The American Statistician, 55*, 244–254.

Hox, J. J., & de Leeuw, E. (1994). A comparison of nonresponse in mail, telephone, and face to face surveys. *Quality and Quantity, 28*, 329–344.

Johnson, R. (1996). Fitting percentage of body fat to simple body measurements. *Journal of Statistics Education, 4*, online journal obtained June 12, 2004 at *http://www.amstat.org/publications/jse/v4n1/datasets.johnson.html*

Jones, M. P. (1996). Indicator and stratification methods for missing explanatory variables in multiple linear regression. *Journal of the American Statistical Association, 91*, 222–230.

Julion, W., Gross, D., & Barclay-McClaughlin, G. (2000). Recruiting families of color from the inner city: Insights from recruiters. *Nursing Outlook, 48*, 230–237.

Kaslow, N. J., Thompson, M. P., Meadows, L. A., Jacobs, D., Chance, S., Gibb, B., Bornstein, H., Hollins, L., Rashid, A., & Phillips, K. (1998). Factors that mediate and moderate the link between partner abuse and suicidal behavior in African American women. *Journal of Consulting and Clinical Psychology, 66*, 533–540.

Kaufman, C. J. (1988). The application of logical imputation to household measurement. *Journal of the Market Research Society, 30*, 453–466.

Kenny, D. A., & Judd, C. M. (1996). A general procedure for the estimation of interdependence. *Psychological Bulletin, 119*, 138–148.

Keppel, G., & Wickens, T. D. (2004). *Design and analysis: A researcher's handbook* (4th ed.). Englewood Cliffs, NJ: Prentice-Hall.

King, G., Honaker, J., Joseph, A., & Scheve, K. (2001). Analyzing incomplete political science data: An alternative algorithm for multiple imputation. *American Political Science Review, 95*, 49–69.

Koss, M. P., Figueredo, A. J., Bell, I., Tharan, M., & Tromp, S. (1996). Traumatic memory characteristics: A cross-validated mediational model of response to rape among employed women. *Journal of Abnormal Psychology, 105,* 1–12.

Kotwall, C. A., Mahoney, L. J., Myers, R. E., & Decoste, L. (1992). Reasons for non-entry in randomized clinical trials for breast cancer: A single institutional study. *Journal of Surgical Oncology, 50,* 125–129.

Krantz, D. H. (1999). The null hypothesis testing controversy in psychology. *Journal of the American Statistical Association, 94,* 1372–1381.

Kreft, I., & de Leeuw, J. (1998). *Introducing Multilevel Modeling.* London: Sage.

Krueger, A., & Zhu, P. (2004).Another look at the New York City school voucher experiment. *American Behavioral Scientist, 47,* 658–698.

Kuhn, T. S. (1970). *The structure of scientific revolutions.* Chicago: University of Chicago Press.

Lakatos, I. (1978). *The methodology of scientific research programmes (Philosophical papers I).* J. Worrall & G. Currie (Eds). Cambridge, UK: Cambridge University Press.

Lavori, P. W. (1992). Clinical trials in psychiatry: Should protocol deviation censor patient data? *Neuropsychopharmacology,* 6(1), 39–48.

Lavori, P. W., Dawson, R., & Shera, D. (1995). A multiple imputation strategy for clinical trials with truncation of patient data. *Statistics in Medicine, 14,* 1913–1925.

Linacre, J. M. (2002). *A users guide to Winsteps Ministep: Rasch model computer programs. www.winsteps.com*

Little, R. J. A. (1988). A test of missing completely at random for multivariate data with missing values. *Journal of the American Statistical Association,* 83, 1198–1202.

Little, R. J. A., & Rubin, D. B. (1987). *Statistical analysis with missing data.* New York: Wiley.

Liu, M., Taylor, J. M. G., & Belin, T. R. (2000). Multiple imputation and posterior simulation for multivariate missing data in longitudinal studies. *Biometrics,* 56, 1157–1163.

Llewellyn-Thomas, H. A., McGreal, M. J., Thiel, E. C., Fine, S., & Erlichman, C. (1991). Patients' willingness to enter clinical trials: Measuring the association with perceived benefit and preference for decision participation. *Social Science and Medicine,* 32, 35–42.

Lord, F. M., & Novick, M. R. (1968). *Statistical theories of mental test scores.* Reading, MA: Addison-Wesley.

McPherson, K., & Britton, A. (2001). Preferences and understanding their effects on health. *Quality in Health Care,* 10(Suppl. 1), 161–166.

Meng, X. L. (1999, October). *A congenial overview and investigation of imputation inferences under uncongeniality.* Paper presented at International Conference on Survey Nonresponse, Portland, Oregon.

Moser, D. K., Dracup, K., & Doering, L. V. (2000). Factors differentiating dropouts from completers in a longitudinal, multicenter clinical trial. *Nursing Research,* 49, 109–116.

Multilevel Models Project. (1996). [MCMC software].

Nesselroade, J. R. (1991). Interindividual differences in intraindividual change. In

J. L. Horn & L. M. Collins, (Eds.), *Best methods for the analysis of change* (pp. 92–195). Washington, DC: American Psychological Association.

Nich, C., & Carroll, K. (1997). Now you see it, now you don't: A comparison of traditional versus random-effects regression models in the analysis of longitudinal follow-up data from a clinical trial. *Journal of Consulting and Clinical Psychology, 65*, 252–261.

Oudshoorn, C. G. M., van Buuren, S., & van Rijckevorsel, J. L. A. (1999). Flexible multiple imputation by chained equations of the AVO-95 survey. *TNO Preventie en Gezondheid, TNO/PG 99.045*. Available online at *http://web.inter.nl.net/users/S.van.Buuren/mi/docs/rapport99045.pdf*

Penrose, K., Nelson, A., & Fisher, A. (1985). Generalized body composition prediction equation for men using simple measurement techniques (abstract), *Medicine and Science in Sports and Exercise, 17*, 189.

Peterson, P. E., Myers, D., & Howell, W. G. (1998). *An evaluation of the New York City scholarships program: The first year*. Washington, DC: Mathematica Policy Research.

Popper, K. R. (1959). *Logic of scientific discovery*. New York: Harper & Row.

Rogosa, D. (1995). Myths and methods: "Myths about longitudinal research" plus supplemental questions. In J. M. Gottman (Ed.), *The analysis of change* (pp. 3–66). Mahwah, NJ: Lawrence Erlbaum Associates.

Rosenthal, R. (1984). *Meta-analytic procedures for social research*. Beverly Hills, CA: Sage.

Roth, P. L. (1994). Missing data: A conceptual review for applied psychologists. *Personnel Psychology, 47*, 537–560.

Rubin, D. (1976). Inference and missing data. *Biometrika, 63*, 581–592.

Rubin, D. B. (1987). *Multiple imputation for nonresponse in surveys*. New York: Wiley.

Rubin, D. B. (1996). Multiple imputation after 18+ years (with discussion). *Journal of the American Statistical Association, 91*, 473–489.

Schafer, J. L. (1997). *Analysis of incomplete multivariate data*. London: Chapman & Hall.

Schafer, J. L. (2001). Multiple imputation with PAN. In A. G. Sayer & L. M. Collins (Eds.), *New methods for the analysis of change* (pp. 355–377). Washington, DC: American Psychological Association.

Schafer, J. L., & Graham, J. W. (2002). Missing data: Our view of the state of the art. *Psychological Methods, 7*, 147–177.

Schafer, J. L., & Olsen, M. K. (1998). Multiple imputation for multivariate missing-data problems: A data analyst's perspective. *Multivariate Behavioral Research, 33*, 545–571.

Schimert, J., Schafer, J. L., Hesterberg, T., Fraley, C., & Clarkson, D. B. (2001). *Analyzing data with missing values in S-Plus*. Seattle, WA: Insightful Corporation.

Schwartz, C. E., & Fox, B. H. (1995). Who says yes? Identifying selection biases in a psychosocial intervention study of multiple sclerosis. *Social Science and Medicine, 40*, 359–370.

Schwartz, N., & Sudman, S. (Eds.). (1996). *Answering questions: Methodology for determining cognitive and communicative processes in survey research*. San Francisco: Jossey-Bass.

Shadish, W. R. (1994). Critical multiplism: A research strategy and its attendant tactics. *New Directions for Program Evaluation, 60*, 13–57.

Shadish, W. R., Cook, T. D., & Campbell, D. T. (2002). *Experimental and quasi-experimental designs for generalized causal inference.* Boston: Houghton-Mifflin.

Sidani, S., McKnight, K., & McKnight, P. (1997). *Modeling subject characteristics in effectiveness research: A comparison of two approaches.* Paper presented at the American Evaluation Association Conference, November 5–8, San Diego.

Simpson, E. H. (1951). The interpretation of interaction in contingency tables. *Journal of the Royal Statistical Society, 13* (Series B), 238–241.

Singer, E., van Thurn, D. R., & Miller, E. R. (1995). Confidentiality assurances and response. A quantitative review of the experimental literature. *Public Opinion Quarterly, 59*, 66–77.

Stanovich, K. (2004). *How to think straight about psychology* (7th ed.). Boston: Allyn & Bacon.

Sudman, S., Bradburn, N., & Schwartz, N. (1996). *Thinking about answers: The application of cognitive processes to survey methodology.* San Francisco, CA: Jossey-Bass.

Tenner, E. (1996). *Why things bite back: Technology and the revenge of unintended consequences.* New York: Knopf.

Thissen, D. (1991). *Multilog user's guide* (Version 6). Chicago: Scientific Software.

Tix, A. P., & Frazier, P. A. (1998). The use of religious coping during stressful life events: Main effects, moderation, and mediation. *Journal of Consulting and Clinical Psychology, 66*, 411–422.

Tomarken, A. J., & Waller, N. G. (2005). Structural equation modeling: Strengths, limitations, and misconceptions. *Annual Review of Clinical Psychology, http://arjournals.annualreviews.org/loi/clinpsy*

Verbeke, G., & Molenberghs, G. (2000). *Linear mixed models for longitudinal data.* New York: Springer-Verlag.

Wade, W. A., Treat, T. A., & Stuart, G. L. (1998). Transporting an empirically supported treatment for panic disorder to a service clinic setting: A benchmarking strategy. *Journal of Consulting and Clinical Psychology, 66*, 231–239.

Wainer, H. (2000). *Computer adaptive testing: A primer.* Mahwah, NJ: Erlbaum.

Ward, T. J., & Clark, H. T. (1991). A re-examination of public-versus private school achievement. The case for missing data. *Journal of Educational Research, 84*, 153–163.

Wiggins, J. S. (1973). *Personality and prediction: Principles of personality assessment.* Reading, MA: Addison-Wesley.

Wiggins, J. S. (1988). *Personality and prediction: Principles of personality assessment* (repr. ed.). Malabar, FL: Krieger Publishing.

Wilkinson, L., & APA Task Force on Statistical Inference. (1999). Statistical methods in psychology journals: Guidelines and explanations. *American Psychologist, 54*, 594–604.

Wilson, K., & Roe, B. (1998). Interviewing older people by telephone following initial contact by postal survey. *Journal of Advanced Nursing, 27*, 575–581.

Winerip, M. (2003, May 7). What some much-noted data really showed about vouchers. *New York Times.*

Wu, M. L., Adams, R. J., & Wilson, M. R. (1997). *ConQuest: Generalised item response modeling software*. Melbourne, Australia: ACER.

Yammarino, F. J., Skinner, S. J., & Childers, T. L. (1991). Understanding mail survey response behavior. A meta-analysis. *Public Opinion Quarterly*, *55*, 613–639.

Yesavage, J. A., & Sheikh, J. I. (1986). Assessment in diagnosis and treatment of geropsychiatric patients. *Psychopharmacology Bulletin*, *24*, 709–711.

Yuan, Y. C. (2000). *Multiple imputation for missing data: Concepts and new development*. In Proceedings of the 25th Annual SAS Users Group International Conference (Paper No. 267). Cary, NC: SAS Institute.

Author Index

Subject Index

B

C

E

F

G

Q

R

S

T